LEGAL HANDBOOK FOR TEXAS NURSES

LEGAL HANDBOOK FOR TEXAS NURSES

Susan Schuerman Murphy

UNIVERSITY OF TEXAS PRESS
AUSTIN

Printed in the United States of America
First edition, 1995

Requests for permission to reproduce material from this work should be sent to Permissions, University of Texas Press, Box 7819, Austin, TX 78713-7819.

∞ The paper used in this publication meets the minimum requirements of American National Standard for Information Sciences — Permanence of Paper for Printed Library Materials, ANSI Z39.48-1984.

Library of Congress Cataloging-in-Publication Data
Murphy, Susan Schuerman, 1961–
Legal handbook for Texas nurses / Susan Schuerman Murphy. — 1st ed.
p. cm.
Includes bibliographical references and index.
ISBN 0-292-75161-3 (cloth : alk. paper). — ISBN 0-292-75176-1 (paper : alk. paper)
1. Nursing — Law and legislation — Texas. 2. Medical laws and legislation — Texas. 3. Nurses — Texas — Handbooks, manuals, etc.
I. Title.
[DNLM: WY 33 AT4 M9L 1995]
KFT1526.N8M87 1995
344.764'0414 — dc20
[347.6404414]
DNLM/DLC.
for Library of Congress 94-27848

Dedicated to my husband and daughter,
who bring much joy to my life.

Contents

TABLES

Preface

At a checkout line at a grocery store in 1992, I ran into a nurse I knew. We had practiced nursing together six years earlier in the Air Force. After catching up on personal news, I accepted her invitation to speak to her graduate nursing class on nursing malpractice. This lecture was the first one I had given to nurses since I had graduated from law school. The urgency and nature of the students' legal questions during the lecture impressed me: the nurses worried about things that should not concern them and did not worry about things that should concern them.

I should not have been surprised, however. Despite governmental regulations imposed on the health care industry and the reality of malpractice litigation, jurisprudence classes were still not mandatory at nursing schools. After researching existing nursing literature, I found there were several good books for nurses regarding the law, but those books tried to tackle the law of all fifty states in under three hundred pages. Because the law is different in every state, those books could only describe trends in the law. It was my opinion that practicing nurses and nursing students needed more specific information to function in the working world. Thus, I sought to provide basic legal information relevant to Texas nurses in one convenient location.

I have several words of caution to the reader, however. First, although every reasonable effort has been taken to ensure that legal information in the book is current and accurate, laws change faster than books can be published. Second, in some instances other lawyers may reach different conclusions and recommendations after reviewing the applicable laws and regulations. Third, not all applicable laws relevant to certain problems that could face a nurse may be included in this book. Finally, it is imprudent to give legal advice without knowing the facts relevant to the situation. For these reasons, this book contains legal information and only one piece of legal advice: the reader should obtain and follow independent legal advice before undertaking any activity that may be within the scope of any law or regulation referenced in this book.

Many people helped me while I was writing this book, and I wish to recognize them.

The manuscript would not have been completed timely if my husband had not dedicated unselfishly a seemingly endless number of hours to supervising our young daughter. Thank you, Kim, for your patience and endurance. My husband thanks Sea World.

I am indebted to those who offered their professional critique of the manuscript.

Thanks to all the nurse attorneys who belong to the Texas chapter of the American Association of Nurse Attorneys for their help and support in so many different ways, especially to Professor Diane Kjervik, Patricia Becker, Vicki Brann, Professor Patricia Gilmore, Penny Hobbs, Joanne Hopkins, Elaine Wright Kasper, Kathleen Viesca, and Karen Zemis. I note specifically and with great fondness Jamie Richardson, who is always armed and ready to contribute a balanced perspective to my opinions from "the other side."

I thank the governmental agencies who contributed information to the book, including the Texas Department of Health, the Texas Board of Vocational Nurse Examiners, and the Texas Board of Nurse Examiners.

Additional thanks go to those who offered their assistance from the Texas Nurses Association, especially to J. L. Brown.

My hope is that the path will be smoothed somewhat for Texas nurses who are armed with the legal information in this book, for nurses indeed travel an already difficult road.

LEGAL HANDBOOK FOR TEXAS NURSES

1

Registered Nurses—Getting and Staying Licensed in Texas

THE TEXAS BOARD OF NURSE EXAMINERS

The Texas Board of Nurse Examiners (TBNE) regulates the practice of professional registered nursing. The TBNE is composed of nine members: six registered nurses (RNs), three of whom must be engaged in professional nurse education, and three public members. Of the three RNs engaged in professional nurse education, one must represent the baccalaureate degree program, one must represent the associate degree program, and the third must represent the diploma program. Members of the TBNE are appointed for six-year terms by the governor; the Texas Senate confirms the appointments.

The powers granted to the TBNE are found in the Texas Nursing Practice Act.[1] The purpose of the TBNE is to protect and promote the welfare of Texas citizens by ensuring that the RN is a safe practitioner. This purpose supersedes the interest of any individual, the nursing profession, or any special-interest group. The TBNE fulfills its mission through two principal areas of responsibility. First, it regulates the practice of professional nursing by licensing RNs. Second, it establishes standards for nursing education.

Rules adopted by the TBNE are published initially in the *Texas Register* and are codified eventually in the Texas Administrative Code.[2] A compilation of TBNE rules and a copy of the Nursing Practice Act can be obtained for a fee from the TBNE. See Appendix I for the telephone numbers of TBNE services.

OBTAINING A TEXAS LICENSE

A person wishing to be licensed as an RN in Texas must apply to the TBNE.[3]

The TBNE is entitled to obtain the criminal-conviction record information maintained by the Texas Department of Public Safety or the Federal Bureau of Investigation identification division to investigate a person who applies for a license, who requests a determination of eligibility for a license, or who is subject to investigation by the TBNE in connection with a complaint or a formal charge filed against the person. The Department of Public Safety may provide the TBNE with criminal-conviction record information concerning the following crimes:

- felonies
- misdemeanors involving moral turpitude
- offenses involving the abuse of drugs, including alcohol
- conduct resulting in revocation of probation imposed under a conviction for the offenses listed above

First-Time Applicant

To qualify for licensure, a person who has never been licensed as an RN in any state must (1) present to the TBNE evidence of successful completion of an accredited program of professional nursing education, (2) present to the TBNE a sworn application, (3) pay the required fees, and (4) pass the TBNE's examination.

Licensure by Endorsement

Registered nurses licensed in other states or foreign countries who seek licensure in Texas are seeking *licensure by endorsement.* Those nurses can obtain a Texas license without taking the Texas examination upon submitting an application under oath and paying a fee established by the TBNE if, in the TBNE's opinion, the board regulating the RN in the other state or foreign country required the same general degree of fitness.

Foreign Nurses

Registered nurses licensed in foreign countries who wish to be licensed in Texas must have:

- graduated from an accredited nursing program in a professional school of nursing (general) of at least two academic years that included theoretical and clinical instruction in medical nursing, surgical nursing, obstetrical nursing, psychiatric nursing, and pediatric nursing
- filed an application for registration by endorsement, which includes the following:

    1. personal data, duly notarized, and the required fee, which is not refundable;

2. certification of graduation from an accredited program;
3. verification of the application by the licensing authority of the foreign country;
4. a recent fade-proof identification photograph, properly identified; and
5. evidence of passing the Commission on Graduates of Foreign Nursing Schools Examination (CGFNSE) or its equivalent

- passed the National Council Licensure Examination for Registered Nurses (NCLEX-RN)

Temporary Permits or Licenses

Temporary permits to practice as an RN in Texas are available to the following candidates:

- graduate nurses who graduated from American or Canadian accredited nursing schools who are taking either the NCLEX-RN or Canadian Nurses' Association Testing Service Examination (CNATSE) for the *first time* if they are scheduled for the first available licensure examination after graduation
- graduate nurses from out-of-state accredited nursing programs who provide evidence that they took the NCLEX-RN for the *first time* in another state
- foreign graduate nurses from a foreign accredited nursing program who have never taken the State Board Test Pool Examination or NCLEX-RN but have passed the CGFNSE and who are enrolled in a board-approved nursing accustomation course and are scheduled for the first available licensure examination

Candidates holding a temporary permit to practice professional nursing as a graduate nurse (GN) must work under the direct supervision of an RN. The temporary license expires on receipt of a permanent license or on receipt of a notice of failing the TBNE examination; the GN must return the temporary license to the TBNE office.

Additionally, temporary licenses are available to RNs seeking licensure by endorsement. The temporary license for the RN by endorsement is good for 90 days and will be issued on receipt of the completed application given under oath and payment of the required fee. The applicant must also have possessed at the time of initial licensing as an RN other qualifications necessary to have been eligible for licensing at that time in Texas and have presented to the TBNE proof of initial licensing by examination and proof that the license and other license or licenses granted to the applicant by any other state have not been suspended, revoked, canceled, surrendered, or otherwise restricted for any reason. The RN holding such a temporary license will receive a permanent license if the nurse has verified her academic and professional credentials and satisfies any other requirement set by statute. The TBNE, however, will either grant or deny the application within 180 days after the TBNE receives all required forms or information. The TBNE may extend the 180-day limit to allow for the receipt and tabulation of examination results.

Registered nurses with inactive or delinquent licenses who have not been practicing nursing for four or more years may be issued a temporary permit for the limited purpose of completing a refresher course, extensive orientation to the practice of professional nursing, or academic courses. The permit is valid for six months and is nonrenewable.

Reactivation from Inactive Status

An RN who has not practiced professional nursing and whose license has been in an inactive status for less than four years may reactivate the license by completing the application form, paying the required reactivation fee and the current licensure fee, and submitting verification of completion of twenty hours of continuing education.

An RN who has not practiced professional nursing in Texas and whose license has been in an inactive status for more than four years must submit the following documents and fees:

- an application for licensure form
- verification of employment as an RN in another jurisdiction or verification of completion of a refresher course, extensive orientation to the practice of professional nursing, or academic courses that meet the TBNE's requirements and were completed within the last year
- evidence of completion of twenty contact hours of continuing education
- a current passport type of photograph
- the required reactivation fee plus the current licensure fee

An RN who has not practiced professional nursing in Texas or another jurisdiction within the last four years and has not participated in a refresher course within the last year must submit an application for a temporary permit limited to completion of a refresher course, extensive orientation to the practice of professional nursing, or academic courses; and the required fee.

The TBNE must adopt rules permitting a nurse on inactive status who is sixty-five years or older to use the title "Registered Nurse Retired" or "RN Retired."

MAINTAINING LICENSE

It is the RN's responsibility to maintain her nursing license. Failure to do so can lead to financial penalties, inconvenience, and possibly licensure discipline.

Registered nurses licenses are renewed every two years. The licensee's birth date determines the time of renewal. Renewal notices are mailed to the addresses shown in the TBNE's records sixty to seventy-five days before the expiration dates.[4] A primary reason for late renewal is that the RN has moved and has failed to inform the TBNE of an address change. It is the RN's duty to notify the TBNE in writing within ten days of a change of address, providing the old address, the new address, and the license number.

It is the RN's responsibility to renew her license whether or not she receives a renewal notice. Any application received by the TBNE after the expiration date will be charged a late fee. If a license has been expired for not more than ninety days, the RN may renew the license by paying the TBNE the required renewal fee and a fee that is one-half the examination fee for the license. If the license has been expired for ninety days but less than one year, the RN may renew the license by paying the TBNE all unpaid renewal fees and a fee that is equal to the examination fee for the license. The TBNE must by rule set a length of time beyond which an expired license may not be renewed. Additionally, the TBNE can establish by rule additional requirements that apply to the renewal of a license that has been expired for more than one year but less than the time limit set by the TBNE beyond which a license may not be renewed.

If an expired license cannot be renewed, an applicant can obtain a new license by submitting to reexamination and complying with the requirements and procedures for obtaining an original license.

If any RN continues to practice professional nursing beyond the time for which the nurse is registered or reregistered, the nurse shall be considered an illegal practitioner and the license may be revoked or suspended. This requirement means an RN with an expired license is not allowed to work as an RN until his license has been renewed.[5]

Name Change

If an RN or candidate for registration should change her name through marriage, divorce, or religious orders or for any other reason, a request for a name change should be sent to the TBNE office within ten days of the name change. The TBNE will mail an affidavit form to the RN or candidate for registration. The RN or candidate must fill out the form and send it back to the TBNE, which will enter the name change on receipt of the duly executed affidavit.

Copying License

The RN has the responsibility to protect her license from loss and potential fraudulent or unlawful use. The RN *must not* copy or allow her license to be copied for any purpose. She may, however, provide her name and license number and the expiration date to employers, other licensing boards, professional organizations, or others needing to verify licensure. These persons or agencies can contact the TBNE office in writing or by telephone to verify licensure.

Inactive Status

Continuing education (CE) is not required for RNs whose licenses are inactive. Making the license inactive is done at the time of license renewal. A licensee who is not practicing nursing and does not want to participate in CE should choose the option of becoming inactive. If a nurse, however, fails to declare inactive status or to renew the license, the license becomes delinquent, which could make the reactivation process more difficult and costly.

If the RN decides to reactivate his license within four years of becoming inactive, he will be required to show proof of twenty hours of CE completion within the previous two years. If the RN has been inactive for more than four years and has not been working in another jurisdiction, he would need to complete, in addition to the CE, a nursing refresher course, extensive orientation, or academic courses before reactivation.[6]

Continuing Education

Requirements for continuing education (CE) have been mandatory since September 1, 1991, in Texas.

To maintain an active Texas license, all RNs must complete twenty hours of CE every two years: ten contact hours must be type I, and ten contact hours must be type II. It is the individual RN's responsibility to select and participate in CE activities that will meet the criteria for acceptable CE credit.

On renewal of the RN's license, the licensee must sign a statement attesting that the CE requirements have been met. The contact hours must have been completed in the two years immediately preceding the license renewal. Contact hours from a previous renewal period will not be accepted. Any additional contact hours that have been earned may not be used for subsequent renewal periods.

Persons licensed by examination or by endorsement are exempt from the CE requirement for the issuance of the initial license and for the immediate renewal period following an initial licensure period. An RN whose license has been revoked and who subsequently applies for reinstatement must show evidence that the CE requirement and other TBNE requirements have been met before the TBNE reinstates the license.

It is the RN's responsibility to maintain a record of CE activities. These records must document attendance as evidenced by original certificates of attendance, contact-hour certificates, academic transcripts, or grade slips. Continuing education certificates or other documentation should not be sent to the TBNE office when the license is renewed. Instead, the nurse retains the documentation in her own files for two renewal periods (four years) and, if audited, must produce them for the TBNE.

AUDITS. The TBNE will audit a random sample of licensees for each renewal month. Audit forms will be sent to selected licensees to substantiate compliance with CE requirements. Within thirty days of audit notification, the RN must submit documentation the TBNE deems necessary to verify compliance with CE requirements for the reporting period being audited. The RN will not avoid audit requirements by failing to inform the TBNE of her current mailing address.

The TBNE will notify the RN of the audit results. Noncompliant RNs will be referred to the TBNE's practice and compliance department for possible disciplinary action. If the TBNE determines that an RN is noncompliant with CE requirements, he may appeal by letter within twenty days of notification of the audit results. The TBNE or its designee shall conduct a review at which the RN may appear in person to present reasons why the audit decision should be set aside or modified. The TBNE's decision after the appeal shall be considered final and binding.

An RN who is audited and is found to be noncompliant will be audited automatically the next reporting period. An RN who falsifies CE records or who fails to complete the audit satisfactorily is guilty of unprofessional conduct and can be disciplined by the TBNE.

TYPE I CONTACT HOURS. The RN can obtain type I contact hours by participating in programs approved by a credentialing agency recognized by the TBNE. A list of these organizations can be obtained from the TBNE office. A nurse must be on the organization's planning committee. Additionally, the program's target audience must include nurses.

Type I programs must meet certain criteria. Activities that may meet these criteria include classroom instruction, individualized instruction, academic courses, self-directed study, and institutional-based instruction. The following activities do not meet CE requirements for license renewal:

- basic cardiopulmonary resuscitation (CPR) courses
- in-service programs—programs sponsored by the employing agency to provide specific information about the work setting and orientation or other programs that address the institution's philosophy, policies, and procedures; on-the-job training; basic CPR; and equipment demonstration
- refresher courses—programs designed to update knowledge or current nursing theory and clinical practice, which consist of a didactic and clinical component to ensure entry level competencies into professional practice
- orientation programs—programs designed to introduce employees to the philosophy, goals, policies, procedures, role expectations, and physical facilities of a specific workplace

A CE program attended outside Texas may be accepted for type I credit if all criteria are met and if it is approved by one of the TBNE's recognized credentialing agencies or organizations.

While the TBNE establishes CE program criteria, the Texas Nurses Association (TNA) approves programs for CE credit. Guidelines for approval can be purchased from the TNA for a nominal price.[7]

TYPE II CONTACT HOURS. The RN can obtain ten type II contact hours by participating in additional type I programs or by participating in activities discussed below.

ADDITIONAL CRITERIA. The following guidelines apply to the selection or planning and implementation of specific CE programs.

Academic Courses. Some academic courses are acceptable for type I CE credit. To qualify, the course must be within the framework of a curriculum that leads to an academic degree in nursing or be any academic course relevant to nursing practice or health care. Course participants, upon TBNE audit, must be able to present an official transcript indicating completion of the course with a "C" grade or better or a "pass" on a pass/fail grading system. No prerequisite courses such as history, government, or biology may be counted for CE credit; only nursing or health-related courses are accepted.[8]

Individualized Instruction. Individualized instruction includes home study and programmed instruction. The program must be developed by a professional group, such as an educational institution, corporation, professional association, or other provider of CE; follow a logical sequence; involve the learner by requiring an active response to the educational materials presented; contain a means to measure achievement of learning objectives of the program; and provide a record of attendance indicating completion of the program.

Up to twenty contact hours of type I or five contact hours of type II credit for one renewal period may be obtained through individualized instruction.

Self-Directed Study. Self-directed study contact hours can be accrued by (1) program development and presentation, (2) auditing of academic courses, (3) specialty certification, or (4) authorship.

An RN who develops and presents a program can get two hours of type II credit per program topic. The program or presentation cannot be part of the licensee's primary employment responsibilities, however. Additionally, credit will be awarded only once regardless of the number of times the program was presented. Upon audit by the TBNE, the RN must submit program objectives and an outline not exceeding one page that includes date and location of the presentation.

Academic courses in nursing or health care can be audited for two hours of type II credit per course. Upon audit by the TBNE, the RN must submit a letter from the course instructor on the academic institution's letterhead indicating that the RN attended the course.

An RN who completes the requirements for certification in a nursing specialty by a national credentialing body can get five type II contact hours. This one-time approval is for initial certification only. Upon audit by the TBNE, the RN must furnish a letter from the national specialty organization indicating initial certification.

An RN who develops and publishes a manuscript related to nursing and health care can get five type II contact hours. Credit for publication will be awarded only once per renewal period, however. Upon audit by the TBNE, the RN must submit a letter from the publisher indicating acceptance of the manuscript for publication or submit a copy of the published work.

DISCIPLINARY PROCEEDINGS

Involvement in any of the following practices can subject a nurse to discipline by the TBNE. Anecdotes of actual cases that led to the revocation of the RN's license follow most of the listed violations.

1. The violation of any of the provisions of this law, any rule, regulation not inconsistent with this law, or order issued hereinunder.

   An RN was issued a reprimand and her license was made subject to stipulations for three years. The RN violated the TBNE-ordered stipulations: (a) she worked in a float pool that led her to work in a critical-care area during the night shift when she was ordered not to do so for one year; (b) the nurse did not present a copy of the TBNE order to two employers and did not cause her employers to submit a notification-of-employment form to the TBNE; (c) when the nurse's supervisor confronted her about a published report of her license stipulations, the RN lied by stating the report was in error; and (d) the nurse failed to notify her employers of the need for random alcohol and drug screens.

2. Fraud or deceit in procuring or attempting to procure a license to practice professional nursing.

   An imposter used the name and license number of an RN in another state to get a Texas license by endorsement. The license that was issued to the imposter was revoked. There was no solace for the RN from another state, however. She testified that the actions of the imposter ruined her credit rating, caused the Internal Revenue Service to threaten to garnishee her bank accounts for back taxes, and forced her to retain an attorney to protect her from legal and financial problems.

3. Conviction of a crime of the grade of felony or a crime of a lesser grade that involves moral turpitude or any conduct resulting in the revocation of probation imposed pursuant to such conviction.

   The TBNE revoked the license of an RN who murdered her son because she thought he was the devil.

   An RN lost his license after he was convicted of three burglaries.

4. The use of any nursing license, certificate, diploma, or permit or transcript of the license, certificate, diploma, or permit that has been fraudulently purchased, issued, counterfeited, or materially altered.
5. The impersonation of, or the acting as a proxy for, another in any examination required by law to obtain a license to practice professional nursing.
6. Aiding or abetting, directly or indirectly, or in any manner whatsoever, any unlicensed person in connection with the unauthorized practice of professional nursing.
7. Revocation, suspension, or denial or any other action relating to the license to practice nursing in another jurisdiction. A certified copy

of the order of denial, suspension, revocation, or any other action shall be conclusive evidence thereof.

An RN's Texas license was revoked after the California nursing board suspended the nurse's license after she was convicted of three counts of attempted murder.

The TBNE revoked an RN's Texas license after another state ratified a voluntary suspension of the nurse's license for eighteen months because she misappropriated or misused drugs.

8. Intemperate use of alcohol or drugs that the TBNE determines endangers or could endanger patients. Intemperate use includes but is not limited to practicing professional nursing or being on duty or call while under the influence of alcohol or drugs.

   An RN admitted, after she was confronted by a nurse manager, that she forged another nurse's signature in the controlled drug administration record, record of waste and spoilage. Additionally, her drug screen tested positive for benzodiazepine on three separate occasions while she was participating in the Texas Peer Assistance Program for Nurses.

   On seven separate occasions from 0745 until 2100, an RN signed out narcotics from the drug floor stock record for a single patient but failed to document medication administration in the PRN medication administration record and the pharmacy patient profile. Additionally, the RN tested positive for morphine four months later.

9. Unprofessional or dishonorable conduct that, in the opinion of the TBNE, is likely to deceive, defraud, or injure patients or the public.

   An RN pilfered forms from a health care institution because she needed the forms to start her own business.

   A nurse falsified an employment application regarding her date of licensure as an RN and periods of employment with various facilities in order to obtain higher pay. Additionally, she provided a prospective employer with an altered Social Security card containing a false Social Security number.

   An RN, employed as a certified registered nurse anesthetist (CRNA), provided his employer with an altered certification card. The nurse's certification had expired years earlier, and he had not been recertified since that date.

   An RN failed to administer Nipride in a responsible manner by increasing the rate of the drip as the patient's blood pressure decreased. The patient's blood pressure had dropped to a dangerous level before the charge nurse intervened and discontinued the medication.

A nurse misrepresented her academic credentials to three prospective employers. The RN graduated from a diploma program yet represented that she possessed B.S.N., M.S.N., and M.B.A. degrees.

A home-services RN accepted money from a client in violation of her employer's policy, coerced a client into naming her as sole beneficiary in the client's will, and became the signatory on several of the client's financial accounts. Additionally, the client executed a durable power of attorney for health care giving the RN power to make medical decisions for the client.

10. Adjudication of mental incompetency.
11. Lack of fitness to practice by reason of mental or physical health that could result in injury to patients or the public.

An RN was observed sleeping for five minutes while standing next to the medication cart. The nurse was awakened and told to step aside while a narcotics count was taken. The nurse, however, fled the hospital without notifying appropriate personnel and never returned to the hospital.

A home health care nurse started exhibiting inappropriate behavior: she was disoriented and wore a cocktail dress during home visits. The RN stated to a nurse manager that she had a cerebral aneurysm, blackouts, and depression and could not remember whether she had completed visits. The TBNE reprimanded the nurse and imposed stipulations on her license that included a mandatory neuropsychiatric evaluation.

12. Failure to care adequately for patients or to conform to the minimum standards of acceptable professional nursing practice that, in the opinion of the TBNE, exposes a patient or other person unnecessarily to risk of harm.

An RN attempted to secure cooperation from a violently combative drug overdose patient by choking him until he became unconscious. This same nurse administered a blood transfusion through the same intravenous access line as a Zantac drip and subsequently with Ringer's lactate solution.

A nurse documented home visits of clients that were never performed. Proof seemed conclusive of one infraction when the nurse documented a visit with a patient who had died more than two weeks earlier.

A GN failed to know the risks and implications involved with interventricular hyperalimentation, failed to properly document and assess a patient, and failed to administer medications or treatments in a responsible manner when he disconnected intravenous tubing from the needle hub in order to change a patient's gown.

In disciplining the RN, the TBNE can either

1. issue a written warning;
2. administer a public reprimand;
3. limit or restrict the RN's license, including limiting the RN's practice to, or excluding it from, one or more specified activities of professional nursing or stipulating periodic TBNE review;
4. suspend the RN's license;
5. revoke the RN's license;
6. require the RN to submit to care, counseling, or treatment by health care providers designated by the TBNE as a condition for the issuance or renewal of a license;
7. require the RN to participate in a program of education or counseling prescribed by the TBNE;
8. require the RN to practice under the direction of an RN designated by the TBNE for a specified period;
9. require the RN to perform public service considered appropriate by the TBNE; or
10. assess a monetary fine.

Additionally, the TBNE may refuse to admit persons to its examinations, refuse to renew a license, or refuse to issue a temporary permit when an individual has been guilty of any behavior listed above. When the TBNE makes a decision, it must notify the person of the basis for its decision. The applicant then is entitled to a hearing before an administrative law judge.

Statistics provided by the TBNE regarding complaints are found in Table 1-1.

Reporting Incompetency

Disciplinary proceedings against an RN begin when a written complaint against the nurse has been filed with the TBNE. Complaints may be made by any person or may be filed by the TBNE on its own initiative.

Each RN having reasonable cause to suspect that an RN has exposed or is likely to expose a patient or other person unnecessarily to a risk of harm, has engaged in unprofessional conduct, has failed to care adequately for a patient, or has failed to conform to the minimum standards of acceptable professional nursing practice or that an RN's practice is or is likely to be impaired by chemical dependency must report in a signed, written report to the TBNE the identity of the nurse and any additional information that the TBNE may require. Alternatively, instead of reporting an impaired or mentally ill nurse to the TBNE, the RN can be reported to a peer assistance program approved by the TBNE.

Table 1-1 *Complaint Information*

	1989	*1990*	*1991*	*1992*
Total complaints				
Pending from prior years	356	495	556	613
Received during fiscal year	954	1,055	1,033	1,063
Total	1,310	1,550	1,589	1,676
Resolution Method[a]				
Informal				
Consent hearing	60	87	118	198
Prehearing conference	43	66	57	53
Board hearing	72	84	114	65
ALJ hearing	N/A	N/A	N/A	24
By appeal	1	5	2	1
Other methods				
Closed by director	90	135	588	419
Referral to other jurisdiction	3	1	20	64
Referral to TPAPN	10	32	66	45
Licensure with conditions	76	63	92	183
Complaint[a] disposition				
No violation	90	135	588	416
Closed—no action	20	39	54	70
Dismissal of charges	2	23	12	6
Warning	1	2	31	73
Reprimand/reprimand with stipulations	56	73	75	82
Suspension/probation	45	33	28	8
Revocation	50	71	87	107
Other methods				
Referral	13	33	86	109
Licensure denial	2	1	4	7
Licensure with conditions	76	63	92	183
Fine	N/A	N/A	N/A	N/A
Time for complaint resolution (days)	135	165	219	174
Reinstatements				
Number of hearings	24	18	27	23
Reinstatement without stipulations	0	1	7	1
Reinstatement with stipulations	18	14	12	9
Reinstatement denial	6	3	8	7

Source: Data are from the Texas Board of Nurse Examiners.

[a]There were 355 cases disposed in 1989, 473 in 1990, 1,057 in 1991, and 1,061 in 1992.

Other persons or institutions will have a duty to report an RN to the TBNE in writing under the following circumstances:

1. each hospital, health science center, nursing home, home health agency, other health care facility, state agency, political subdivision, school of professional nursing, temporary nursing service, or person that employs, hires, or contracts for the services of RNs and terminates, suspends for more than seven days, or takes other substantive disciplinary action as defined by the TBNE against an RN because the RN has exposed or is likely to expose a patient or other person unnecessarily to a risk of harm, has engaged in unprofessional conduct, has failed to care adequately for a patient, or has failed to conform to the minimum standards of acceptable professional nursing practice or because the RN's practice is or is likely to be impaired by chemical dependency;
2. a certifying or accrediting professional association that expels, decertifies, or takes any other substantive disciplinary action because the RN fails to conform to minimum standards of acceptable professional nursing practice;
3. each state agency that licenses, registers, or certifies hospitals, nursing homes, health science centers, home health agencies, or other health care facilities or agencies or that surveys such facilities or agencies with respect to quality of professional nursing care provided and has reason to believe that an RN exposed or is likely to expose patients or other persons unnecessarily to a risk of harm, engaged in unprofessional conduct, or failed to conform to the minimum standards of acceptable professional nursing practice or has reason to believe that the RN's practice is or is likely to be impaired by chemical dependency;
4. a professional liability insurance company that must report an RN when a suit has been filed against the nurse for damages or a suit has been settled for medical malpractice damages;
5. the RN, who must report herself when a suit has been filed against her for medical malpractice and she is not covered by liability insurance or is insured by a nonadmitted carrier;[9]
6. the state prosecutor when an RN is convicted of a felony, a misdemeanor involving moral turpitude, a violation of state or federal controlled substance laws, or an offense involving fraud or Medicare/Medicaid program abuse or if an RN is adjudged mentally ill or mentally incompetent; and
7. the professional nursing peer review committee that finds an RN exposed or is likely to expose a patient or other person unnecessarily to a risk of harm, engaged in unprofessional conduct, failed to care adequately for a patient, or failed to conform to the minimum stan-

dards of acceptable professional nursing practice or that an RN's practice is or is likely to be impaired by chemical dependency.

The TBNE will be adopting rules to minimize unnecessary duplicative reporting and the reporting of minor incidents.[10] Additionally, the TBNE is not required to investigate a report filed by an insurer but must maintain a record of the report and investigate if it receives two or more reports involving separate incidents on a nurse in any five-year period.

An individual, organization, agency, or facility is not liable in any civil action for failure to file a report against an RN, but the appropriate state licensing agency can take action against any of these for not reporting as required.

An individual, organization, agency, or facility making a report without malice that is permitted or required or reasonably believed to be required or permitted is immune from civil liability and may not be subject to any other retaliatory action as a result of making the report. If retaliatory action does occur, the person or institution can counterclaim for defense costs, reasonable attorney's fees, and actual and punitive damages if the suit or retaliatory action is determined to be frivolous, unreasonable, or taken in bad faith. A person fired as a result of making the report is entitled to reinstatement in the employee's former position or to severance pay in an amount equal to three months of the most current salary and compensation for wages lost during the period of suspension or termination.

A nurse's license is a valuable property right. Consequently, a nurse who has a complaint filed against her may wish to hire an attorney to help protect her license. Generally, it is better for a nurse to have legal representation as soon as the nurse is informed that a complaint has been filed, which means before she talks to the TBNE's investigator. In choosing an attorney, the nurse should find an attorney who has knowledge of nursing practice and experience representing nurses before the TBNE. The Texas chapter of the American Association of Nurse Attorneys (TAANA) is an excellent resource for finding an attorney (see Appendix II).

Preliminary Investigation

When a complaint is filed against a nurse, the identity of the nurse is often unclear. For instance, the name of the nurse and whether he is an RN rather than a licensed vocational nurse (LVN) is often misrepresented. Consequently, upon the filing of a complaint, the TBNE may conduct a preliminary investigation into the identity of the person named or described in the complaint.

The TBNE must make an initial investigation of the complaint to determine whether formal charges should be filed against the RN for prohibited acts. The first consideration of the TBNE must be whether the RN's continued practice poses a risk of harm to clients or other persons. Unless otherwise provided, all investigations must be conducted by the TBNE or persons authorized by the TBNE to conduct them. Each complaint against an RN that requires a determination of professional nursing competency must be reviewed by a TBNE member, consultant, or employee with professional nursing background considered sufficient by the TBNE. Typically, the RN who is the subject of the investigation will be interviewed.

A complaint and investigation concerning an RN and all information and materials compiled by the TBNE are confidential and not subject to disclosure, discovery, subpoena, or other means of legal compulsion for their release to anyone other than the TBNE or its employees or agents involved in licensee discipline, except this information may be disclosed to

1. persons involved with the TBNE in a disciplinary action against the RN,
2. professional nursing licensing or disciplinary boards in other states,
3. TBNE-approved peer assistance programs,
4. law enforcement agencies, and
5. persons engaged in bona fide research, if all individual-identifying information has been deleted.

If the majority of TBNE members or a three-member committee of TBNE members designated by the TBNE determines from the evidence or information presented to it that an RN by continuation in practice would constitute a continuing and imminent threat to the public welfare, the TBNE or the three-member committee shall temporarily suspend the license of the RN. The license may be suspended without notice or hearing on the complaint, provided institution of proceedings for a hearing before the State Office of Administrative Hearings is initiated simultaneously with the temporary suspension and provided that a hearing is held as soon as can be accomplished. The State Office of Administrative Hearings shall hold a preliminary hearing not later than the fourteenth day after the date of the temporary suspension to determine if there is probable cause that a continuing and imminent threat to the public welfare still exists. A final hearing on the matter must be held not later than the sixty-first day after the date of temporary suspension.

Investigatory Letter

After the preliminary investigation, unless the investigatory letter to the nurse would jeopardize the investigation, the TBNE must notify the RN that a complaint has been filed against her and the nature of the complaint. An information file about each complaint against a licensee will be maintained by the TBNE. The parties to the complaint will be notified at least quarterly about the status of the file until final disposition of the complaint unless notice would jeopardize the investigation.

Most complaints that are filed against nurses are dismissed without the TBNE disciplining the nurse. If it dismisses a complaint, the person who filed the complaint must be informed of the dismissal and the reasons.

Informal Settlement

The TBNE will make a timely and appropriate preliminary investigation of the complaint and can issue a warning or reprimand to the person against whom the complaint was filed. If the investigation reveals probable cause for further disciplinary action, the TBNE shall either attempt an informal disposition of the complaint or file formal charges against the RN, stating the rules that have been violated and briefly describing the acts or omissions that constitute the violation.

During informal settlements, the TBNE openly shows the nurse nonprivileged evidence it has to support its charges. The RN is given an opportunity to show compliance with all requirements of law for the retention of the license either in writing or through an informal meeting. The TBNE can dispose of any complaint by stipulation, agreed settlement, agreed order, or dismissal. An agreed disposition is considered a disciplinary order and is a public record.

Formal Hearing

If the TBNE's initial investigation reveals probable cause that the RN committed an act or acts prohibited by the Nursing Practice Act and if there is no agreed disposition of the complaint, the TBNE shall file formal charges against the RN. A copy of the formal charges must be served on the RN or the RN's attorney of record.

Not later than the thirtieth day after receiving a written request from the RN or the RN's attorney, except for privileged information, the TBNE must provide the RN with access to all known exculpatory information in its possession and all information in its possession that it intends to offer into evidence in presenting its case-in-chief at the contested hearing on the complaint.

Eventually a formal hearing will be held in front of an administrative law judge (ALJ). The hearing will be governed by the Administrative Procedure and Texas Register Act. In prosecuting the formal charges, the TBNE has the power to issue subpoenas, compel the attendance of witnesses, and administer oaths to persons giving testimony at hearings. At the close of the hearing, the ALJ will file findings, conclusions, and recommendations. Based on these conclusions, the TBNE will impose sanctions on the RN.

The filing of formal charges against an RN by the TBNE, the nature of those charges, disciplinary proceedings of the TBNE, and final disciplinary actions (including warnings and reprimands) are not confidential and are subject to disclosure, however. In fact, if the TBNE takes a final disciplinary action, including a warning or reprimand, against an RN, the TBNE must immediately send a copy of its final order to the nurse and to the last known employer of the RN.

The TBNE, however, can probate any penalty imposed on the RN. The TBNE has the right and may, upon majority vote, probate any order denying an application for a license or suspending any license as long as the probated practitioner conforms to the orders and rules that the TBNE may set out in the terms of probation. Probationary terms may include but are not limited to restricting the practice of the person to, or by excluding, one or more specified activities of professional nursing or requiring the person to submit to supervision, care, counseling, or treatment by a practitioner designated by the TBNE. At the time of probation, the TBNE must set out the time that constitutes the probationary period. The TBNE, however, may at any time while the probationer remains on probation hold a hearing and upon majority vote rescind the probation and enforce the TBNE's original action by denying or suspending the RN's license. The hearing to rescind the probation must be called by the president of the TBNE, who must issue notice of the time and place for the hearing to the RN or her attorney at least twenty days before the hearing. The notice must contain the charges or complaints against the probationer. The TBNE can send the notice by registered or certified mail to the RN's most recent address as shown in the records of the TBNE.

A person is entitled to a hearing before the TBNE if it proposes to refuse to admit a person to its examination; to refuse to issue a temporary permit, license, certificate of registration or of reregistration; or to suspend or revoke a person's permit, license, or certificate. The hearing may be before a subcommittee of the TBNE, a majority of which is composed of RNs. If the RN requests, however, a hearing before the entire TBNE must be granted. Proceedings for a disciplinary action is an administrative hearing governed by the Administrative Procedure and Texas Register Act.

If the RN is found to have violated TBNE rules, the RN can be charged with the costs of the administrative hearing. If the RN voluntarily surrenders her license to the TBNE and executes a sworn statement that she no longer desires to be licensed, the TBNE can revoke her license without the necessity of formal charges, notice, or opportunity of hearing.

Any person whose license or certificate to practice nursing has been revoked or suspended or who has been otherwise disciplined by the TBNE may appeal the decision to any of the district courts in the county where the nurse resides; a trial will be held to determine whether the TBNE's decision was arbitrary and capricious. The TBNE's decision shall not be enjoined or stayed, however, except on application to the district court after notice to the TBNE.

License Reinstatement

A suspended or revoked license may be reinstated upon application to the TBNE. If the license was revoked, however, application cannot be made until one year after the revocation was issued. The TBNE may not reinstate a surrendered license unless it determines the RN is competent to resume practice.

2

Licensed Vocational Nurses—Getting and Staying Licensed in Texas

THE TEXAS BOARD OF VOCATIONAL NURSE EXAMINERS

The Texas Board of Vocational Nurse Examiners (TBVNE) regulates the practice of licensed vocational nursing. The TBVNE is composed of fifteen members: seven licensed vocational nurses (LVNs), one registered nurse (RN), one physician, one hospital administrator, and five public members. Members are appointed for six-year terms by the governor; the Texas Senate confirms the appointments.

The powers granted the TBVNE are found in the Vocational Nurse Act.[1] The chief legal responsibility of the TBVNE is to safeguard public welfare by ensuring that the LVN is a safe practitioner. The TBVNE ensures public safety by regulating vocational nurse education and by licensing vocational nurses. Rules adopted by the TBVNE are published initially in the *Texas Register* and eventually codified in the Texas Administrative Code. A compilation of TBVNE rules and a copy of the Vocational Nurse Act can be obtained for a fee from the TBVNE.

OBTAINING A TEXAS LICENSE

A person wishing to be licensed as an LVN in Texas must apply to the TBVNE.[2] To qualify for licensure, the applicant must have (1) successfully completed the program at an approved vocational nurse school, (2) at least two years of high school education or its equivalent, (3) passed the TBVNE examination, and (4) paid the nonrefundable examination and application fees by cash, cashier's check, money order, individual institutional check, or state warrant (no personal checks).

Disabled[3] candidates, who are otherwise qualified, shall not be deprived of the opportunity to take the licensing examination solely by reason of a disability. If testing accommodations are required, they must be submitted to the TBVNE at least 130 days before the examination date. The request must include (1) a letter from the candidate requesting specific modifications, including a description of the candidate's disability and when it was diagnosed; (2) a letter from the candidate's nursing education program director explaining what modifications were made by the nursing program to accommodate the candidate during her program of study; and (3) a written evaluation of the disability from an appropriate professional confirming the diagnosis of a disability and suggesting what test modifications are warranted based on the candidate's condition. If a learning disability is identified, a detailed report must be submitted by a professional certified or trained in the area of learning disabilities. These costs are the responsibility of the candidate. The request for consideration of special testing accommodations must occur before the candidate takes the National Council Licensure Examination for vocational nurses (NCLEX-PN) for the first time. The TBVNE will bear the costs of modifications to the testing procedure.

A vocational nurse student who has had a criminal conviction must send the TBVNE a copy of the charges and disposition of the case for evaluation before graduation. If the conviction involved drugs, evidence of rehabilitation (counseling, drug program, psychiatric treatment, etc.) must be submitted for presentation to TBVNE members according to rules governing administrative hearings (Administrative Procedure and Texas Register Act). A vocational nurse who seeks licensure by endorsement and who has a criminal conviction or disciplinary action by a board of nursing must send a copy of the charges and disposition of the case with the application for licensure by endorsement. A vocational nurse on probation or with a restricted license will be presented to the TBVNE according to the Administrative Procedure and Texas Register Act.

An applicant will be issued a license or notified of ineligibility for licensure within ten working days from the date the TBVNE receives a completed application. An application is considered complete when all required documents have been submitted, the national examination results have been received (if applicable), and the endorsement application has been approved (if applicable). If the application is not completed within six months, the application, related documents, and processing fees must be resubmitted by the applicant.

Temporary Permits

An applicant for an LVN license may be entitled to a temporary permit while awaiting the issuance of a license. Temporary permits will not be issued to any examination or endorsement applicant under investigation. Holders of temporary permits must practice under the direct supervision of an RN or LVN or a physician. Temporary permits will expire on the date the applicant receives the license or on the date indicated on the permit for an applicant who fails the examination.

For graduates of approved LVN programs in Texas or other states, temporary permits will be issued for the first scheduled examination only; permits will not be issued to applicants who have previously failed examinations by the TBVNE or boards of other states.

Temporary permits may be issued to RN education applicants for the first scheduled examination if they meet certain criteria.

Temporary permits will be issued to endorsement applicants who (1) meet licensure requirements, (2) are approved by the TBVNE's division of education, (3) are educated in the United States or its territories, (4) hold active or current licenses to practice vocational nursing in another state, and (5) present satisfactory sworn evidence of requirements listed in (1)–(4).

Licensure for RN Students

Persons who have completed two or more years of professional nursing school in an accredited school in Texas or in another state can apply for an LVN license after passing the TBVNE examination. Additionally, a graduate of a professional nursing program will be eligible to take the examination for vocational nurse licensure after the graduate has failed the RN licensure examination one time. The professional nurse graduate will be allowed four opportunities for the licensing examination (one initial and three reexaminations) within two years of being notified of failing the RN examination.

Licensure by Endorsement

A person licensed as an LVN in a state other than Texas can obtain a Texas LVN license by endorsement without taking the TBVNE examination if the applicant

1. has completed satisfactorily theory and clinical practice as evaluated by the TBVNE,
2. has graduated from an approved vocational nursing program or has completed at least two years in a professional nursing program,
3. has achieved a passing score acceptable to Texas on the NCLEX-PN,
4. holds a current vocational nurse license in another state,
5. shows employment in the nursing profession within the past five years or evidence of a refresher course or completion of supervised employment for a specified period, and
6. pays the application fee.

Reactivation of License

A vocational nurse who has been on inactive status or whose license has been delinquent, revoked, or suspended for more than five years must meet the following criteria for licensure:

1. submit request form and affidavit;
2. submit verification of employment as an LVN in another state or employment as an RN in Texas or another state within the last twelve months; or
3. submit evidence of successful completion of a refresher course or an agreement to supervised employment or an agreement to complete a refresher course, with verification of such submitted to the TBVNE office before the issuance of a license; and
4. submit required fees.

MAINTAINING LICENSE

It is the LVN's responsibility to maintain his nursing license. Failure to do so can lead to financial penalties, inconvenience, and possibly licensure discipline.

The LVN licensee must renew his license every two years. The TBVNE will mail an application for renewal to the last known address of every currently licensed LVN at least thirty days before the license's expiration date. Absent renewal, the license shall become invalid on the day following the expiration date and remain invalid until the date the TBVNE receives the licensee's renewal and penalty fee. A person who practices vocational nursing after his or her license is expired is an illegal practitioner, and the TBVNE may suspend or revoke the license.

Address and Name Change

It is the licensee's responsibility to notify the TBVNE of a change of address within ten days of change. The TBVNE will not charge for updating address information.

A sworn affidavit, marriage license, divorce decree, or legal court order setting out a name change must be submitted to the TBVNE by the licensee, as appropriate. The TBVNE will charge a fee for a name change and an additional fee for a duplicate license or temporary permit reflecting the change. If the change occurs at the time of renewal, no additional charge will be taxed on top of the renewal fee.

Copying License

Employers may not copy an employee's LVN license; copies of LVN licenses may not be kept in personnel files. Licenses may be copied only under the following circumstances: (1) state-to-state licensure endorsement process, (2) investigative processes involving a license, and (3) any exception deemed appropriate by the executive director acting as an agent for the TBVNE. If schools or employers wish to verify licensure status, they may present the name, license number, and Social Security number of the LVN to the TBVNE office. Status of the license and expiration date will be confirmed.

Inactive Status

An LVN who is not actively engaged in the practice of vocational nursing may be placed on an inactive-status list by the TBVNE at the expiration of the person's license upon written request to the TBVNE in the manner it requires. An LVN on the inactive-status list may neither practice vocational nursing nor violate the Vocational Nurse Act or TBVNE rules. A person desiring to reenter the active practice of vocational nursing must notify the TBVNE. On payment of fees and compliance with other TBVNE rules, the TBVNE will remove the person's name from the inactive-status list.

Continuing Education

To maintain an LVN license, the licensee must complete twenty contact hours of continuing education (CE) within the two years immediately preceding renewal of registration. Surplus credit cannot be carried forward for a subsequent reporting period. One contact hour measures fifty consecutive minutes of participation in an approved learning activity. Continuing education is measured also by CE units. One CE unit equals ten contact hours.

Persons licensed by examination are exempt from CE requirements for issuance of the initial license and for the immediately succeeding renewal period following initial licensure.

Continuing education is not required for endorsement in Texas. A licensee who is endorsed in Texas shall be exempt from CE requirements for issuance of the initial license and for the immediately succeeding renewal period following initial licensure.

A licensee who has been delinquent for less than five years may renew her license by showing evidence of having completed twenty contact hours of acceptable CE within two years immediately preceding the application for licensure. The licensee shall then be exempt from CE requirements for the immediately succeeding renewal period following relicensure. A licensee who has been delinquent for five or more years may renew her license only after completing an acceptable refresher course or such other requirements as the TBVNE may indicate.

A licensee on inactive or emeritus status[4] for less than five years must submit verification of having completed at least twenty contact hours of CE within the past two years immediately before applying for reactivation. The licensee shall be exempt from the CE requirements for the immediately succeeding renewal period following reactivation. A nurse on inactive or emeritus status for more than five years must (1) submit verification of employment as an LVN or RN in another state within the past five years immediately before application or (2) submit evidence of successful completion of a refresher course or an agreement to complete a refresher course or an agreement to supervised employment, with verification of such submitted to the TBVNE office before issuance of a license. The nurse will be exempt from CE requirements for the biennium in which the license is reactivated and the immediately succeeding renewal period.

A license that has been revoked, suspended, or voluntarily surrendered may be reinstated if authorized by the TBVNE. The licensee shall be exempt from the CE requirements for the immediately succeeding renewal period following reinstatement.

A written request for an exception to the mandatory CE requirement may be sent to the executive director of the TBVNE by a licensee who falls into any of the following categories:

1. Requesting inactive status.
2. Requesting emeritus status.
3. Is renewing an emeritus license.
4. Had been delinquent and applied for relicensure before July 1, 1993.
5. Had been on inactive status for less than five years and applied for reactivation before July 1, 1993.
6. Can show evidence, satisfactory to the executive director, of any of the following conditions:
   a) The licensee had overseas active military duty during the immediately preceding biennium. Short periods of active duty such as summer or weekend drills by a member of the armed forces reserves and duty in the United States Public Health Service are not included in this exemption. A copy of the orders or discharge papers upon the licensee's completing military service shall be required as evidence.
   b) The licensee's spouse is a member of the armed forces, and the licensee was caused to be absent from the United States for more than six months during the biennium because of the spouse's duties with the armed forces.
   c) The licensee had overseas nursing employment for one year or

more or overseas residence for one year or more and current employment.

d) The licensee had a total physical or mental disability up to two years immediately before applying for relicensure, and the licensee has verification of readiness and ability to work if relicensed.

e) The licensee had a missionary assignment overseas for one year or more.

f) The licensee had a sabbatical or educational leave overseas for one year or more.

g) The total disability of an immediate family member for whom the licensee had total responsibility existed for one year or more but did not exceed two years.

Each request will be reviewed individually to determine if a true exclusion exists. If not, a decision to waive or defer the CE requirement to the immediately succeeding renewal period will be made. A licensee whose CE requirement has been deferred shall submit with the next renewal application substantiation of participation in the required number of CE contact hours for that renewal period as well as the number of contact hours that were deferred from the previous renewal period.

The following activities are not accepted in meeting CE requirements:

- In-service programs — programs sponsored by the employing agency to provide specific information about the work setting and orientation or other programs that address the institution's philosophy, policies, and procedures; on-the-job training; and equipment demonstration.
- Refresher courses — programs designed to update knowledge or current nursing theory and clinical practice, which consist of a didactic and clinical component to ensure entry-level competencies into professional practice.
- Orientation programs — programs designed to introduce employees to the philosophy, goals, policies, procedures, role expectations, and physical facilities of a specific workplace.

The activities that may meet CE criteria are discussed below.

CERTIFICATION. A licensee who completes the requirements for certification in a nursing specialty by a national credentialing body may receive five hours of credit. This one-time approval is for initial certification only. A maximum credit of one contact hour per renewal period may be obtained for certification in basic cardiopulmonary resuscitation.

INDIVIDUALIZED INSTRUCTION (HOME STUDY/PROGRAMMED INSTRUCTION). Programs for individualized instruction, including home study and programmed instruction, must be developed by a professional group, such as an educational institution, corporation, professional association, or other provider of CE. Additionally, these programs must follow a logical sequence, involve the learner by requiring an active response to the educational materials presented, contain a means to measure achievement of learning objectives of the program, and provide a record of attendance as required by the TBVNE. No more than five contact hours may be obtained for one renewal period.

ACADEMIC COURSES. An academic course must be within the framework of a curriculum that leads to an academic degree in nursing or be any academic course relevant to nursing practice or health care. Participants, upon audit by the TBVNE, must be able to present an official transcript indicating completion of the course with a grade of "C" or better or a "pass" on a pass/fail grading system.

AUDITING OF ACADEMIC COURSES. Academic courses in nursing or health care may be audited. The licensee must submit a letter, upon request by the TBVNE, from the course instructor indicating that the licensee attended the course. Two hours of credit per course may be obtained through this means.

SELF-DIRECTED STUDY. The development and presentation of a program that is not part of the licensee's primary employment responsibilities may be considered for CE credit. Credit shall be awarded only once regardless of the number of times the program or work was presented. The licensee must submit, upon request, program objectives and an outline not to exceed one page. Five hours of credit per renewal period may be obtained through this means.

AUTHORSHIP. The licensee may develop and publish a manuscript for statewide or nationally distributed journals or books. Proof of acceptance from the editor or the published work documents achievement of this type of credit. Credit shall be awarded only once per topic per renewal period. Five contact hours may be obtained through this means.

Programs attended or provided out of state may be accepted for CE credit if they meet TBVNE criteria and documentation is available for presentation to the TBVNE by the licensee upon request.

The TBVNE evaluates an educational program according to certain criteria in determining whether participation in the program will earn CE credit. The program must be at least fifty consecutive minutes in length and target nurses. It is the responsibility of every licensee to select and participate in CE activities that will receive credit. Consequently, the LVN in selecting programs and the provider in planning and presenting CE programs should contact the TBVNE concerning criteria for credit, including learners' objectives, content, instructors' qualifications, teaching methods, and evaluation.

The provider must furnish each participant a record of attendance specifying the provider's name and number; title, date, and location of the program; number of contact hours; participant's grades; and organization granting approval, if applicable. The LVN must retain these records for a minimum of four years from the date of completion. The records are not mailed to the TBVNE every renewal period. Instead the nurse attests under penalty of perjury that during the preceding renewal period the licensee has completed the required number of CE credits. The records are mailed to the TBVNE only if the licensee is audited.

The provider must retain records concerning the target audience; program planning materials, content, and objectives; an outline of the instructor's qualifications; teaching methods and materials; evaluation tools; and a list of participants. The provider must keep these records for a minimum of four years from the date of completion.

The TBVNE audits a random sample of licensees to substantiate compliance with CE requirements. Failure to notify the TBVNE of a current mailing address will not absolve the licensee of an audit. If audited, the LVN has thirty days after notification to submit documentation to the TBVNE showing compliance with CE requirements. The TBVNE will notify the nurse of the audit results. A nurse found in noncompliance will automatically be audited in the subsequent reporting period. Additionally, she will be referred to the TBVNE's investigation division for possible disciplinary action; failure to complete the audit satisfactorily or falsification of records constitutes unprofessional conduct and provides grounds for disciplinary action.

Any licensee who wishes to appeal a decision of noncompliance with CE requirements must submit a letter of appeal within thirty days of notification of the audit results. The TBVNE or its designee must conduct a review in which the nurse may appear in person to present reasons why the audit decision should be set aside or modified. The decision of the TBVNE after the appeal shall be considered final and binding.

DISCIPLINARY PROCEEDINGS

An LVN can be disciplined by the TBVNE for involvement in any of the practices listed in Appendix to Chapter 2. Disciplinary action may include reprimand, suspension, probation of suspension, or revocation of a license.

A nurse's license is a valuable property right. Consequently, a nurse who has a complaint filed against him may wish to hire an attorney to help protect his license. Generally, it is better for a nurse to have legal representation as soon as the nurse is informed that a complaint has been filed. In choosing an attorney, the nurse should find an attorney who has knowledge of nursing practice and experience representing nurses before the TBVNE. The Texas chapter of the American Association of Nurse Attorneys (TAANA) is an excellent resource for finding an attorney (see Appendix II).

Proceedings for a contested case are initiated when some person files a complaint with the TBVNE against an LVN. The complaint is a sworn statement of the allegations and includes a statement of the matters asserted and a reference to the particular sections of the statutes and rules involved. The TBVNE maintains an information file about each complaint relating to a licensee. The TBVNE at least as frequently as quarterly and until final disposition of the complaint will notify the parties to the complaint of its status unless the notice would jeopardize an undercover investigation.

Once a complaint is filed, the TBVNE investigates the allegations. If the TBVNE proposes to refuse a person's application for a license, to reprimand a licensee, to place on probation a person whose license has been suspended, or to suspend or revoke a person's license, the person is entitled to a hearing before the TBVNE. The hearing will be held in Travis County. The licensee will be served notice of hearing or investigation; notice will be sent by registered, certified, or regular mail to the licensee's most recent address as shown in the investigative records of the TBVNE.

Not all disciplinary actions against licensees result in a hearing. The executive director of the TBVNE may negotiate an agreed order with the nurse.

If a hearing is held, the proceedings are governed by administrative hearing rules (Administrative Procedure and Texas Register Act).[5]

In reviewing a complaint that the applicant has been convicted of a crime that directly relates to the duties and responsibilities of an LVN, the TBVNE shall consider the following evidence in determining the applicant's present fitness to practice vocational nursing:

1. the extent and nature of the person's past criminal activity;
2. the age of the person at the time of the commission of the crime;
3. conduct and work activity of the person before and after criminal activity;
4. documentation of rehabilitation while the person is incarcerated or after release;
5. notarized letters of recommendation from prosecution, law enforcement, and correctional officers who prosecuted, arrested, or had

custodial responsibility for the person; letters from the sheriff or chief of police in the city where the person resides; and letters from other persons having contact with the convicted person; and
6. records of steady employment; provision for dependents; payment of all court costs, supervision fees, and fines; and restitution if ordered as a result of the person's conviction.

The applicant bears the burden and expense of providing and presenting relevant documentation.

In reviewing a complaint that the applicant has a history of voluntary or involuntary psychiatric hospitalization, the TBVNE shall consider the following evidence in determining the applicant's present fitness to practice vocational nursing:

1. conduct and work activity of the person before and after hospitalization;
2. documentation to indicate that the person is presently in good mental health, specifically a current psychological or psychiatric evaluation that shall include any information that the TBVNE may require;
3. a current status report from a counselor, therapist, or physician; and
4. notarized letters of recommendation.

The applicant has the responsibility to provide the supportive documentation.

In reviewing a complaint of intemperate use of drugs or alcohol by a licensee, the TBVNE shall consider the following evidence in determining the licensee's present fitness to practice vocational nursing:

1. documentation demonstrating the degree of sobriety obtained;
2. documentation showing completion of a drug or alcohol rehabilitation program;
3. evidence of participation in Alcoholics Anonymous (AA), Narcotics Anonymous (NA), or other twelve-step program or aftercare;
4. a current status report from a drug- and alcohol-abuse counselor or AA/NA sponsor; and
5. notarized letters of recommendation.

The licensee has the burden to provide supportive documentation.

In reviewing a complaint that the licensee defaulted on a guaranteed student loan, the TBVNE shall consider the following evidence in determining the licensee's present fitness to practice vocational nursing: (1) a certificate issued by the student loan corporation certifying that the applicant has entered a repayment agreement on the defaulted loan or (2) a certificate issued by the student loan corporation certifying that the licensee is not in default on a loan guaranteed by the corporation. The licensee has the burden to provide the relevant documentation.

An order disciplining a licensee may be appealed to the district court in the county where the licensee resides.

REINSTATEMENT

A former licensee can request reinstatement of the license one year from the date of revocation or suspension or upon the conclusion of any specified period of suspension. The applicant must submit to the TBVNE in writing a short and plain statement of the reasons why the license should be reinstated. The applicant has the burden of proof to show present fitness or rehabilitation to practice vocational nursing. If the license was revoked, suspended, or voluntarily surrendered based on a finding, admission, or allegation that the applicant was unfit to practice by reason of intemperate use of alcohol or drugs, misappropriation of controlled substances, an adjudication of mental incompetence, or the existence of any mental disorder, the applicant must submit a written psychiatric or psychological evaluation and a written medical evaluation. The evaluations must be obtained solely at the applicant's expense and forwarded directly to the agency by the examiner. The psychiatric or psychological evaluation must be prepared by a licensed psychiatrist or psychologist, and the medical evaluation must be prepared by a licensed physician.

Once the TBVNE receives the request for reinstatement and medical reports, the applicant will be notified of a date and time of an appearance before the TBVNE. If the applicant fails to appear, another appearance date will not be authorized before the TBVNE for another six months, unless good cause is shown to the executive director of the TBVNE.

In considering reinstatement, the TBVNE will consider

1. the severity of the act that resulted in revocation or suspension of the license,
2. the conduct of the applicant subsequent to the revocation or suspension of the license,
3. the lapse of time since the revocation or suspension,
4. the degree of compliance with all conditions the TBVNE may have stipulated as a prerequisite for reinstatement,
5. the degree of rehabilitation attained by the applicant as evidenced by sworn notarized statements sent directly to the TBVNE from qualified people who have personal and professional knowledge of the applicant, and
6. the applicant's present qualifications to practice vocational nursing based on the applicant's history of nursing-related employment or education.

After evaluation the TBVNE may

1. deny reinstatement of a suspended or revoked license;

2. reinstate a suspended or revoked license and probate the practitioner for a specified time under certain conditions;
3. authorize reinstatement of the suspended or revoked license,
4. require the satisfactory completion of a specific program of remedial education approved by the TBVNE, and
5. require monitoring of the applicant's practice as specified by the TBVNE.

If the request for reinstatement is denied by the TBVNE, it may not consider a subsequent application until the expiration of one year from the date of denial of the prior application.

APPENDIX TO CHAPTER 2
UNPROFESSIONAL CONDUCT LIKELY TO DECEIVE, DEFRAUD, OR INJURE THE PUBLIC

(1) Misappropriating supplies, equipment, or medications or personal items of the patient/client, employer, or any other person or entity.

(2) Administering medications and treatments in a negligent manner.

(3) Inaccurately recording, falsifying or otherwise altering patient/client or employee records.

(4) Obtaining or attempting to obtain or deliver medication(s) through means of misrepresentation, fraud, forgery, deception, or subterfuge.

(5) Practicing vocational nursing in Texas without a current Texas license.

(6) Practicing as a vocational nurse while the individual's ability to practice is impaired by alcohol, drugs, physical or mental disability.

(7) Aiding and abetting the practice of vocational nursing by any person not licensed to practice vocational or practical nursing.

(8) Impersonating a licensee, or permitting another person to use an individual's vocational nursing license for any purpose.

(9) Failing to report facts known to an individual regarding the incompetent, unethical, or illegal practice of any other licensed health care professional.

(10) Failing to cooperate with the agency by not furnishing any papers or documents requested or not responding to subpoenas issued by the agency.

(11) Knowingly engaging in a profession involving contact with the public while suffering from an infectious and communicable disease which presents a serious risk to public health.

(12) Knowingly performing an exposure-prone procedure while suffering from an infectious and communicable disease which presents a serious risk to public health, without counsel from a personal physician with knowledge of infectious disease, infection control, the epidemiology of the disease and procedures performed by the LVN.

(13) Knowingly failing to adhere to universal precautions for infection control.

(14) Refusing to treat a patient/client, or other person who suffers from an infectious and communicable disease involving serious risk to public health.

(15) Willfully betraying a practitioner-patient/client privilege as recognized by law.

Source: 22 Texas Administrative Code § 239.11.

(16) Interfering with an investigation or disciplinary proceeding by willful misrepresentation of facts before the agency or the Board, or by the use of threats or harassment against any patient/client or witness to prevent them from providing evidence in a disciplinary proceeding or any other legal action.

(17) Knowingly causing or permitting physical or emotional injury to any person, or engaging in sexual contact with a patient/client.

(18) Knowingly and willfully referring any individual for treatment/rehabilitation with the express intent of receiving remuneration, either directly or indirectly.

(19) Knowingly falsifying or forging a physician's order or prescription.

(20) Failing to repay a guaranteed student loan, as provided in the Texas Education Code.

(21) Failing to conform to the minimal standards of acceptable prevailing practice, regardless of whether or not actual injury to any person was sustained, including but not limited to:

(A) Failing to assess and evaluate a patient's status or failing to institute nursing intervention which might be required to stabilize a patient's condition or prevent complications.

(B) Performing or attempting to perform nursing techniques or procedures or both in which the nurse is untrained by education or experience.

(C) Delegating nursing care functions or responsibilities to an individual lacking the ability or knowledge to perform the function or responsibility in question.

(D) Causing suffering, permitting or allowing physical or emotional injury or impairment of dignity or safety to the patient, or failing to report same in accordance with the incident reporting procedure where the vocational nurse is employed or working.

(E) Knowingly or consistently failing to follow the policy and procedure for the wastage of medications in effect at the facility at which the nurse is employed or working.

(F) Leaving a nursing assignment without notifying appropriate personnel.

(G) Engaging in unnecessary violence towards any person in connection with the practice of vocational nursing.

(H) Failing to comply with a supervisor's valid directives.

(I) Negligently or intentionally violating a physician's order addressing patient care.

(22) Being convicted of a crime which relates to the practice of vocational nursing. Those crimes which the Board considers to be directly related to the duties and responsibilities of an LVN shall include, but are not limited to:

(A) Any felony or misdemeanor which involves an act of fraud, dishonesty, or deceit.
(B) Any criminal violation of the Vocational Nurse Act or other statutes regulating or pertaining to nursing or the medical profession.
(C) Any crime involving moral turpitude.
(D) Murder.
(E) Assault.
(F) Burglary.
(G) Robbery.
(H) Theft.
(I) Rape or sexual abuse.
(J) Patient abuse.
(K) Injury to an elderly person.
(L) Child molestation, abuse, endangerment, or neglect.
(M) Felony conviction for driving while intoxicated.
(N) Sale, distribution, or illegal possession of narcotics, controlled substances, or dangerous drugs.
(O) Tampering with a governmental record.
(P) Offenses which include attempting or conspiring to commit any of the offenses listed above.
(23) Violating state or federal laws relative to drugs, including controlled substances and dangerous drugs.
(24) In determining whether a crime not listed above relates to vocational nursing, the Board will consider:
(A) The nature and seriousness of the crime.
(B) The relationship of the crime to the purposes for requiring a license to practice vocational nursing.
(C) The extent to which a license might offer opportunities to engage in further criminal activity of the same type as that in which the person was previously engaged.
(D) The relationship of the crime to the ability, capacity, or fitness required to perform the duties and to discharge the responsibilities of an LVN.

3

Scope of Practice

Registered professional nurses (RNs) and licensed vocational nurses (LVNs) must know the scope of practice as defined by Texas law so that they may meet minimum acceptable levels of practice. Meeting minimum practice standards is accomplished by nurses' not accepting responsibility for delegated tasks outside the scope of their practice, by not delegating to others tasks that are outside the scope of their professional practice, and by independently and safely performing nursing tasks within the scope of nursing practice. Failing to meet minimum practice standards can result in licensure discipline, employment discipline, and nursing negligence liability.

REGISTERED NURSES

The scope of practice for Texas RNs can be gleaned from many sources, including but not limited to the Texas Nursing Practice Act (NPA), the regulations of the Texas Board of Nurse Examiners (TBNE), the Texas Medical Practice Act, and state and federal health and safety laws. This section will establish the framework of the Texas RN's scope of practice.

Texas Nursing Practice Act

The Texas NPA defines the RN's practice very broadly as the performance for compensation of any nursing act

1. in the observation, assessment, intervention, evaluation, rehabilitation, care and counsel, and health teachings of persons who are ill, injured, or infirm or are experiencing changes in normal health processes;
2. in the maintenance of health or prevention of illness;
3. in the administration of medications or treatments as ordered by a licensed physician, including a podiatric physician licensed by the Texas State Board of Podiatry Examiners, or a dentist;

4. in the supervision or teaching of nursing;
5. in the administration, supervision, and evaluation of nursing practices, policies, and procedures; or
6. in the requesting, receiving, and signing for professional samples and distributing the samples to patients at a site serving underserved populations.

The NPA clarifies, however, that the foregoing must not be deemed to include acts of medical diagnosis or prescription of therapeutic or corrective measures.[1]

Roles and Responsibilities Generally

The TBNE has defined more specifically the roles and responsibilities of RNs by establishing minimum acceptable levels of professional nursing practice.[2] The RN shall

- know and conform to the Texas NPA and the TBNE's rules and regulations, as well as all federal, state, or local laws, rules, or regulations affecting the RN's current area of nursing practice, and
- provide, without discrimination, nursing services regardless of the age, disability, economic status, gender, national origin, race, religion, or health problems of the client served.

GOAL-DIRECTED NURSING CARE. The RN shall

- use a systematic approach to provide individualized, goal-directed nursing care by
    1. performing nursing assessments regarding the health status of the client,
    2. making nursing diagnoses that serve as the basis for the strategy of care,
    3. developing a plan of care based on assessment and nursing diagnosis,
    4. implementing nursing care, and
    5. evaluating the client's responses to nursing interventions.
- institute appropriate nursing intervention that might be required to stabilize a client's condition and prevent complications.
- clarify any order or treatment regimen that the nurse has reason to believe is inaccurate, nonefficacious, or contraindicated by consulting with the appropriate licensed practitioner and notifying the ordering practitioner when the RN makes the decision not to administer the medication or treatment.

- know the rationale for and the effects of medications and treatments and shall correctly administer the same.
- accurately report and document the client's symptoms, responses, and status.

PROVIDING FOR SAFE ENVIRONMENT. The RN shall

- implement measures to promote a safe environment for clients and others.
- implement measures to prevent exposure to infectious pathogens and communicable conditions.
- respect the client's right to privacy by protecting confidential information unless obligated or allowed by law to disclose the information.

COORDINATION OF CLIENT CARE. The RN shall

- collaborate with the client, members of the health care team and, when appropriate, the client's significant others in the interest of the client's health care.
- consult with, utilize, and make referrals to appropriate community agencies and health care resources to provide continuity of care.

DELEGATION AND SUPERVISION. The RN shall

- when acting in the role of nurse administrator ensure that adequate strategies are in place to verify the current Texas licensure and credentials of personnel for whom the RN is responsible.
- make assignments to others that take into consideration client safety and that are commensurate with the educational preparation, experience, knowledge, and ability of the persons to whom the assignments are made.
- supervise nursing care provided by others for whom the RN is administratively or professionally responsible.
- accept only those nursing assignments that are commensurate with the RN's own educational preparation, experience, knowledge, and ability.
- obtain instruction and supervision as necessary when implementing nursing procedures or practices.

EDUCATION. The RN shall

- be responsible for her own continuing competence in nursing practice and individual professional growth.
- promote and participate in client education and counseling based on health needs.

REPORTS OF UNSAFE PRACTICE. The RN shall

- report unsafe nursing practice by an RN who a nurse has reasonable cause to suspect has exposed or is likely to expose a client unnecessarily to risk of harm as a result of failing to provide client care that conforms to the minimum standards of acceptable and prevailing professional practice.
- report unsafe-practice conditions or other practitioners to the appropriate authority or licensing board.

Nursing Acts Delegable and Nondelegable by Registered Nurses

The TBNE has spoken more specifically about what nursing tasks an RN may delegate to unlicensed persons[3] and the type of supervision the delegating RN must provide. The full utilization of the services of an RN may require the nurse to delegate selected nursing tasks to unlicensed personnel. The scope of delegation and the intensity of supervision by the RN may vary depending on the setting, the complexity of the task, the skills of the unlicensed person, and the client's condition, ability, and willingness to be involved in the management of his own care. Although unlicensed personnel may be used to complement the RN in the performance of nursing functions, these personnel cannot be used as substitutes for the RN.[4]

The following rules do not apply to RNs who supervise or instruct others in the gratuitous nursing care of the sick, who are qualified nursing faculty or preceptors directly supervising or instructing nursing students in the performance of nursing tasks while the students are enrolled in accredited nursing programs, and who instruct or supervise an unlicensed person in the proper performance of nursing tasks as a part of an education course designed to prepare persons to obtain a state license, certificate, or permit that authorizes the person to perform such tasks.[5]

GENERAL CRITERIA FOR DELEGATION. The RN delegating nursing tasks to unlicensed persons shall comply with the following requirements. The RN must practice in accordance with these rules as well as any other regulations related to the RN's specific area or practice setting.

1. The RN must assess the client's nursing-care needs. The RN should, when the client's condition allows, consult with the client to identify the client's nursing needs before delegating nursing tasks.
2. The nursing task must be one that a reasonable and prudent RN would find is within the scope of sound nursing judgment to delegate.
3. The nursing task must be one that, in the opinion of the delegating RN, can be properly and safely performed by the unlicensed person

involved without jeopardizing the client's welfare. The RN delegates nursing tasks based on the needs of the client and on the knowledge and skills of the individual selected to perform those tasks.

4. The nursing tasks must not require the unlicensed person to exercise nursing judgment or intervention except in emergency situations.
5. The unlicensed person to whom the nursing task is delegated must be adequately identified. The identification may be by individual or, if appropriate, by training, education, or certification of the unlicensed person.
6. The RN shall have either instructed the unlicensed person in the delegated task or verified the unlicensed person's competency to perform the nursing task.
7. The RN shall adequately supervise the performance of the delegated nursing task.
8. The RN shall be accountable and responsible for the delegated nursing task.[6]

If a licensed practitioner delegates tasks to an unlicensed person over whom the RN has supervisory responsibilities, the RN is responsible for verifying the training of the unlicensed person and verifying that the unlicensed person can properly and adequately perform the delegated task without jeopardizing the client's welfare.

If the RN cannot verify the unlicensed person's capability to perform the delegated task, the RN must communicate this fact to the licensee who delegated the task.

When the course of study for nursing students has included appropriate instruction to prepare them to perform the tasks that will be delegated, certain nursing tasks may be delegated to RN students working as unlicensed personnel in agencies, facilities, or institutions. The nursing students, however, must be currently enrolled in accredited professional nursing programs or on semester breaks from those programs. Delegation must be consistent with the delegation rules listed below.[7]

DELEGABLE NURSING TASKS. When the general criteria for delegation have been met, by way of example and not in limitation, the following nursing tasks can be delegated regardless of the setting:

- Noninvasive and nonsterile treatments (unless otherwise prohibited as listed under "Routinely Nondelegable Nursing Tasks" below).
- The collecting, reporting, and documenting of data including but not limited to

  1. vital signs, height, weight, intake and output, clinitest, and hematest results;

2. changes from baseline data established by the RN;
3. environmental situations;
4. client or family comments relating to the client's care; and
5. behaviors related to the plan of care.

- Ambulation, positioning, and turning.
- Transportation of the client within a facility.
- Personal hygiene and elimination, including vaginal irrigations and cleansing enemas.
- Feeding, cutting up of food, or placing of meal trays.
- Socialization activities.
- Activities of daily living.
- Reinforcement of health teaching planned or provided by the RN.

In independent living environments, when the client has stable and predictable health care needs, the RN can delegate activities of daily living and nursing tasks required for maintenance of the client's status. These tasks may be delegated only when the general criteria and supervision criteria have been met and when the RN has assessed the client's available support systems and the client has expressed, through traditional or nontraditional means of communication, his ability and willingness to share in the management of his care. Delegable tasks, in addition to those identified above, include by way of example and not in limitation the following tasks:

- Medication administration in compliance with the rules relating to the administration of medications.
- Assistance with feeding, including tube feeding through permanently placed tubes.
- Assistance with elimination, including intermittent catheterization.
- Assistance with other activities necessary to maintain the independence of the client, such as maintenance of skin integrity and mobility.[8]

NONDELEGABLE NURSING TASKS. By way of example and not in limitation, the following nursing tasks are not within the scope of sound professional nursing judgment to delegate:

- Physical, psychological, and social assessments that require professional nursing judgment, intervention, referral, or follow-up.
- Formulation of nursing-care plan and evaluation of the client's response to the care rendered.
- Specific tasks involved in the implementation of the plan of care that require professional nursing judgment or intervention.
- The responsibility and accountability for client health teaching and

health counseling that promote client education and involve the client's significant others in accomplishing health goals.
- Administration of medications, including intravenous fluids, except when allowed by administration of medication regulations.[9]

ROUTINELY NONDELEGABLE NURSING TASKS. By way of example and not in limitation, the following are nursing tasks that are not usually within the scope of sound professional nursing judgment to delegate:

- Sterile procedures: those procedures involving a wound or an anatomical site that could potentially become infected.
- Nonsterile procedures, such as dressing or cleansing penetrating wounds and deep burns.
- Invasive procedures: inserting tubes in a body cavity or instilling or inserting substances into an indwelling tube, unless allowed by other regulations.
- Care of broken skin other than minor abrasions or cuts generally classified as requiring only first-aid treatment.

The tasks listed above may be delegated to an unlicensed person only in accordance with the following guidelines:

- Under circumstances in which a reasonably prudent RN would find that the delegation does not jeopardize the client's safety or welfare.
- If, in the judgment of the RN, the unlicensed person has the appropriate knowledge and skills to perform the nursing tasks in a safe and effective manner.
- If the delegation is in compliance with the general criteria for delegation.
- If the RN delegating the task is directly responsible for the nursing care given to the client.
- If the agency, facility, or institution employing unlicensed personnel follows a current protocol for the instruction and training of unlicensed personnel performing nursing tasks under section 218.10 of the Texas Administrative Code and the protocol is developed with input by RNs currently employed in the facility and includes

    1. the manner in which the instruction addresses the complexity of the delegated task.
    2. the manner in which the unlicensed person demonstrates competency of the delegated task.
    3. the mechanism for reevaluation of the competency.
    4. an established mechanism for identifying those individuals to whom nursing tasks under section 218.10 may be delegated.

- If the protocol recognizes that the final decision on what nursing tasks can be safely delegated in any specific situation is within the specific scope of the RN's professional judgment.[10]

SUPERVISION. When the RN delegates nursing tasks to unlicensed personnel, the RN must supervise the tasks. The degree of supervision required must be determined by the RN after evaluating appropriate factors including but not limited to (1) the stability of the client's condition, (2) the training and capability of the unlicensed person to whom the nursing task is delegated, (3) the nature of the nursing task being delegated, and (4) the proximity and availability of the RN to the unlicensed person when the nursing task will be performed.

A candidate holding a temporary permit to practice professional nursing as a graduate nurse (GN) must work under the direct supervision of an RN who is working on the same unit and is readily available to the GN for consultation and assistance. The GN shall not be placed in a charge position or work in an independent practice setting.[11]

The degree of proximity and the availability of the RN to the unlicensed person when the nursing task will be performed depend on the health care setting.

Health Care Institutions. In acute care, long-term care, rehabilitation centers, or clinics providing public health services, the delegating RN must be readily available to supervise the unlicensed person in the performance of delegated tasks.

Clients' Residences. In group homes, foster homes, and clients' residences, the RN must be responsible for the nursing care rendered and shall make supervisory visits at least every two weeks when the RN is required to assess, plan, intervene, and evaluate the client's unstable and unpredictable condition and need for skilled nursing services.

Independent Living Environments. In hospice care, group homes, foster homes, and the client's residence, school, and place of work, if the client has stable and predictable health care needs, the RN must make supervisory visits when, in consultation with the client and, if appropriate, family and significant others, the RN determines it is necessary to ensure that safe and effective services are provided. The ability or desire of the client to participate in the supervision of the care provided by the unlicensed person should be considered when the RN establishes the frequency of supervisory visits.[12]

MEDICATION ADMINISTRATION. The RN may *never* delegate the following tasks to any medication provider:

- Calculation of any medication doses except for measuring a prescribed amount of liquid medication and breaking a tablet for administration, provided the RN has calculated the dose.
- Administration of the initial dose of a medication that has not been previously administered to the client.
- Administration of medications by any injectable route.
- Administration of medications used for intermittent positive pressure breathing or other methods involving medication inhalation treatments.
- Administration of medications through a tube inserted in a cavity of the body except in independent living environments.
- Responsibility for receiving verbal or telephone orders from a physician, dentist, or podiatrist.
- Responsibility for ordering a client's medication from the pharmacy.

The aspects of medication administration that may be delegated by the RN depend on the practice setting.

In settings in which the RN's regularly scheduled presence is required to perform ongoing assessment, intervention, and evaluationof the client's health status and stability, the RN may only delegatemedication administration in compliance with the following requirements:

1. An RN may delegate the administration of medications to unlicensed persons working in a long-term care setting and holding valid medication aide permits issued by the Texas Department of Health under the Health and Safety Code, chapter 242, subchapter F. The RN must be knowledgeable regarding the rules of the Texas Department of Health governing medication aides and must ensure that the medication aide is in compliance with the statute.
2. An RN may delegate the administration of medications to unlicensed persons working in a home health setting and holding valid home health medication aide permits issued by the Texas Department of Health under the Health and Safety Code, chapter 142, subchapter B. The RN must be knowledgeable regarding the rules of the Texas Department of Health governing home health medication aides and must ensure that the home health medication aide is in compliance with the statute. The RN must make a supervisory visit at least weekly or when any change in medication regimen is ordered while the medication aide is in the client's residence.

The RN may delegate the administration of medications in independent living environments when (1) the client's clinical and behavioral status is stable and predictable, does not require the regular presence and assessment, intervention, and evaluation by an RN and (2) the client has expressed his ability and willingness to participate in the management of his care. This setting includes hospice settings if the client's deteriorating condition is predictable. The delegation can occur only after the RN has trained or verified the training of the unlicensed person to administer the medication. The RN may delegate only medications that are administered orally or via permanently placed feeding tubes; sublingually; or topically, including eye, ear, and nose drops and vaginal or rectal suppositories.[13]

Medical Acts Delegable to Registered Nurses

Physicians can delegate to any *qualified and properly trained* RN any medical act that a reasonable and prudent physician would find is within the scope of sound medical judgment to delegate if, in the opinion of the delegating physician, the act can be *properly and safely performed* by the RN and the act is performed in its *customary manner,* not in violation of any other statute, and the RN does not hold herself out to the public as being authorized to practice medicine. The Texas Board of Medical Examiners (TBME) has the authority to determine whether any medical act may or may not be properly or safely delegated by physicians.[14]

The TBNE may only recommend to the TBME the adoption of rules relating to physicians delegating medical acts to RNs.[15] The TBNE, however, has the authority to regulate the practice of nursing. Consequently, while the TBME has the authority to decide when a medical act will be delegated to RNs, the TBNE, through its power to discipline nurses, has the power to regulate when RNs will accept the delegation of medical acts by physicians.

The TBNE has ruled that an RN can accept only those nursing assignments commensurate with her educational preparation, experience, knowledge, and ability. The TBNE has issued position statements on the delegation of certain medical acts.

EPIDURAL/INTRATHECAL PAIN CONTROL. The TBNE has determined that it is within the scope of practice of an RN to administer analgesic and anesthetic agents via the epidural route to control pain. The RN, however, must be knowledgeable about the pharmacological effects of the drugs, the physiology of the route, the monitoring and nursing care of the patient, and emergency procedures.

Additionally, there must be documentation that the nurse has participated in educational activities to gain and maintain the knowledge and skill. The RN should be educated as to

- anatomy and physiology of the spinal cord and column.
- purpose of the epidural and intrathecal catheter for pain management.
- catheter placement and signs and symptoms of misplacement.
- effects of medication administered epidurally or intrathecally.
- nursing management of untoward effects of medications.
- associated complications.
- nursing care, which includes

  1. observation — monitoring of sedation levels and other patient parameters;
  2. procedures — administration of medication, catheter maintenance, and site care and checking of placement; and
  3. emergency interventions.

Appropriate nursing policies and procedures that address the education and skills of the nurse and nursing care of the patient should be developed to guide the nurse in the administration of epidural and intrathecal medications. The nurse needs to ensure that practice is guided by agency policies and procedures. Standing medical orders and protocols approved by the medical staff of the facility should include but not necessarily be limited to

- the purpose and goal of treatment.
- the dosage range of medication to be administered including the maximum dosage.
- intravenous access.
- treatment of respiratory depression and other side effects including an order for a narcotic antagonist.
- options for inadequate pain control.
- physician/certified registered nurse anesthetist (CRNA) availability and backup.[16]

TATTOOS. It is the TBNE's position that micropigment implantation (the technique of depositing pigment under the skin using a micro-tattooing probe) is not within the scope of practice of RNs as defined in the Nursing Practice Act.[17]

LASER THERAPY. The TBNE views the use of lasers as a type of surgery. As such, an RN *may not* perform the delivery of laser energy to a patient as an independent nursing function. The TBNE, however, recognizes that RNs play many important roles in the care of patients undergoing procedures performed with lasers and may appropriately be involved with (1) preparing and educating the patient preoperatively and postoperatively, (2) operating the laser equipment while the physician performs the procedure, and (3) maintaining a safe environment. Further, an RN who has documented education and experience may, under the delegation and direct supervision of the physician, assist with the direct delivery of laser energy to the patient. There must be, however, approved policies and procedures to guide the RN who performs this delegated medical act.[18]

Intravenous Conscious Sedation

The TBNE has determined that it is within the scope of practice of an RN to administer pharmacological agents via the intravenous (IV) route to produce conscious sedation. Optimal anesthesia care is best provided by qualified anesthesiologists and CRNAs. The TBNE, however, recognizes that the demand in the practice setting necessitates non-CRNAs providing IV conscious sedation. Employing facilities should have policies and procedures to guide the RN.[19]

The American Association of Nurse Anesthetists[20] and the American Nurses Association[21] have developed excellent guidelines for RNs providing IV conscious sedation. These guidelines are treated in Chapter 9, "Drug Therapy."

ALLIED HEALTH PROFESSIONALS

The TBNE has ruled that RNs must make assignments to others that take into consideration client safety and that are commensurate with the educational preparation, experience, knowledge, and ability of the persons to whom the assignments are made.[22] Thus, it is important for RNs to be knowledgeable about the scope of practice of allied health professionals in order to know when and to whom nursing tasks may be properly delegated.

Licensed Vocational Nurses

The Vocational Nurse Act does not define clearly the scope of the vocational nurse's practice. Vocational nursing is defined as "nursing services that generally require experience and education in biological, physical, and social sciences sufficient to qualify for licensure as a Licensed Vocational Nurse."[23] So that nurses can begin to understand this definition of vocational nursing, experiential and educational licensure requirements for LVNs will be explored.

To qualify for licensure, applicants must have (1) successfully completed the program at an approved vocational nurse school, (2) at least two years of high school education or its equivalent, and (3) passed the Texas Board of Vocational Nurse Examiners (TBVNE) examination. See the discussion under "Obtaining a Texas License" in Chapter 2.

To be approved, vocational nurse schools must be at least twelve months in length. The program must have a minimum total of 1,398 clock hours: 558 hours for classroom instruction and 840 for clinical practice. The curriculum plan must enable students to acquire knowledge, skills, and abilities to develop competence in the following activities:

1. understanding and providing for essential human needs as related to health and therapeutics;
2. gathering, recording, and communicating information;
3. participating as a team member in planning, implementing, and evaluating nursing care of individuals in all age groups;
4. developing and implementing safe practices in meeting health needs;
5. understanding the impact of hygienic and environmental influences on the health status of individuals; and
6. influencing health status through promotion of hygiene, self-awareness, and individual participation in improving or maintaining a state of health or wellness.

Instruction must be provided in biological, physical, social, behavioral, and nursing sciences, including body structure and function, microbiology, pharmacology, and nutrition; signs of emotional health; and human growth and development. In summary, experiences should include the administration of medications; health promotion and preventive aspects; nursing care of persons with acute, chronic, and age-related illnesses; and rehabilitative care.

Correlated theory and clinical practice must be provided in the areas discussed below but not necessarily in separate courses.

NURSING CARE OF CHILDREN. Experiences must include care of children and meeting their needs in a variety of age groups in the acute-care setting. Day care and clinical settings may be utilized as supplementary experience. Common health deviations; physical, psychological, and neurological handicaps; and nutritional needs shall be emphasized. Students shall have opportunities to develop understanding of normal growth and development and the influences of the family, home, church, school, and community. Student practice in caring and understanding the needs of newborn infants shall also be included.

MATERNITY NURSING. Opportunities shall be provided for students to gain an understanding of the psychological and physiological aspects of pregnancy, labor, and puerperium. Assisting mothers in the care of their infants shall be emphasized. A variety of settings, including clinics, organized maternity units, and maternity cases in nonsegregated units, may be used for providing maternity nursing experience.

NURSING CARE OF THE AGED. Opportunities shall be included for the care of individuals experiencing specific changes related to aging. Students shall develop an understanding of the physical and mental changes associated with aging and the implications of aging in planning nursing care.

NURSING CARE OF ADULTS. Opportunities shall be provided to the student through the use of various resources to care for adults who have health deviations. Resources used shall include learning experiences to illustrate the individual as a member of the family, the responsibilities and functions of the community in providing nursing care, and the types of agencies where nursing is practiced. Preventive, therapeutic, and rehabilitative aspects shall be provided. Experiences shall also include the physical, psychological, and spiritual components of health and disease. Experiences shall include but not be limited to the acute-care settings.

NURSING CARE OF INDIVIDUALS WITH MENTAL HEALTH PROBLEMS. Learning opportunities shall include an understanding of personality development, human needs, common mental mechanisms, and factors influencing mental health and mental illness. Common mental disorders and related therapy shall be included. Clinical experience in a unit or facility specifically designed for psychiatric care is optional.

According to the Medical Practice Act, physicians can delegate to any qualified and properly trained LVN acting under the physician's supervision any medical act that a reasonable and prudent physician would find is within the scope of sound medical judgment to delegate if, in the opinion of the delegating physician, the act can be properly and safely performed by the LVN and the act is performed in its customary manner, not in violation of any other statute, and the LVN does not hold herself out to the public as being authorized to practice medicine.

Nursing tasks that are delegable to LVNs may best be surmised by considering the experience and educational background of the LVN in light of the delegation and supervision criteria established earlier in this chapter for RNs.

Nurse Aides

Registered nurses should know the training and competency evaluation requirements of Texas nurse aides who are employed in Medicare/Medicaid nursing facilities.[24] (Private-duty aides and sitters hired by residents of facilities do not have to meet these requirements, although facilities are encouraged to develop their own policies regarding these individuals.)

The Texas Department of Health (the Department) maintains a registry of all individuals who qualify as nurse aides. Upon inquiry, the Department must verify if an individual is listed and shall disclose any information concerning a finding of abuse,[25] neglect,[26] or misappropriation of a resident's property[27] by the individual. The Department must also disclose any statement by the individual related to the finding or a clear and accurate summary of such a statement.

To qualify as a nurse aide in Texas, a person must complete satisfactorily a nurse aide training and competency evaluation program (NATCEP) or a competency evaluation program (CEP) approved by the Department or qualify by waiver[28] or reciprocity.[29] An individual must be so qualified within four months of working as a nurse aide on either a full- or part-time basis. Additionally, facilities may not employ individuals who have had a finding entered into the registry concerning abuse, neglect, mistreatment of a resident, or misappropriation of a resident's property.

Each NATCEP must teach a minimum of seventy-five clock hours of training: (1) at least fifty-one clock hours must be classroom and skills training that does not involve direct care of residents, and (2) at least twenty-four clock hours must be clinical training defined as hands-on care of residents by trainees under the direct supervision of a licensed RN or LVN.

At least sixteen introductory hours of training must be in the following areas before any direct contact with a resident:

1. communication and interpersonal skills,
2. infection control,
3. safety and emergency procedures including the Heimlich maneuver,
4. promoting of residents' independence, and
5. respect of residents' rights.

Each NATCEP must teach a curriculum established by the Department including:

1. personal-care skills,
2. basic nursing skills,
3. mental health and social service needs,
4. care of cognitively impaired residents,
5. basic restorative services, and
6. residents' rights.

At the completion of the NATCEP, the trainee will receive a copy of his performance record of major duties and skills taught. The record will consist of, at a minimum, a listing of the duties and skills expected to be learned in the NATCEP, space to record when the trainee performs this duty or skill, spaces to note satisfactory or unsatisfactory performance, and the name of the instructor supervising the performance.

The CEP is a two-part test; the applicant must pass both parts of the examination. The first part is a skills examination that includes a demonstration by the trainee of a minimum of five randomly selected skills drawn from a pool of skills generally performed by nurse aides and listed on the performance record. This pool of skills includes all the personal-care skills listed in the curriculum. The second part is a written or oral examination that includes fifty multiple-choice questions selected from a pool of test items addressing each course requirement in the curriculum. A person who fails may retest twice. After failing the examination three times, the person must complete the training portion of the NATCEP before retesting.

A criminal-conviction check for certain misdemeanor and felony offenses must be completed on nurse aide trainees. The trainee will not be allowed to take or complete the clinical experience portion of the program or the competency evaluation program if the criminal check reveals that a trainee will be permanently barred by law from employment as a nurse aide.

Medication Aides

Generally, medication aides are nurse aides who hold a permit that enables them to administer medication under the authority and direct supervision of a licensed RN or LVN who is either on duty or on call by the employing facility.[30]

There are certain eligibility requirements for medication aides. They must

1. be able to read, write, speak, and understand English;
2. be at least eighteen years of age;
3. be free of communicable diseases and in suitable physical and emotional health to safely administer medications;
4. be a graduate of a high school or have a general equivalency diploma;
5. be currently employed in a facility as a nurse aide or nonlicensed direct-care staff person; and
6. have been employed in a facility for ninety days as a nurse aide or nonlicensed direct-care staff person. This employment must have been completed within the twelve-month period preceding the first official day of the applicant's medication aide training program.

To obtain a medication aide permit, the individual must file an application with the Texas Department of Health (the Department),[31] complete a medication aide training program (unless a waiver or reciprocity is granted), and pass an examination that evaluates the applicant's knowledge of accurate and safe drug therapy. To maintain the license, the medication aide must complete seven clock hours in a continuing education program approved by the Department every year.

The medication aide training program must include at least 140 hours of training: (1) 100 hours of classroom instruction and training; (2) 20 hours of return skills demonstration laboratory; (3) 10 hours of clinical experience, including clinical observation and skills demonstration under the direct supervision of a licensed nurse in a facility; and (4) 10 more hours in the return skills demonstration laboratory in the order above in (1)–(3). The program must last from 60 to 180 days. The program must include, at a minimum, the following instruction and training:

1. Procedures for preparation and administration of medications
2. Responsibility, control, accountability, storage, and safeguarding of medications
3. Use of reference materials
4. Documentation of medications in resident's clinical records, including PRN medications
5. Minimum licensing standards for facilities covering pharmaceutical service, nursing service, and clinical records
6. Federal and state certification standards for participation under Medicare and Medicaid pertaining to pharmaceutical service, nursing service, and clinical records
7. Lines of authority in the facility, including facility personnel who are immediate supervisors
8. Responsibilities and liabilities associated with the administration and safeguarding of medications
9. Allowable and prohibited practices of permit holders in the administration of medication
10. Drug reactions and side effects of medications commonly administered to facility residents
11. Rules covering the medication aide program

A medication aide *may* do the following things:

1. Observe and report to the facility's charge nurse reactions and side effects to medication shown by a resident.
2. Take and record vital signs before the administration of medication that could affect or change the vital signs.
3. Administer regularly prescribed medication that the permit holder has been trained to administer only after personally preparing (setting up) the medication to be administered. The medication aide

must document the administered medication in the record's clinical record.

4. Administer oxygen per nasal cannula or a nonsealing mask only in an emergency. Immediately after the emergency, the permit holder must verbally notify the licensed nurse on duty or on call and appropriately document the action and notification.
5. Apply specifically ordered ophthalmic, otic, nasal, vaginal, and rectal medication.

A medication aide *may not* do the following things:

1. Administer medication by the injection route, which includes intramuscular, intravenous, subcutaneous, intradermal, and hypodermoclysis routes.
2. Administer medication used for intermittent positive pressure breathing (IPPB) treatments or any form of medication inhalation treatments.
3. Administer previously ordered PRN medication unless authorization is obtained from the facility's licensed nurse on duty or on call. If authorization is obtained, permit holders must

    a) document in the resident's records the symptoms indicating the need for the medication and the time the symptoms occurred;
    b) document in the resident's records that the facility's licensed nurse was contacted, symptoms were described, and permission was granted to administer the medication and the time of contact;
    c) obtain permission to administer the medication each time the symptoms occur in the resident; and
    d) ensure that the licensed nurse who gave permission cosigns the resident's record by the end of the nurse's shift or, if the nurse was on call, by the end of the nurse's next tour of duty.

4. Administer the initial dose of a medication that has not been previously administered to a resident. Whether a medication has been previously administered shall be determined by the resident's current clinical records.
5. Calculate a resident's medication doses for administration except that the permit holder may

    a) measure a prescribed amount of a liquid medication to be administered and
    b) break a tablet for administration to a resident provided the licensed nurse on duty or on call has calculated the dosage. The resident's medication card or its equivalent shall accurately

document how the tablet must be altered before it is administered.

6. Crush medication unless authorization is obtained from the licensed nurse on duty or on call. The authorization to crush the specific medication must be documented on the resident's medication card or its equivalent.
7. Administer medications or feedings through a tube inserted in a cavity of the body.
8. Receive or assume responsibility for reducing to writing a verbal or telephone order from a physician, dentist, or podiatrist.
9. Order a resident's medications from a pharmacy.
10. Apply topical medications that involve the treatment of skin that is broken or blistered or when a specified aseptic technique is ordered by the attending physician.
11. Steal, divert, or otherwise misuse medication.
12. Violate any provision of the Health and Safety Code of the medication aide provision.
13. Fraudulently procure or attempt to procure a medication permit.
14. Neglect to administer appropriate medications, as prescribed, in a responsible manner.
15. Administer medications if the person is unable to do so with reasonable skill and safety to residents by reason of drunkenness, excessive use of drugs, narcotics, chemicals, or any other type of material.

Physician Assistants

In Texas, physician assistants (PAs)[32] are persons who have graduated from PA training programs accredited by the Committee on Allied Health Education and Accreditation of the American Medical Association or have passed the examination given by the National Commission on the Certification of PAs and who are licensed as PAs with the TBME. While engaged in professional activities, the PA must wear a name tag identifying the person as a physician assistant.

The TBME regulates PAs. They augment the physician's data-gathering abilities necessary to reach decisions and institute patient-care plans. The PA has no authority to independently supplant the physician in the integration of medical data or in the decision-making process required to establish a final diagnosis and formulate a therapeutic plan. In fact, every physician who wishes to supervise a PA must obtain TBME approval; the supervising physician assumes responsibility and legal liability for the PA's services. Generally, a physician can supervise no more than two full-time PAs.

The supervising physician must continuously supervise the PA, which does not necessarily require the constant physical presence of the supervising physician. A PA may have more than one supervising physician. Telecommunications must always be available. Physician assistants must utilize mechanisms that provide medical authority when such mechanisms are indicated, including but not limited to standing delegation orders, standing medical orders, or protocols.

When supervising physicians delegate medical tasks, PAs must provide medical services within their education, training, and experience. These services include but are not limited to

1. obtaining patient histories and performing physical examinations
2. ordering or performing diagnostic and therapeutic procedures
3. formulating a working diagnosis
4. developing and implementing a treatment plan
5. monitoring the effectiveness of therapeutic interventions
6. assisting at surgery
7. offering counseling and education to meet patient needs
8. making appropriate referrals
9. requesting, receiving, and signing for professional samples and distributing the samples to patients at a site serving medically underserved populations

Lay Midwives

A lay midwife[33] is a person who, having met the requirements of the midwifery board, conducts a normal delivery of a child; gives the necessary supervision, care, and advice to a woman during normal pregnancy, labor, and the postpartum period; and gives newborn care. Lay midwives are neither nurses nor natural childbirth trainers who, although not present at birth, counsel expectant mothers in the techniques of giving birth without artificial or mechanical assistance. Their practice is regulated through the midwifery board and the Texas Board of Health.

A lay midwife can be distinguished from a certified nurse midwife. Certified nurse midwives are RNs who are recognized as advanced nurse practitioners by the TBNE and are certified by the American College of Nurse-Midwives. As nurses they can perform tasks delegated by physicians. They also have the authority to watch for and recognize abnormal symptoms of pregnancy.[34]

Lay midwives, after successfully lobbying the Texas legislature, are now called "midwives" instead of the previous title of "lay midwives." In this book, however, midwives will be called "lay midwives" to avoid confusing them with certified nurse midwives.

EDUCATION. Historically there were no mandatory educational courses or continuing education (CE) requirements for a lay midwife (LM). Effective September 1, 1992, however, an LM, at the time of her initial documentation, must have taken the mandatory basic midwifery education course. An LM training course, which is approved by the Texas Department of Health (the Department), may be offered by a local health department, an accredited postsecondary educational institution, an adult education program, or any other entity approved by the Texas Board of Health.

The LM training course shall be taught in Spanish if that is the only language a participant understands. If other students do not understand Spanish, the course will then be taught in English and Spanish.

Applicants will receive a letter of documentation from the Department when they fulfill the educational requirements.

Basic information manuals and instructor manuals are provided by the midwifery board to any person who requests them. The manual must include at least the following information: (1) the knowledge necessary to practice as an LM, (2) the basic education and CE requirements for an LM, (3) legal requirements and procedures pertaining to midwifery, and (4) standards of practice for an LM. The fee for the manual, which is available in English and Spanish, may not be greater than ten dollars.

DOCUMENTATION. Before individuals can practice as LMs in Texas, they must first fulfill documentation requirements. They must provide satisfactory evidence to the Department midwifery program coordinator that they (1) are trained to perform newborn screening tests or that they have made arrangements for those tests, (2) hold a current certificate issued by the American Heart Association in basic life-support cardiopulmonary resuscitation (CPR) for adults and children, and (3) have met all the requirements for the mandatory basic midwifery education course.

Each person who practices midwifery must apply to the Department annually to be documented as an LM. The completed application must be accompanied with a nonrefundable fee. There is a sixty-day grace period for late registrations, but a late filing fee may be charged.

With this identifying information, the Department will keep a roster of all LMs.

DISCLOSURE REQUIREMENT. Each LM must disclose in oral and written form to a prospective client the limitations of the skills and practices of an LM. The disclosure shall include the following information:

1. statistics of the LM's experience as a midwife;
2. the date of the expiration of the LM's documentation;

3. the date of the expiration of the LM's CPR certification;
4. the LM's compliance with CE requirements;
5. medical backup arrangements;
6. the LM's legal requirements, including statements concerning newborn blood screening, ophthalmia neonatorum prevention, and prohibited acts; and
7. a statement that state law requires every newborn child to be tested for certain heritable diseases[35] and hypothyroidism.

The LM must disclose if she is approved to collect blood specimens that are to be used in the performance of tests. If she is not approved, she must inform the client of her duty to refer the client to an appropriate health care facility or physician for the collection of the specimens.

The midwifery board will prescribe the disclosure form that will be used. The written disclosure may not be more than five hundred words and must be in English and Spanish. Additionally, the LM must disclose to a prospective or actual client the procedure for reporting complaints to the Department.

The LM must encourage a client to seek prenatal care. Also, if the LM recognizes a sign or symptom of a childbirth complication, she must encourage the client to seek medical care.

PROHIBITED ACTS. An LM may not do the following things:

1. except for a prophylaxis approved by the Department to prevent ophthalmia neonatorum, administer a prescription drug to a client except under the supervision of a licensed physician in accordance with the laws of Texas;
2. use forceps or surgical instruments for any procedure other than cutting the umbilical cord or providing emergency first aid during a delivery;
3. remove placenta by invasive techniques;
4. advance or retard labor or delivery by using medicines or mechanical devices;
5. use in connection with her name a title, abbreviation, or any designation tending to imply that she is a "registered" or "certified" midwife as opposed to a lay midwife;
6. assist at an other than normal childbirth except in an emergency situation that poses an immediate threat to the life of the mother or newborn;
7. advertise or otherwise represent that the LM is a physician or a graduate of a medical school;
8. use in combination with the term "midwife" the term "nurse" or other titles, initials, or other designations that imply the midwife is an RN or an LVN; or

9. make a false statement or record false information on a birth certificate.

Municipalities can adopt local ordinances that further regulate LM practice.

PENALTIES. An LM commits a class C misdemeanor if she knowingly or intentionally (1) practices as an LM without the proper documentation, (2) commits a prohibited act, (3) fails to comply with the disclosure requirement, or (4) fails to comply with requirements relating to the collection of blood specimens for the screening of newborns.

Additionally, if an LM intentionally or knowingly falsifies a birth certificate document, she commits a third-degree felony.

Civil penalties may be taxed against an LM for prohibited acts, also. The Texas attorney general or a district, county, or city attorney may seek an injunction against an LM to restrain the LM from violating the Midwifery Act if the violation creates an immediate threat to the health and safety of the public. Also, a penalty of up to $250 per each day of the violation may be assessed.

NEWBORN SCREENING. Each LM shall perform blood-screening tests for phenylketonuria, hypothyroidism, and other heritable diseases according to chapter 33 of the Health and Safety Code; other heritable diseases include galactosemia, sickling hemoglobinopathies, and congenital adrenal hyperplasia.[36] The LM may draw the blood specimen herself if the Department approves her. If the LM is not approved, she must refer her client and newborn to an appropriate health care facility or physician for testing. Once approved by the Department, an LM does not practice medicine by drawing blood.

If the blood tests are abnormal, the Department will notify the LM. If the screening test indicates that the newborn is at high risk, the Department shall recommend that the newborn be placed under the care of a licensed physician for diagnosis and will provide the name of a consulting pediatric specialist in the newborn's geographic area. The Department, the health authority, and the consulting pediatric specialist may follow up a positive test with the parents of the newborn since the child was not attended by a physician at birth.[37]

The Department, local health departments, public health districts, and local health units owned, operated, or leased by a political subdivision of Texas must provide clinical and laboratory support services to pregnant women and their newborns who are clients of LMs. The support services to be provided include prenatal, postpartum, and child health care and family planning. A woman and her newborn may not be denied services because of an inability to pay.

SYPHILIS SCREENING. An LM is entitled to attend a woman during her normal pregnancy, labor, and postpartum period. Consequently, if she is attending a woman during her prenatal or postnatal period, the LM must submit or cause to be submitted the syphilis blood examinations according to the provisions of chapter 81 of the Health and Safety Code. These provisions are explored more fully in Chapter 4, "Advanced Nurse Practitioners."

4

Advanced Nurse Practitioners

In Texas, advanced nurse practitioners (ANPs) are professional registered nurses who have additional training and education in a practice area that prepares them for advanced nursing practice. Although ANPs can perform nursing functions without the supervision of physicians, accreditation as an ANP by the Texas Board of Nurse Examiners is not a license to practice medicine. Consequently, the ANP cannot independently perform medical functions, such as diagnosing illnesses and prescribing treatments; physicians still must delegate medical acts to ANPs and supervise the implementation. Because of their additional training, however, ANPs can perform delegated medical tasks with less supervision.

ADVANCED NURSE PRACTITIONER DEFINED

The Texas Board of Nurse Examiners (TBNE) defines the advanced nurse practitioner (ANP) as a currently licensed registered professional nurse in Texas who is prepared for advanced nursing practice because of an advanced educational program of study. The ANP is prepared to practice in an expanded role to deliver health care services either independently or in collaboration with other health care professionals.[1]

Four categories of ANPs are generally recognized in Texas: (1) nurse anesthetist, (2) nurse midwife, (3) nurse practitioner, and (4) clinical nurse specialist. An ANP who wishes to use another title must first get approval from the TBNE. Also, any subcategory title must be approved by the TBNE.[2] For example, if a nurse wants to refer to himself as a pediatric nurse anesthetist, the pediatric subcategory would have to be approved by the TBNE.

The TBNE has ruled that an ANP "shall wear a name tag which identifies her or him as a registered nurse and the appropriate category of approval."[3]

CREDENTIALING

Before a registered nurse (RN) can hold herself out as being an ANP or can use titles that so imply, she must have her credentials approved by the TBNE. To be credentialed as an ANP in Texas,[4] the applicant must be a qualified Texas RN and have the appropriate educational training. The educational training should be appropriate to the practice area and at least one academic year in length at the certificate or master's degree level; it may include a formal preceptorship. The ANP program of study should be accredited by the TBNE. If the ANP program is not accredited, the program must meet certain requirements adopted by the TBNE.

To have credentials approved, an RN must submit evidence necessary to ensure compliance with the educational requirements. This evidence may include but is not limited to (1) current registration as an RN in Texas, (2) a transcript and a course description from the ANP program of study, (3) evidence of current certification in the area of practice by a national or state organization approved by the TBNE,[5] and (4) a nonrefundable credentialing fee that is currently twenty-five dollars.

If a nurse attended an ANP program outside Texas, the program must meet certain educational requirements and should be approved by the appropriate licensing body in that state or be accredited by a national accrediting body recognized by the TBNE.

A nurse can be credentialed in more than one ANP category but must submit a separate application and fee for each category. Additionally, the nurse must have completed additional education in the desired area of approval in an approved program.

> *Example 4.1: An RN has submitted her ANP credentialing application and fee but her job as an ANP is supposed to start next week. What should the nurse do?*
>
> *Answer: The nurse should apply for interim approval.*

An RN cannot hold herself out to be an ANP or use titles that so imply until her credentials have been approved by the TBNE. The TBNE, however, may grant interim approval for a period not to exceed thirty days while the application is pending. To apply for interim approval, the nurse must submit to the TBNE an affidavit swearing that she meets all the ANP requirements and that she has completed and mailed the application to the appropriate educational program; an appropriate individual associated with the program will then complete the back page of the application. The nurse is eligible for interim approval only once. The TBNE will send a letter to the nurse if the TBNE grants ANP interim approval.

Example 4.2: An ANP just realized that his license was granted three years ago and that he has not renewed his license. What is the status of his license?

Answer: His license is expired. He can reinstate his ANP license by reinstating his RN license, submitting a completed recredentialing form, and paying the recredentialing fee to the TBNE.

An ANP must be recredentialed every two years in conjunction with renewing her RN license. If she does not renew her RN license or does not complete and send in the required recredentialing form and payment, then the TBNE's approval of the RN as an ANP shall expire.

If the ANP status has lapsed within four years, a nurse may reinstate her ANP status by sending the completed recredentialing form and fee to the TBNE. If the ANP status has lapsed for four years or more, then the nurse must reinstate her RN license and reapply for credentialing; she must meet the *current* requirements for credentialing approval.

SCOPE OF PRACTICE

Generally

The ANP's scope of practice can be gleaned from a variety of state laws.

The TBNE has adopted some rules concerning ANPs.[6] It has stated broadly that an ANP "provides a broad range of personal health services, the scope of which shall be based upon educational preparation, continued experience, and the accepted scope of professional practice of the particular specialty area."[7] In describing an ANP's function, the TBNE states that the ANP "acts *independently* or in collaboration with the health care team in the observation, assessment, *diagnosis,* intervention, evaluation, rehabilitation, care and counsel, and health teachings of persons who are ill, injured, or infirm or experiencing changes in normal health processes; and in the promotion and maintenance of health or prevention of illness."[8]

Does this description mean that an ANP can diagnose illness independently? An ANP is an RN with specialized training in a certain practice area. The ANP's scope of practice must be authorized by the Nursing Practice Act and other applicable state laws.[9] The Nursing Practice Act's definition of nursing does not include the diagnosis of disease. In fact, the statute states that the definition of nursing "shall not be deemed to include acts of medical diagnosis or prescription of therapeutic or corrective measures."[10] Practicing medicine has been defined as diagnosing, treating, or offering to treat any disease, disorder, deformity, or injury.[11] Consequently, there is no statute that gives ANPs or any nurse the authority to independently diagnose the ill, injured, or infirm or independently prescribe a medical treatment. Therefore, the TBNE's definition of ANPs should not be read as giving ANPs the authority to independently diagnose patients or to independently prescribe medical treatment. An ANP's observation and assessment may aid the physician with his diagnosis and choice for a treatment modality; the nurse, under a physician's supervision, may then carry out the resulting physician's order.[12]

Generally, a physician can delegate a medical act to any qualified and properly trained person acting under the physician's supervision if the act can be properly and safely performed in its customary manner.[13] Because an ANP has received further training and education, a physician should be able to delegate more medical tasks to an ANP than could be delegated to a general RN. Also, decreased instruction and supervision by a physician will be needed with delegated medical functions for which the ANP has been properly trained.[14]

The Texas Board of Medical Examiners (TBME) has the authority to determine when and how physicians may delegate medical acts to nurses.[15] The TBNE regulates when and how nurses may accept responsibility for medical tasks delegated to nurses by physicians.

The TBNE has ruled that ANPs must utilize mechanisms that provide medical authority when such mechanisms are indicated. These mechanisms may include but are not limited to protocols, policies, or other orders. This provision shall not be construed as requiring authority for nursing aspects of care. The protocols and policies should be (1) jointly developed by the ANP and the appropriate physicians, (2) signed by both the nurse and physicians, and (3) reviewed at least annually. The scope and detail of the protocols and policies may vary in relation to the complexity of the situations covered and the area of practice and educational preparation of the individual ANP.[16]

The Texas attorney general has ruled specifically how an ANP may function in a finite number of situations. An ANP *may* (1) take a patient's medical history and perform a physical examination if she is educated in these procedures; (2) note health status and deviations from normal within the limits of her educational preparation; and (3) perform simple laboratory tests under a physician's orders but should not diagnose an illness from the test; instead she must report the result to the physician who will then make the diagnosis. An ANP *may not* (1) generally provide medications to patients under standing and written orders unless the physician has prescribed them for an individual patient and (2) diagnose a patient's disease.[17]

Medically Underserved Populations

An ANP will have potentially greater authority to perform medically delegated tasks with less physician supervision in medically underserved populations. These tasks include carrying out presigned prescription drug orders and diagnosing and treating patients according to protocols.

The Medical Practice Act states that "[a]t a site serving a *medically underserved population,* a [licensed] physician . . . shall be authorized to delegate to a registered nurse or physician assistant acting under adequate physician supervision, the act or acts of administering, providing, or *carrying out a prescription drug order* . . . through physician's orders, standing medical orders, standing delegation orders, or other orders or protocols as defined by the [Texas Board of Medical Examiners]."[18]

MEDICALLY UNDERSERVED POPULATION DEFINED. A site serving a medically underserved population means a site that is located in either (1) a medically underserved area;[19] (2) a health manpower shortage area;[20] (3) a clinic designated as a rural health clinic under the Rural Health Clinic Services Act;[21] (4) a public health clinic or a family planning clinic under contract with the Texas Department of Human Services or the Texas Department of Health; (5) a site located in an area in which the Texas Department of Health determines there exists an insufficient number of physicians providing services to eligible clients of federal, state, or locally funded health care programs; or (6) a site the Texas Department of Health determines serves a disproportionate number of clients eligible to participate in federal, state, or locally funded health care programs.[22]

CARRYING OUT A PRESCRIPTION DRUG ORDER. The Medical Practice Act defines "carrying out a prescription drug order" as completing a prescription drug order that is presigned by the delegating physician by providing the following information: (1) the patient's name and address; (2) the drug and dosage to be dispensed; (3) directions to the patient for taking the drug; (4) the name, address, and telephone number of the physician; (5) the name, address, and telephone and identification numbers of the RN completing the prescription drug order; (6) the date; and (7) the number of refills permitted.[23]

The RN who carries out the prescription drug order must be recognized by the TBNE as having specialized education and training, including pharmacology, to carry out such an order.[24]

GUIDELINES. The TBME has been given authority to adopt additional methods to carry into effect, or put into force, a physician's prescription under a physician's orders, standing medical orders, standing delegation orders, or other orders or protocols.[25] The TBME has exercised this authority by adopting minimum standards for the supervision of RNs so that they can diagnose and prescribe treatment in medically underserved populations according to protocols.[26]

Supervision of Registered Nurses.[27]

Example 4.3: An ANP is interviewing for a job at a clinic in a medically underserved area. The ANP asks the supervising physician how many clinics she supervises. The physician answers that she supervises two busy clinics. If the ANP accepts the job, will he be adequately supervised?

Answer: It depends on how many combined business hours per week the clinics log. If the combined business hours equal more than eighty hours per week, the physician must have approval from the TBME.

A physician may not supervise more than three clinics without the approval of the TBME. Also, a physician may not supervise any number of clinics with combined regular business hours in excess of eighty hours per week without the approval of the TBME.

Example 4.4: The ANP next asks the supervising physician how often she visits the clinics and for what reasons. The physician answers that she visits whenever she needs to supervise the care of patients, which tends to be at least once a week. If the ANP accepts the job, will he be adequately supervised?

Answer: Maybe. The supervising physician must visit the clinic in person at least once a week during regular business hours. Also, during visits, the physician must not only supervise the care of patients but also must be involved in a quality assurance plan.

The delegating physician must visit the clinic in person at least once a week during regular business hours to observe and to provide medical direction and consultation. The observation and consultation must at least include (1) reviewing with the ANP the case histories of patients with problems or complications that are not covered by protocol; (2) personally diagnosing or treating patients who require physician follow-up; and (3) verifying that patient care is provided by the clinic in accordance with a written quality assurance plan on file at the clinic, including randomly reviewing and countersigning at least 10 percent of patient charts.

Additionally, the physician's supervision must be documented through a log that is kept at the clinic. The log must include (1) the names or identification numbers of patients who are discussed during daily status reports; (2) the times when the physician is on site; (3) a summary of what the physician did while on site; and (4) a description of the quality assurance activities that were conducted, including the names of any patients who were seen or whose case histories were reviewed with the nurse. The supervising physician shall sign each log at the conclusion of each site visit.

Example 4.5: During the interview, the physician states that she is available by cellular phone for emergencies at any time. Will the ANP be adequately supervised?

Answer: Maybe. The ANP would be adequately supervised for emergencies, but the physician must also receive daily status reports.

The delegating physician must be available by telephone or direct telecommunications for consultation, assistance with medical emergencies, or patient referrals at all times that the clinic is open. Additionally, the physician must receive daily status reports, to be conveyed in person, by telephone, or by radio, from the ANP on any complication or problem encountered that is not covered by protocol.

Example 4.6: The ANP feels comfortable that he will be supervised adequately, so he accepts the job. Then the physician states that she will be going on vacation for two weeks. Will the ANP be supervised adequately?

Answer: Maybe. The vacationing physician must make arrangements for another physician to supervise the ANP. The substitute physician must be familiar with the protocols of the clinic.

If a delegating physician is unavailable to supervise an ANP, arrangements must be made for another physician to provide supervision. The substitute physician must affirm in writing that he is familiar with the protocols or standing delegation orders in use at the clinic and is accountable for adequately supervising the care that is provided.

It is possible to get special exceptions from the TBME for (1) the percentage of charts that are to be reviewed, (2) the limitation on the number of clinics supervised, or (3) the limitation on the number of working hours. The request must state the special circumstances and needs prompting the exception, the names and locations of the clinics and hours to be supervised, and the plan for supervision. If the TBME grants the exception, it shall state the percentage of charts that must be reviewed and the number of clinics or combined clinic hours that can be supervised.

Prescribing Medications. At sites serving medically underserved populations, an ANP may use prescriptions that are presigned by a supervising physician according to protocols.[28] Such protocols may authorize the diagnosis of a patient's condition and treatment, including a prescription for dangerous drugs; no prescriptions for controlled substances may be authorized or issued, however.

The proper use of protocols requires the integration of clinical data that is gathered by an ANP by means of the supervising physician's preexisting written plan for determining a diagnosis and appropriate treatment. This authority, however, does not authorize the exercise of independent medical judgment by ANPs. The supervising physician will remain responsible to the TBME and to his patients for acts performed under his delegated authority. Additionally, the ANP remains professionally responsible for her actions that are performed under the scope and authority of her own license.

The delegating physician is responsible for devising and enforcing a system to account for and monitor the use of presigned prescriptions. When the physician authorizes an ANP to complete and issue a presigned prescription, the prescription form must comply with the rules adopted by the Texas State Board of Pharmacy. The delegating physician must maintain at his usual place of business a list of ANPs who are authorized to carry out prescription drug orders. At the pharmacist's request, the physician must provide the pharmacist with a copy of the physician's written authorization for the ANPs.[29]

Advanced nurse practitioners can telephonically prescribe medication for a patient to a pharmacy if the delegating physician authorizes this method in writing. This authority must be maintained in the usual place of business and available for inspection.[30]

> *Example 4.7: According to protocol, a patient needs a prescription drug. The patient, however, can afford only a generic drug. What should the ANP do?*
>
> *Answer: The protocol should answer when and under what circumstances a generic drug can be substituted.*

A prescription has two signature lines: one is printed "PRODUCT SELECTION PERMITTED," whereas the other says "DISPENSE AS WRITTEN." The physician must communicate dispensing instructions to the pharmacist by signing on the appropriate line. Generally, if the practitioner's signature does not clearly indicate that the prescription must be dispensed as written, generically equivalent drug selection is permitted.[31] If the physician proposes to authorize a generic substitution through protocol, however, the protocol shall provide direction to the ANP whether and under what circumstances product selection will be permitted by the pharmacist.[32] No prescription form can contain a preprinted order for a drug product by the brand name, generic name, or manufacturer's name.[33]

A practitioner physician must maintain a record of each acquisition and disposal of a dangerous drug for two years after the date of acquisition or disposal.[34] For a first-time conviction, the practitioner commits a class B misdemeanor if records are not maintained in the manner they are supposed to be maintained.[35] The dangerous-drug records must be available for inspection and copying by the Department of Public Safety at all reasonable hours. Additionally, the Department of Public Safety has the authority to inventory all stocks of dangerous drugs that are on hand.[36]

If a physician violates the TBME rules on delegating acts to ANPs, the physician's authority to supervise ANPs can be canceled. Also, the physician can be subject to disciplinary action by the TBME. If an ANP violates these rules, the TBME shall promptly notify the TBNE of the violation.[37] Consequently, the nurse could be subject to disciplinary action by the TBNE.[38]

NURSING NEGLIGENCE

If an ANP is sued for nursing negligence, her conduct will be judged against what a reasonable and prudent nurse would have done under the same or similar circumstances.[39] Because an ANP is a nurse specialist, she can expect to be held to a higher standard of care than a general nurse is held.[40] Consequently, the standard to which the ANP will likely be held is what a reasonable and prudent ANP in her area of practice would have done under the same or similar circumstances.

If an ANP practices outside the bounds of the Nursing Practice Act and is found to have practiced medicine, if she is sued under a negligence cause of action, she may be judged against a reasonable and prudent physician standard.[41]

NURSE MIDWIVES

In Texas, the act of delivering a baby in an uncomplicated pregnancy is not the practice of medicine. It could become the practice of medicine, however, if the patient has a disease, disorder, deformity, or injury that requires the services of a physician.[42]

The Texas attorney general has answered some questions about the range of services a nurse midwife may provide without engaging in the practice of medicine. A nurse midwife *may* (1) perform and repair an episiotomy or suture lacerations if these services are generally performed in connection with normal childbirth and (2) dispense a controlled substance if the nurse midwife is the agent or an employee of a registered physician or a hospital. A nurse midwife *may not* diagnose a disease or obstetrical complication.[43]

Disease Prevention and Detection

Texas law may impose duties for disease prevention and detection on the nurse midwife.

SYPHILIS. A pregnant woman must have her blood tested for syphilis during her first examination and visit. The test for syphilis must be a "standard serologic test" that is submitted to a laboratory. The physician or person who is attending the woman must keep the laboratory report for nine months and must deliver the report to any successor.

Additionally, a blood sample for syphilis testing must be obtained within twenty-four hours of delivery; the sample of blood can be taken from the mother or from the umbilical cord of the infant. Once again, the blood must be submitted for a "standard serologic test."

The prenatal syphilis blood sample must be submitted by "[a] physician or other person permitted by law to attend a pregnant woman during gestation or at delivery of an infant." The postnatal syphilis blood sample must be submitted by a "physician or other person in attendance at a delivery."[44] Considering the scope of an ANP's practice, generally this task should be delegated to a nurse by a physician. If, however, the ANP is practicing in a medically underserved population, the ANP could submit the blood sample via a protocol.

OPHTHALMIA NEONATORUM. A nurse or midwife in attendance at childbirth shall use or cause to be used a prophylaxis approved by the Texas Board of Health to prevent ophthalmia neonatorum.[45] The midwife is responsible for the administration of the prophylaxis to each infant she delivers by either administering the prophylaxis under standing delegation orders issued by a licensed physician or requiring it to be administered by an appropriately licensed and trained individual under standing delegation orders issued by a licensed physician. If a physician is not available to issue a standing delegation order or if no physician will agree to issue a standing delegation order, a midwife shall administer or cause to be administered the prophylaxis by an appropriately trained and licensed individual approved by the Texas Board of Health.

The proper administration and possession by a midwife of the prophylaxis does not violate the Texas Dangerous Drug Act. The nurse or midwife in attendance at the delivery who fails to give the prophylaxis commits a class B misdemeanor.

A free prophylaxis may be available from the Texas Department of Health if the newborn's financially responsible adult is unable to pay.[46] Subsequently, the health care provider may not charge the mother for the free prophylaxis.

NEWBORN SCREENING. When not assisted by a physician at delivery of the newborn, the nurse midwife must perform blood-screening tests[47] for phenylketonuria, hypothyroidism, and other heritable diseases; "other heritable diseases" includes galactosemia, sickling hemoglobinopathies, and congenital adrenal hyperplasia.[48] The tests must be performed by a laboratory either established or approved by the Texas Department of Health.

If the newborn's parents, managing conservator, or guardian, because of any religious tenets or practices of an organized church of which any of them are adherents, objects to the blood tests, the tests may not be administered. Consequently, the nurse midwife who is not assisted by a physician must enter the objection of the parents, managing conservator, or guardian into the newborn's medical record and have them sign it. The nurse midwife will not be held liable or responsible for the failure of the parents, managing conservator, or guardian to consent to the tests. If a screening test result is abnormal, the Texas Department of Health shall provide the test result to the person who submitted the test.

Birth Certificates

A physician, midwife, or person acting as a midwife, in attendance at birth must file a birth certificate no later than the fifth day after the date of birth; it must be filed with the local registrar of the registration district in which the birth occurs.[49] If the birth occurs in a hospital or birthing center, the hospital administrator, the birthing center administrator, or a designee of the appropriate administrator may file the birth certificate in lieu of the attending physician, midwife, or person acting as a midwife.

The birth certificate item relating to the child's father shall be completed only if

1. the child's mother was married to the father at the time of the child's conception, at the time of the child's birth, or after the child's birth;
2. paternity is established by order of a court of competent jurisdiction; or
3. the father signed the birth certificate or consented in writing, on a form prescribed by the Texas Department of Health, to be named as the father of the child on the child's birth certificate.[50]

If the items relating to the child's father are not completed on a birth certificate filed with the state registrar, the state registrar must notify the attorney general.[51] Alternatively, when the paternity consent forms are signed, the local registrar must transmit them to the state registrar, who must transmit them to the attorney general, who can use the forms for any purpose connected with the provision of child-support services.[52]

The "For Medical and Health Use Only" section of the birth certificate is not part of the legal birth certificate. Consequently, the information in that section is confidential and may not be released or made public; its only use is for anonymous statistics. The Social Security numbers and signatures of the parents are also not part of the legal birth certificate. Therefore, they may not be used or disseminated for any purpose other than to establish and enforce child-support orders.[53]

When a nurse does not have a duty to file the birth certificate, she may be asked by the local registrar to submit information necessary to complete the birth certificate when the person filing it could not obtain the information through a diligent inquiry. The nurse must then answer correctly to the best of her knowledge. Additionally, she may be required to verify her statements by signing them.[54]

It is a third-degree felony for a nurse to do the following things:

1. intentionally or knowingly make a false statement or direct another person to make a false statement on a birth certificate;
2. intentionally or knowingly supply false information or create a false record or direct another to do these things for use in preparing a birth certificate;
3. without lawful authority and with the intent to deceive, make, counterfeit, alter, amend, or mutilate or direct another to do these things to a birth certificate;
4. for purposes of deception, intentionally or knowingly obtain, possess, use, sell, or furnish to another (or direct or attempt to direct another to commit these acts) a birth certificate that is made, counterfeited, altered, amended, or mutilated without lawful authority or is false in whole or in part or relates to the birth of another individual, whether living or deceased; or
5. intentionally or knowingly fraudulently identifies herself to obtain or return a birth certificate.[55]

If a nurse is convicted, the court will order as a condition of probation that the nurse can never again obtain a birth certificate and cannot practice midwifery; a condition of parole will be that the nurse can never again obtain a birth certificate.[56]

It is a class C misdemeanor for a nurse to (1) refuse or fail to furnish correctly any information in her possession affecting the birth certificate or (2) fail, neglect, or refuse to fill out the birth certificate and file it with the local registrar or deliver it on request to the person with the duty to file it as required by statute.[57]

DEATH CERTIFICATES

Statutory duties concerning death certificates may be imposed on some ANPs, especially those working at sites serving medically underserved populations. Accordingly, these nurses should follow their protocols when dealing with patients who have died. These protocols should reflect the following requirements.

The physician who was in attendance when the death occurred must provide medical certification for the death certificate within ten days after the death.[58]

The person in attendance at a fetal death (stillbirth) must provide the medical certification for the fetal death certificate;[59] a fetal death certificate is required when the fetus is at least twenty weeks of gestation.[60]

Sudden Infant Death Syndrome (SIDS) is recognized in Texas as a primary cause of death for death certificate purposes.[61] In Texas, the death of a child younger than two years of age must be reported immediately to the proper authorities if the child dies suddenly or is found dead and the cause of death is unknown.[62] In counties that do not have a medical examiner's office, an inquest must be held by the justice of the peace if an infant who is younger than eighteen months of age is suspected of dying from SIDS.[63]

A nurse who suspects that a child died from abuse or neglect must report this belief, within forty-eight hours, to the Texas Department of Protective and Regulatory Services; any local or state law enforcement agency; the state agency that operates, licenses, certifies, or registers the facility in which the alleged abuse or neglect occurred; or the agency designated by the court that was to be responsible for the protection of the child. The report can be oral but must be followed up within five days in writing. All reports are confidential, and there is immunity from civil and criminal liability for persons reporting in good faith.[64]

If a person had a certain communicable disease at death, the person's body (preferably a great toe) should be tagged with the message "Communicable Disease—Blood/Body Fluid Precautions Required" along with the patient's name. The tag should be on card-stock paper no smaller than five centimeters by ten centimeters; the letters cannot be smaller than six millimeters in height. Patients' diseases that require this tagging are AIDS, anthrax, brucellosis, Creutzfeldt-Jakob disease, viral hepatitis (types B, C, and D), HIV infection, plague, Q fever, rabies, Rocky Mountain spotted fever, syphilis, tuberculosis, tularemia, and viral hemorrhagic fevers.[65]

5

Nursing Negligence Insurance

Insurance is a vehicle for redistributing risk. By purchasing professional liability insurance, a nurse can transfer the financial risk to her insurance company if she makes a professional mistake that injures a patient. The transfer of risk is not complete, necessarily. First, the insurance policy limit must be high enough to compensate fully a patient for his injury. Second, the nurse and her injurious act must fall under the policy's provisions.

THE INSURANCE CONTRACT

A contract is established between the nurse and the insurance company when the nurse purchases professional liability insurance: the nurse promises to pay an insurance premium in exchange for the insurance company's agreement to assume a defined amount of financial risk if a nurse is sued for damages by her patient. There are three parts to the insurance contract: (1) the insuring agreement, (2) the contract conditions, and (3) the exclusionary clauses.[1] Because insurance contracts may vary, the nurse should read the contract before purchasing insurance or before relying on another person's policy (no matter how boring it is). Additionally, the nurse should seek clarification of terms or conditions that remain unclear.

Insuring Agreement

Most insurance policies state that they will pay for the defense of any suit seeking "damages" and will pay damages up to the policy limits through settlement or as awarded as a judgment. If a suit is filed against a nurse solely to enjoin her from the unlawful practice of medicine (injunctive relief), the insurance company will not pay for her defense. If the suit is for damages, the insurance company will hire an attorney and pay the attorney's fees, the costs of preparing for trial, and any court costs.[2]

Contract Conditions

The second part of the insurance contract sets forth the rights and obligations of the insurance company and the nurse. A nurse's failure to uphold an obligation or to protect a right may result in a breach of contract, which means that the nurse has no insurance coverage.[3]

Most insurance contracts demand that a nurse report, either orally or in writing, an unexpected incident or unusual happening, threats of litigation made by the patient or family, and any legal papers or letters from an attorney.[4] The nurse should use her professional judgment in deciding what to report to the insurance company, although it is better to err on the side of caution by reporting claims that never result in a lawsuit. Subject to the dictates of the insurance contract, the nurse should report generally any occurrence for which nursing judgment could be questioned, bad outcomes resulting from professional nursing services, and any complaints from patients about the nurse to the health care institution's administration.[5]

A nurse must also assist in the defense of the claim. This duty includes the right to participate in discovery and trial and to avoid jeopardizing the defense.

Most insurance contracts specify that the insurance company gets to select the attorney. If for some reason a nurse is not happy with the assigned attorney, the nurse should inform the insurance company in writing. If the insurance company does not hire a new attorney and the problem has not been addressed, the nurse should confer with her professional nursing organization or seek the advice of an independent attorney.[6] Additionally, the insurance company generally retains the right of full control of the defense of the case and the right to authorize settlement.

Policy Exclusions

Most nursing negligence policies will exclude the following from coverage: criminal acts, gross negligence, intentional torts, punitive damages, acts outside the scope of nursing practice (unlawful practice of medicine), and injuries induced by a drug- or alcohol-impaired nurse. The insurance company may defend the nurse against these charges, but if he is found guilty, he will be required to reimburse the insurance carrier for all legal fees, expenses, judgment, and court costs.

The law recognizes an inherent conflict of interest in this triangle since the insurance company pays the attorney, who is supposed to represent zealously a nurse's interest. Texas law dictates that if a conflict of interest arises, the attorney is supposed to put the nurse's interest above that of the insurance company. If the conflict cannot be resolved, however, the nurse may have to hire an attorney at her own expense to represent her interest.

A problem can arise, also, if the insurance policy limits are not high enough to compensate fully the injured patient (excess verdict). If the insurance company expects that there may be an excess verdict, it should counsel the nurse to hire his own attorney to represent his interest for the amount over the policy limits. The insurance company in Texas, however, has a duty to try to settle the case within policy limits if, through its contract with the nurse, it retains complete control over the defense and the right to authorize settlement. If the insurance company breaches its duty and an excess verdict results, the nurse has a cause of action against the insurance company for the excess verdict.[7] Frequently in Texas the nurse will assign her right to sue to the plaintiff, who will sue the insurance company for the judgment above the insurance policy limit.

TYPES OF INSURANCE

Claims-Made versus Occurrence

There are two types of insurance policies: claims-made and occurrence.[8] *Claims-made* policies will cover patient claims against nurses that are reported while the policy is in force. An *occurrence* policy will cover a nurse for acts or omissions that occurred during the contract's policy period, even if the claim is not reported until after the contract is through.

> *Example 5.1: A nurse has a claims-made policy. Before the nurse had the policy, she had no insurance even though she was a practicing nurse. She was just sued by a patient for an incident that happened before the nurse had insurance. Her claims-made policy will cover her.*

> *Example 5.2: A nurse has an occurrence policy. Six months later he cancels the policy because he thinks it is too expensive. He does not purchase more insurance. One year after canceling his insurance he is sued by a patient for an act that he allegedly performed while the occurrence policy was in force. He is covered by the occurrence policy.*

A nurse who switches from a claims-made policy to an occurrence policy must buy what is called "tail" insurance if future claims are brought by a patient for the nurse's actions that occurred when the claims-made policy was in force. Most institutional medical malpractice policies are written on a claims-made basis. Therefore, a nurse who relies on the institution's policy probably will need to purchase tail coverage on leaving employment.

Individual versus Institutional Policy

Professional liability insurance policies can be purchased either by individual nurses or by health care institutions.

An *individual policy* is purchased in the name of, and premiums are paid by, the nurse. Except for any policy exclusions, the insurance policy will cover the nurse for specifically defined professional acts that are performed at any time and any place that are within the scope of nursing practice. An *institutional policy*, however, is purchased by and in the name of a health care institution. A nurse may also be an "additional insured" under the policy, but she will have limited policy rights. For instance, a nurse will be covered only for acts within the scope of nursing practice and within the scope of employment. Additionally, she may not have a right to a separate defense, that is, separate counsel assigned to the nurse if she is sued. Consequently, if a conflict were to arise between the defense of the hospital's interest versus the nurse's interest, the nurse would have to hire her own attorney at her own expense, which may become quite costly.

A *group insurance policy* is a type of institutional policy that partnerships and professional corporations buy frequently. These policies do not typically cover nurse employees as "additional insureds" without a specific endorsement by the nurse's name.

Before a nurse relies on an institutional policy, she must investigate through her employer and possibly the insurance carrier whether she is covered by the policy and, if so, what her rights are under the policy.

SHOULD NURSES CARRY INSURANCE?

The American Association of Nurse Attorneys (TAANA) has taken the position that all professional nurses engaged in the practice of nursing *should be insured* against liabilities to third parties arising out of the nurses' professional practice,[9] and TAANA reasons that the public expects professionals to remedy the harm they cause through their errors; insurance creates a fund that can satisfy that expectation. It is also TAANA's policy position that picking insurance should be an informed decision based on the following factors: nature of the nurse's practice, impact of prevailing state and federal laws on the nurse's exposure to loss, and the reasonableness of the options available.

No law requires Texas nurses to carry professional liability insurance. The Texas nurse should consider the following factors, however, when making an informed choice about whether to purchase professional liability insurance.

Nature of Nurse's Practice

Some studies have shown the following areas as more risky for suit: maternity-obstetrics, intensive care (neonatal, pediatric, adult), and hospital-based medical-surgical nursing.[10]

A nurse's area of practice is also relevant when a nurse picks a policy limit if liability coverage is purchased. For instance, a pediatric patient who sustains permanent injury from a nurse's negligent act or omission will likely have larger damages than a terminal cancer patient since the pediatric patient has a longer life span.

Texas Homestead Laws

Under the Texas homestead laws,[11] a patient cannot take the following assets if she successfully sues a nurse who has no insurance or if the verdict is above the insurance policy limits:

1. one or more burial lots;
2. house plus (*a*) one acre of land if the house or location of the house is urban, (*b*) one hundred acres if it is rural and the nurse is single, or (*c*) two hundred acres if it is rural and the nurse has a family;
3. the following personal property up to a value of $60,000 if the nurse has a family but only up to a value of $30,000 if the nurse is single:

   a) home furnishings, including family heirlooms;
   b) food;
   c) farming or ranching vehicles and implements;
   d) tools, equipment, books, and apparatus, including boats and motor vehicles used in a trade or profession;
   e) clothes;
   f) jewelry not to exceed 25 percent of the limits listed above in (3);
   g) two firearms;
   h) athletic and sporting equipment, including bicycles;
   i) a two-, three-, or four-wheeled motor vehicle for each member of a family or single adult who holds a driver's license or who does not hold a driver's license but who relies on another person to operate the vehicle for the benefit of the nonlicensed person;
   j) the following animals and their food that is on hand: two horses, mules, or donkeys and a saddle, blanket, and bridle for each; twelve head of cattle; sixty head of other types of livestock; and 120 fowl;
   k) household pets; and

l) the present value of any life insurance policy to the extent that a member of the family of the insured or a dependent of a single insured adult claiming the exemption is a beneficiary of the policy;

4. current wages for personal services;
5. professionally prescribed health aids of the nurse or of her dependents;
6. unpaid commissions for personal services not to exceed 25 percent of aggregate limitations of either $30,000 or $60,000; and
7. any retirement funds, whether vested or not, that are recognized by section 403(b) of the 1986 Internal Revenue Code.

A nurse whose present equity in property is exempt from any potential forfeiture should consider other factors before forgoing insurance. A patient who successfully sues a nurse can attempt to collect the judgment from nonexempt property for ten years after perfection of the judgment. Thus, a nurse who acquires nonexempt property for ten years after the judgment, perhaps through inheritance, frugal saving, or winning the Texas lottery, could lose it to the patient allegedly injured. This prospect is especially troubling if the nurse is close to retirement and does not have many working years to rebuild a financial portfolio.

A nurse who suffers a judgment in excess of her insurance policy limit or who has no professional liability insurance could file for bankruptcy. This option may not be available if the nurse filed bankruptcy within the past ten years. Additionally, the nurse should weigh the effect of this decision on her credit rating.

Immunity From Liability

All federally employed nurses are immune from work-related professional liability.[12] This immunity extends to Veterans Affairs, military, and United States Public Health Service nurses. Federally employed nurses who volunteer as nurses or who advise their neighbors on health issues should consider purchasing insurance for these activities, which are outside the scope of their employment.

Nurses employed by state or county hospitals and clinics are immune from liability for their acts or omissions if the patient receives a judgment or settlement from the employer. Suit may not be barred, however, if the patient first sues the nurse.[13] Generally, nurses employed by state or county hospitals or clinics have immunity from suit and liability for discretionary acts in some circumstances. Liability exposure for nurses employed by state or county hospitals and clinics may be expanding, however: a nurse will likely not enjoy immunity from liability if the nurse's duties are not uniquely different from those duties of nurses engaged in the same duties in the private sector or if no function unique to government is being exercised.[14]

Deep Pockets

Some people argue that if nurses purchase professional liability insurance, they will attract suits because a pot of money has been created that is attractive to lawyers and their clients. There may be some truth to this philosophy, but its logic is not fail-safe.

Other people do not know whether a nurse has professional liability insurance unless he tells them. *Nurses should not tell anyone that they have professional liability insurance.* If a patient and the patient's lawyer do not know whether a nurse has nursing negligence insurance, there is no attraction to sue; a lawyer who files suit against a nurse is gambling on whether the nurse has coverage. If a nurse broadcasts to his colleagues and patients that he has insurance, then he certainly may attract a lawsuit.

Once suit is filed, whether a nurse has nursing negligence insurance is discoverable, including her policy limits. (The policy behind this law is that knowing the policy limits helps to settle lawsuits.) Thus, if a nurse has insurance, once the patient discovers this fact after suit is filed, the continuance of the suit may be fueled by the fact that insurance money exists.

The fact that a nurse does not have insurance, however, will probably not encourage a patient to drop the lawsuit. While it will be more difficult for a successful litigant to collect a judgment, the patient can still satisfy the judgment by taking the nurse's property that is not protected by Texas homestead laws. The patient will not know until the judgment is final whether the nurse has nonexempt property to satisfy the judgment. Additionally, once an attorney has accepted the patient as a client, the attorney has a general obligation to continue representation. Consequently, once suit is filed, it will probably not be dropped once it is discovered that the nurse has no insurance.

Another reason that a suit will likely not be dropped once it is discovered that the nurse has no insurance is that many plaintiffs' attorneys assume that the nurse is judgment proof. The nurse is sued as a conduit to reach the deep pockets of the nurse's employer: employers are liable vicariously for the negligent acts of their employees. It seems logical that since the employer and the nurse will have the same interest, which is to prove that the nurse did not act negligently, the nurse should not need to finance her own defense: the nurse could rely on the defense provided by the employer.

Indeed many attorneys for responsible, solvent health care institutions prefer that employees not have insurance: the health care institution feels responsible for taking care of its employees and fears that if all defendants to the suit have their own representation, the defense becomes too complicated and fractional. Consequently, one could conclude that a nurse who is judgment proof should not buy insurance and should rely on the employer for a legal defense. The problem with this conclusion is that not every employer feels the same sense of loyalty to its nurse employees and not every employer is financially solvent or adequately insured.

Additionally, defense attorneys will attest to cases when the employer's defense strategy is not consistent with a strategy most beneficial to the nurse. Nurses have to be concerned about not only financially ruinous judgments but also judgments finding that the nurse's acts or omissions fell below the minimum standard of care. Judgments are reported to the TBNE, which has the power to discipline nurses for such conduct. Thus, nurses have incentives to ensure that they can afford a legal defense that puts a nurse's interest first.

A solution that may balance these concerns is for the nurse to purchase a nursing negligence insurance policy that has low policy limits: the nurse will be afforded a legal defense but will not have created a large sum of money that will attract or fuel a suit. This compromise may not be advantageous to a nurse who is not judgment proof.

Last, juries generally are not told whether a nurse has professional liability insurance. Consequently, juries will not give larger judgments to nurses who have insurance policies and will not go easy on nurses who do not have insurance. Juries, however, are free to assume that a nurse has professional liability coverage.

Can a Nurse Afford a Legal Defense?

A nurse's professional liability insurance premium buys a legal defense if the nurse is ever sued. Depending on the case's proceeding, a legal defense can cost between $10,000 and $100,000 or more. In deciding whether to purchase professional liability insurance, a nurse needs to determine whether he can finance personally the cost of a legal defense. These costs will be incurred on the average over a two-year period. Most attorneys, however, will require a large retainer before accepting the nurse as a client. Additionally, the nurse must take the time to find an attorney who has the expertise to handle his case; insurance companies hire attorneys for their nurse clients and screen carefully those they hire.

Do Employers Require Nurses to Carry Insurance?

Some employers require their nurse employees to carry professional liability insurance as a condition of employment. This practice is more common with advanced nurse practitioners and nurse educators. Thus, some nurses may have no choice about whether they must carry liability insurance if they want a certain job. State or county hospitals and clinics that carry liability insurance, however, cannot themselves require their nurse employees to carry professional liability insurance as a condition of employment.[15]

Does the Employer's Insurance Provide Adequate Coverage?

As previously explained, some nurses will be covered on their employer's institutional insurance policy. Typically the policy will cover the nurse only for nursing acts done for the benefit of the employer. Thus, if a nurse desires to volunteer her nursing services, she may desire further protection from liability through her own policy. Additionally, the nurse may desire the added protection of her own attorney if she is sued rather than relying on an attorney who was hired to protect mainly her employer's interest. Thus, the nurse may desire to purchase insurance that will afford her this right.

Peace of Mind

An intangible but important benefit that professional liability insurance affords is peace of mind. All humans make mistakes. Knowing this fact, a nurse may be somewhat relieved that if the unthinkable happens and a patient is injured by the nurse's act or omission, the nurse has a legal defense free of charge with some protection against a financially ruinous adverse judgment. This peace of mind may add confidence to the nurse in her work and ease tensions in the relationship between the nurse and her patients.

Nurses need to make informed decisions about whether to purchase professional liability insurance. Each nurse needs to weigh for herself the factors outlined above to determine if the benefits of having insurance outweigh the cost of purchasing insurance.

6

Nursing Negligence

It is commonplace for nurses to fear being sued by their patients. Fear is fueled not only by a recognition of the litigious nature of American society but also by misconceptions about the legal system. A nurse's fear of suit may be eased somewhat through a better understanding of the legal system.

AN OVERVIEW OF THE LEGAL SYSTEM

Just as medicine is divided into medicine and surgery specialties, the law can be categorized into civil and criminal law. Generally, the law is different for each. Nurses are susceptible to being involved in both systems.

Criminal Law

Criminal law governs crimes against the state or the United States. Crimes are acts committed and omitted in violation of duties created by statutes. Upon conviction, individuals who commit crimes generally pay back society by paying fines and/or serving prison sentences. Crimes can be classified into misdemeanors and felonies. Misdemeanors under Texas state law carry penalties of fines up to $4,000 and/or jail terms up to one year. Excluding capital offenses and state jail felonies, felonies under Texas state law generally carry penalties of fines up to $10,000 and/or prison terms from two to ninety-nine years. A more complete treatment of criminal punishments is found in Appendix III.

There are many state and federal penal statutes applicable to a nurse's practice, some of which are explored throughout this book. A nurse who is convicted of a criminal offense is not immune from being sued by an injured party on a civil cause of action. Nurses convicted of crimes may also lose their jobs and their nursing licenses.

Civil Law

Two specialty areas of civil law are tort law and contract law. Contract law concerns obligations that arise from agreements between two or more persons. For instance, contract law governs the relationship between a nurse and a nurse's employer. Tort law remedies wrongs that result when one party breaches a duty imposed by law rather than a duty imposed by agreement.

A negligence cause of action is a tort. *Negligence* is the failure to use such care as a reasonably prudent person would use under the same or similar circumstances. It is characterized by inadvertence or thoughtlessness.

Gross negligence is the intentional failure to perform a duty in reckless or conscious disregard of the consequences. It differs from negligence in the degree of inattention. Punitive damages are recoverable for gross negligence. There is no clear distinction between gross negligence and *intentional torts*.

Medical malpractice is a subspecialty of negligence and is defined as negligence performed by a professional. Medical malpractice occurs when one rendering medical professional services fails to exercise the degree of skill commonly applied in the community by the average prudent member of the profession.

Nursing negligence is a term used in this chapter to refer to the situation in which a nurse fails to use such care as a reasonably prudent nurse would use in the same or similar circumstances.

NURSING NEGLIGENCE CAUSE OF ACTION

There are multiple civil causes of action that conceivably could arise from the nurse-patient relationship. The most common cause of action, however, is that of nursing negligence. This cause of action will be explored more fully.

To win a negligence cause of action against a nurse, the patient must prove four elements: (1) the nurse owed the patient a *duty*, (2) the nurse *breached her duty*, (3) the patient was *injured*, and (4) the breach of duty was the *proximate cause* of the patient's injury.

Duty

A nurse owes her patient many duties. Before liability can attach, however, the law must recognize a duty. The duty a nurse owes to her patient is expressed at least partially through the Texas Nursing Practice Act, rules and regulations of the Texas Board of Nurse Examiners (TBNE) and the Texas Board of Vocational Nurse Examiners (TBVNE), state and federal health and safety laws, and Texas case law. The nurse's duty is explored throughout this book. A nurse should know what is and is not her duty. A nurse can be sued successfully only for breaching *the nurse's* duty. For example, she is not legally liable for a physician's misdiagnosis of a patient, because the nurse has no duty to diagnose.

Proximate Cause

Proximate cause is a term of art in the legal profession. It has two distinct elements: causation in fact and proximate cause.

CAUSATION IN FACT. Before a nurse can be found guilty of negligence, the patient must prove that her conduct *in fact* caused the injury. The most common test in determining causation in fact is the "but for" test: the injury would not have occurred but for the act. For instance, a nurse breached her duty of providing a safe environment by failing to raise the side rails while the patient ate his lunch. The patient did not fall out of bed. Instead the patient died from food poisoning. Failing to raise the side rails did not cause the death; hospital food caused the death. Therefore, the nurse's breach of duty did not *in fact* cause the injury, and she is not legally liable.

PROXIMATE CAUSE. The patient must also prove that the nurse's breach of duty was the proximate cause of the injury. This doctrine limits liability to only foreseeable consequences of a nurse's acts. For instance, a nurse provides an unsafe environment in a patient's room by leaving a trash can in the walking path. A nurse aide who is carrying a patient's food tray does not see the trash can and trips, running into an unused intravenous (IV) pole. The IV pole pitches into the hallway and trips a medical student who is running down the hall while holding a pair of scissors. As the medical student braces for a fall, the scissors go flying down the hall and injure the eye of a patient who is sitting outside his room in a wheelchair.

Will the nurse who misplaced the trash can be liable for the patient's injured eye? This scenario illustrates not only that mothers are right when they warn their children against running while holding scissors but also that such an unlikely sequence of events is not foreseeable. Consequently, the nurse would not be liable for the patient's injured eye.

All four elements must be satisfied before liability is imposed. A physician orders a nurse to administer a pain medication to his pediatric patient. The nurse misplaces a decimal point in his calculations and administers ten times the correct amount. The child suffers respiratory arrest. The child is resuscitated but is brain damaged.

The nurse has a duty to administer correctly medication that is ordered by a physician. The nurse breached that duty when he administered the wrong dosage of medication. The child suffered an injury—brain damage. The nurse's breach of duty proximately caused the injury: the wrong dosage of medication in fact caused the respiratory arrest, and it was foreseeable that it would. The nurse is guilty of nursing negligence.

Not all mistakes, however, satisfy the requirements for a nursing negligence cause of action. Suppose a physician orders a nurse to administer one Colace capsule (a mild stool softener) to her adult patient. By mistake the nurse administers two Colace capsules. Instead of having one bowel movement that day, the patient has two. The nurse had a *duty* to administer the medication properly. She *breached that duty* when she administered the wrong dosage of medication. There was no injury, however. Therefore, the nurse is not legally liable for her mistake.

DEFENSES, AVOIDANCES AND MITIGATING FACTORS

If the care a nurse provides is ever questioned, some available laws may either protect her from being sued or, if sued, protect her from or limit a damage award.

Statute of Limitations

A patient must sue the nurse within a certain period from when the negligence occurred. If the patient waits too long, he will be barred from suing. In legal terminology, this period is called the statute of limitations. Generally, an adult patient must sue the nurse within two years from the occurrence of negligence.[1]

Sometimes the patient will have longer than two years in which to sue. The first instance is when the patient did not know or reasonably could not have known about the negligence within the two-year period.[2]

> *Example 6.1: A surgical nurse miscounted the number of surgical sponges used during an operation. Consequently, a surgical sponge was left in the patient's abdomen. Three years later the patient approached his doctor about an abdominal mass. Exploratory surgery revealed that a surgical sponge had been left in his abdomen. Can the patient sue?*
>
> *Answer: The patient can sue the surgical nurse when the patient discovered the sponge three years after the operation if he did not know or could not reasonably have known about it before then.*

The Texas Supreme Court has not answered how long a patient will have to sue once he discovers the negligence after the two-year statute-of-limitations period has run, although one court gave a patient thirteen months to file his suit.[3] Second, a patient may have longer than two years in which to sue if the nurse fraudulently conceals his negligence.

Example 6.2: A nurse injures his patient when he administers the wrong dosage of medication. The nurse alters the hospital records to hide the mistake. When the patient's family questions him about the cause of the injury, the nurse lies, telling them that the patient suffered a rare hypersensitivity reaction to the medication. The patient and his family learn four years later the real cause of injury. Can the patient sue the nurse?

Answer: The patient has two years from discovering the negligence to sue the nurse since the nurse fraudulently concealed his negligence.

When a nurse has a duty to disclose his negligence but fraudulently conceals it, the two-year statute of limitations will not begin to run until the negligence is discovered or in the exercise of reasonable diligence should be discovered.[4]

While a nurse should not fraudulently conceal her negligence, she should not be naive about what she tells the patient about possible acts of negligence. For instance, a patient falls and the nurse, who feels responsible, exclaims in a room full of people, "I am sorry I let you fall." A nurse's admission is admissible in court to prove liability.

While it is safe to say that a nurse should never admit liability to a patient, what a nurse says to a patient concerning possible negligent acts must be determined on a case-by-case basis. Some factors that should be considered include the nurse's relationship with the patient, the patient's personality, and the magnitude of the injury. If at all possible, before a nurse talks to a patient concerning possible negligent acts, she should consult an attorney. If the nurse has professional liability insurance, she should contact her insurance carrier about any possible claim (the policy probably requires her to do so); the insurance carrier may provide her with free legal advice. Additionally, the health care institution's legal counsel should be consulted.

Living minors under the age of twelve years have until their fourteenth birthday to file a health care liability suit. Living minors older than twelve years have two years in which to file a suit.[5] Because of the longer statute-of-limitations period, obstetrical and pediatric nurses who desire insurance coverage should be wary. For instance, an obstetrical nurse who purchased a claims-made insurance policy and who quits practicing nursing today will need insurance coverage for an additional fourteen years to cover all potential lawsuits.

Immunity from Suit and Liability

All federally employed nurses are immune from work-related professional liability. Federally employed nurses include military, United States Public Health Service, and Veterans Affairs nurses. Nurses employed by state or county hospitals or clinics have immunity from suit and liability in some circumstances: (1) if judgment or settlement of a claim is obtained against the governmental entity or (2) for discretionary acts (as opposed to ministerial acts) performed in good faith within the scope of their authority. Because a nurse's exposure to liability is circumstance dependent in state or county employment, the nurse should consider obtaining professional liability insurance. Nurses working as independent contractors of a governmental entity will not be immune from liability. This situation may apply to nurses working as temporary nurses.

Good Samaritan Laws

Generally, all nurses who administer emergency care at the scene of an accident that they did not cause will be protected by the Texas Good Samaritan law.[6] Under the Texas Good Samaritan law, any person who in good faith administers emergency care at the scene of an emergency and who is not in a hospital or other health care facility or means of medical transport is not liable in civil damages for an act performed during the emergency *unless* the act is willfully or wantonly negligent.

A nurse who helps an emergency victim will lose immunity from suit if the nurse asks for or accepts any payment for nursing services provided.

Comparative Responsibility

A patient cannot win damages in a negligence cause of action against a nurse when the patient is more responsible for the injury than the nurse.[7]

> *Example 6.3: A patient sues a nurse on one legal theory—negligence. The patient's sciatic nerve was injured when the nurse administered a drug parenterally. Despite the nurse's instruction to the patient not to move, the patient moved, which caused the nurse to place the needle outside the safe administration zone, injuring the patient. The jury found the patient 51 percent responsible for the injury and the nurse 49 percent responsible. Can the patient recover damages from the nurse?*
>
> *Answer: The patient cannot recover damages from the nurse.*

When a patient sues a nurse to recover damages for negligence resulting in personal injury, property damage, or death, the patient can recover damages only if his percentage of responsibility is *less than or equal to*

50 percent. In Example 6.3 the patient cannot recover damages from the nurse, because the patient is more than 50 percent responsible for the injury.

A patient can win damages with a higher percentage of fault in some situations.

Example 6.4: A patient was injured when her IV infusion pump malfunctioned and delivered all her medication in a bolus. The patient sued two entities on two separate legal theories in the same lawsuit. The attending nurse was sued for negligence in monitoring the patient's condition adequately, and the manufacturer of the infusion pump was sued on the legal theory of strict products liability. The jury found the pump manufacturer 40 percent negligent, the nurse 5 percent negligent, and the patient 55 percent negligent because the patient saw the pump's warning light flashing but did not inform the nurse of her predicament. Can the patient win damages since she is more than 50 percent responsible for the injury?

Answer: The patient can win damages.

A patient can recover damages for personal injury, property damage, or death when her percentage of responsibility is *less than 60 percent* if at least one defendant is found liable on a basis of strict tort liability, strict products liability, or breach of warranty. In Example 6.4 the manufacturer was found liable on the theory of strict products liability. Therefore, the patient could recover damages as long as her negligence was less than 60 percent, which it was.

If a patient wins a damage award that the patient is entitled to recover, the court will reduce the award by a percentage equal to the patient's percentage of responsibility.[8] For instance, in Example 6.3, suppose the patient was found only 50 percent liable for his sciatica, which would allow him to recover for his injuries. The jury found his damages were $10,000. The court will reduce his damage award by $5,000 (50 percent of $10,000). The nurse, therefore, would only be liable for $5,000 in damages.

A nurse who is sued successfully along with other people in the same lawsuit will only be liable for damages to the degree reflected in the percentage of responsibility found by the jury (or the court). For instance, in Example 6.4, if the jury found damages were $100,000, the nurse would only be responsible for $5,000 (5 percent of $100,000). However, the nurse can be liable for the full damage award in the following situations:

1. the percentage of responsibility attributed to the nurse is greater than 20 percent and the percentage of responsibility attributed to the nurse is greater than the percentage of responsibility attributed to the patient when the patient does not win either a strict tort li-

ability, strict products liability, or breach-of-warranty cause of action against any defendant or
2. the patient is found blameless and the nurse's percentage of responsibility is greater than 10 percent.[9]

If the nurse pays any of the damage award on behalf of another defendant, however, she can recover the amount paid by that defendant (right of contribution).[10]

Reasonable and Prudent Standard

It is likely that, if a nurse is sued for negligence, her acts or omissions will be judged according to what a reasonable and prudent member of the nursing profession would have done under the same or similar circumstances.[11] Therefore, the nurse's experience and educational background will be considered along with the circumstances surrounding the incident.

Respondeat Superior

A nurse's employer can be held legally liable for the nurse's actions when the nurse is acting within the scope of employment. If a patient wins a judgment against the employer and the patient's judgment is paid fully by the employer, the patient cannot get any money subsequently from the nurse. If the nurse was sued along with the employer, however, the employer can seek contribution from the nurse. It seems remote that an employer would seek contribution from a nurse employee.

WHEN A PATIENT SUES

In Texas, before a patient can sue a nurse on a health care liability claim, the patient must give the nurse written notice of the claim by certified mail, return receipt requested, at least sixty days before filing the lawsuit.[12]

A nurse who receives this notice of an impending lawsuit and has professional liability insurance should contact her insurance company *immediately* and provide it with a copy of the notice, including a copy of the certified mail receipt. The importance of informing the insurance company immediately is twofold. First, the professional liability insurance contract probably specifies that the nurse has a duty to inform the insurance company of any possible claim against her with the penalty of losing insurance coverage if the nurse does not comply. Second, the insurance company will be appointing the nurse a defense attorney (free of charge to the nurse), who should be provided with as much time as possible to prepare a defense and possibly prevent the lawsuit from being filed.

If the nurse does not have professional liability insurance coverage and she receives notice of an impending lawsuit, she should carefully choose and hire an attorney as soon as possible. The attorney should have experience in defending nurses against nursing negligence claims. Most large towns have a few law firms that specialize in this field. Nurses in rural areas may have to travel to the nearest large town to get this type of specialized representation. In choosing the best attorney, the nurse can start by calling the local bar association's referral service and asking for names of attorneys or law firms specializing in defending health care professionals. Additionally, if she knows another health care professional who defended against a lawsuit in the past, she can ask whether legal representation was adequate. After getting names of defense attorneys, the nurse should interview them. She should ask how many trials they have handled, how many cases they have worked on, and how much they charge per hour. When the nurse has hired an attorney, she should expect to pay a retainer to the attorney, typically higher than $10,000 initially. Subsequently, the nurse will probably be billed monthly for legal services.

There is one situation of which the nurse should be wary.

> *Example 6.5: A physician has been sued recently for medical malpractice, and the nurse was working when the incident happened. The nurse has not been sued, but she has been asked to be deposed or interviewed by the patient's attorneys involved with the case. What should the nurse do?*
>
> *Answer: A nurse who has been subpoenaed for a deposition must attend the deposition or face being held in contempt of court. I believe that a nurse should neither attend the deposition nor be interviewed without being represented by her own attorney. If the nurse has professional liability insurance, she should contact her insurance company immediately. If the nurse does not have insurance coverage, she should immediately hire an attorney who specializes in medical malpractice defense.*

Any statement made by a nurse is considered an "admission" and is admissible in a court of law. Frequently a patient's attorney will ask the nurse in these situations if she has professional liability insurance. If the nurse answers affirmatively, she will likely be joined as a defendant in the lawsuit. As long as the statute of limitations has not run out, there is nothing to prevent the nurse from being sued subsequent to the physician. If the nurse participates in a deposition, her testimony is sworn and she cannot change it without subjecting herself to perjury charges or being made to look like a liar on the witness stand or a witness whose testimony cannot be believed. Nurses have been sued after giving deposition testimony. Therefore, a nurse should have her own adequate legal representation before she is deposed or interviewed. The nurse's attorney can prevent the nurse from waiving any privileges she may have and prevent her from admitting liability.

ANATOMY OF A LAWSUIT

Assume that the nurse received a sixty-day notice letter and a lawsuit is filed against the nurse for nursing negligence. There are three general stages of a lawsuit: (1) pretrial, (2) trial, and (3) appeals. Not every stage will be reached necessarily in every lawsuit. For instance, most cases are settled in the pretrial stage. Additionally, not all the cases that reach a final judgment at the trial phase are appealed.

Pretrial

The most important aspect of the pretrial phase is *discovery*. Through discovery, both the patient and the nurse through their attorneys attempt to find information to either build their case (for the plaintiff) or to build their defense (for the defendant).

There are three discovery tools used against the opposing party: (1) *interrogatories*, which ask the other party to answer certain questions in writing; (2) *admissions*, which ask the other party either to admit or to deny certain statements in writing; and (3) requests for *production of documents*, which ask the other party to produce certain documents or tangible items. These discovery requests have important deadlines. While it is the attorney's responsibility to ensure that the requests are properly and timely filed, the nurse may have to assist her attorney in answering the requests and must observe deadlines imposed by her attorney.

A discovery tool that can be used against both the opposing party and other individuals not parties to the lawsuit are *depositions*. During a deposition, an individual who may have information relevant to the lawsuit is posed questions. A court reporter will transcribe the questions and the answers, and the meeting may be videotaped. The individual being deposed is under oath to tell the truth. Attorneys for both sides will attend the deposition. Testimony gathered from the deposition can be admitted into evidence during a trial without the deposed person being there. Alternatively, deposition testimony can be used to impeach a witness testifying in person at a trial; that is, inconsistent testimony is admitted to show either that the witness is lying or that his testimony is not reliable. Each person is given the chance to review his testimony for accuracy once the court reporter transcribes the deposition testimony. If deposed, the nurse should review the transcription for accuracy and have transcription errors corrected.

Most cases are settled during the pretrial stage. If not, the case will go to trial. There is a trend for cases to go to mediation before trial to enhance the chances of settlement. In mediation a mediator, who is a neutral party, helps parties move toward a settlement by helping them realize the strengths and weaknesses of their cases and thus find common ground.

Trial

Most trial dates in Texas state courts are set for about eighteen to twenty-four months after a lawsuit is filed, depending on how busy the court docket is where the case is filed. It takes even longer to get a court date in federal court. If discovery is not finished by the trial date or if one attorney has a conflict with the initial trial date, a continuance may be granted, further postponing the trial date.

A case may be tried before either a judge or a jury. The trial will be before a jury if either the nurse or the patient timely requests one; most patients request a jury trial. In jury trials, both sides select a certain number of jurors from a larger group of potential jurors. Both sides pose questions to potential jurors and strike those from the panel who seem to be prejudicial to their side of the case.

After a jury is selected, the trial begins with opening statements, during which both sides, beginning with the plaintiff, will present an overview of the case from their perspectives to the jury (or judge if there is no jury). The plaintiff may say incriminating things that may incite or anger the nurse. The nurse should remain calm and not react. The nurse's turn to paint events as they happened occurs when the nurse's attorney makes an opening statement.

Next come two important phases of the trial. First is the case-in-chief, in which the plaintiff, who has the burden of proof, admits evidence to support every element of his cause of action. The plaintiff must prove nursing negligence by a preponderance of the evidence, meaning that it is more likely than not that the nurse committed nursing negligence. During this phase of the trial, the defendant will try to keep evidence out by objecting according to the rules of evidence. After the plaintiff has presented his evidence, he will close and it is the defendant nurse's turn to present her evidence to rebut the patient's evidence. During this second phase of the trial, the plaintiff will be trying to keep out evidence by objecting according to the rules of evidence. Once the defendant is finished presenting evidence, the defendant closes.

The trial judge and attorneys in state court will develop a *jury charge*.

The jury charge applies the law to the facts of the case and poses questions for the jury to answer. Once a charge is drafted, both sides make *closing statements*. The patient's attorney will begin and end since the patient has the burden of proof. During closing statements both sides summarize the evidence and present their theories of the case. The jury will retire until its verdict is rendered. The jury's verdict will be read in open court.

Once judgment is rendered, the losing party may have a right to appeal the verdict. In state court trials, the verdict is first appealed to one of fourteen intermediate appellate courts, depending on where the trial court is located. Sometimes large verdicts will be reduced by the appellate court. Once the appellate court renders its verdict, the party who is unhappy with this verdict may have the right to appeal to the Texas Supreme Court. Appellate courts can either affirm the trial court judgment, reverse and send the case back to the trial court for a new trial, or reverse and render judgment.

If a judgment becomes final, the patient will try to collect the judgment. If an insurance policy exists, the insurance company will pay the judgment up to its policy limits. If there is no insurance policy or if the judgment exceeds the policy's limit, the patient will try to satisfy the judgment by attaching the nurse's nonexempt property (property not protected under the Texas Homestead Act).

TESTIFYING

There are many situations in which a nurse may have to testify in court. First, a nurse may be called as a *lay witness* to testify to occurrences he witnessed or observed. Second, a nurse may be called as an *expert witness*. Expert witnesses testify about their opinions after it is established that they possess special skill or knowledge on a subject.

Testimony is presented in court through a question-and-answer format. The questions posed by the attorney who calls a nurse as a witness is called *direct examination*. Unless the court considers the witness hostile, the attorney will ask open-ended questions. When the attorney has completed direct examination, the opposing attorney will complete *cross-examination*. During cross-examination the attorney will ask unfriendly, leading questions. The nurse should ignore the attorney's attitude. The nurse should be forthright and truthful when he answers cross-examination questions. Upon *redirect examination* the attorney friendly to his side will have the opportunity to rehabilitate his testimony. The nurse will be able to round out his cross-examination answers, for instance, by admitting that while anything is possible, the possible did not happen in this case.

When testifying, it is important that the nurse follow a few rules:

1. *Prepare for testimony.* Your attorney or the attorney who asks you to testify should help you prepare for testimony. Preparation should include reviewing relevant documents and practicing testifying.
2. *Answer the question.* Answer the question as asked but go no further. Do not worry about how the answer may distort your story, because your attorney has time to rehabilitate your answer later on.
3. *Keep testimony simple.* The jury is composed of laypeople. Consequently, the witness should explain technical terms and keep the testimony as simple as possible to keep the jury's attention.
4. *Do not worry about objections.* The attorney representing the other side may object claiming your response was "unresponsive," raise her voice, twist your words, and limit your testimony to try to make you look like an incompetent, uncaring nurse. You should understand the game and stay calm and collected. When an attorney stands to lodge an objection, stop talking until after the judge rules on the objection; do not try to finish your answer while the attorney is speaking.
5. *Ask for clarification.* If you do not understand the question, ask for clarification.
6. *Dress professionally.* Dress professionally but comfortably.
7. *Enunciate.* Speak loudly and clearly enough so that the court reporter, the judge, and the jury can hear you. Answer questions verbally rather than nonverbally; a court reporter cannot transcribe a nod of the head.

7

Consent

CONSENT DEFINED

"Consent" means the permission that a patient gives to a health care provider to perform a certain procedure or treatment.

"Informed consent" means consenting to medical treatment after the patient is advised of the probable results if he gets treated or remains untreated, the alternative treatments, and the risks or hazards inherent in the procedure or treatment that could influence a reasonable person in deciding whether or not to consent.

The difference between these related terms can be illustrated. A physician orders a nurse to administer a shot of penicillin. The patient *consents* to the medical treatment when he lets the nurse inject the antibiotic. The patient gives his *informed consent* when he lets the nurse inject the antibiotic after he considers the probable result that his infection will worsen if he remains untreated and his infection will be cured if he gets treated, alternative antibiotic treatments, and the inherent risk of an allergic reaction to the drug.

If a patient does not give a nurse consent to administer a procedure or treatment and the nurse administers it anyway, the nurse could be sued by the patient for civil negligence, disciplined by the licensee's regulatory board for unprofessional conduct, and prosecuted by the state of Texas for criminal assault, aggravated assault, or reckless conduct. A nurse's defense to criminal charges would be that the patient consented to or the nurse reasonably believed that the patient consented to the nurse's conduct, assuming that the conduct did not threaten or inflict serious bodily injury or that the patient knew the conduct was a risk of a recognized medical treatment or a scientific experiment conducted by recognized methods.

A patient's consent can be implied from behavior. For example, a nurse informs a patient that the nurse needs to take the patient's blood pressure. The patient's consent is implied when she rolls up her sleeve and holds out her arm.

Alternatively, a patient expressly consents to the administration of medication when he asks the nurse, "Can I have my Demerol shot now, please?"

PROBLEM AREAS

Driving While Intoxicated

Any person who operates a motor vehicle or a watercraft in a public place in Texas is deemed, by state law, to have given consent to the taking of one or more specimens of his *breath* or *blood* for analysis to determine the alcohol concentration or the presence of a controlled substance, dangerous drug, or other substance in his body if the person was arrested for any offense arising out of acts alleged to have been committed while he was driving or in actual physical control of a motor vehicle or a watercraft while intoxicated.[1]

> *Example 7.1: A police officer enters an emergency room with an apparently drunken man in handcuffs. The police officer asks the nurse to draw a blood specimen to determine the prisoner's blood-alcohol level. When the man in custody hears the officer's request, the man states loudly in slurred speech, "You will not draw my blood." The police officer says that the man was involved in a one-car accident on IH-10, no one else was injured, and the arrested man refused to take a Breathalyzer test. Does the nurse have the legal authority to draw the blood specimen despite the drunken man's request?*
>
> *Answer: The nurse does not have legal authority to draw the blood specimen.*

It is implied in Example 7.1 that the apparently drunken motorist gave consent to have his blood analyzed for the presence of alcohol since he was under arrest for driving while intoxicated in a public place. The specimen must be taken at the request of a peace officer who has reasonable grounds to believe that the person had been driving or was in actual physical control of a motor vehicle or a watercraft while intoxicated in a public place in Texas.

Upon the request of a peace officer, if a person *under arrest* refuses to give a breath or blood specimen, then *no specimen shall be taken*. There is one exception to this rule, however. A person *shall be required* to give a specimen if

1. the person was arrested for an offense involving the operation of a motor vehicle or a watercraft under chapter 49 of the Texas Penal Code;[2]
2. the person was the operator of a motor vehicle or a watercraft in-

volved in an accident that the officer reasonably believes occurred as a result of the offense;
3. at the time of the arrest, the officer reasonably believes that a person has died or will die as a direct result of the accident; and
4. the person refuses the officer's request to voluntarily give a specimen.

Because the exception does not apply to Example 7.1—since no one other than the drunken man was injured and the officer could not reasonably believe that the arrested man will die as a direct result of the accident—the nurse has no legal authority to take a blood specimen since the patient refused.

Example 7.2: After the police officer talks to the arrested man, it is discovered that the man is deathly afraid of needles but will consent to a urinalysis. The police officer orders the nurse to obtain a urinalysis on the arrested man. Should the nurse comply with the order?

Answer: The nurse should obtain a urinalysis pursuant to a physician's order if hospital policy permits.

An arrested person is deemed to have given consent to only breath and blood tests. An arrested person, however, can consent to giving any other type of specimen to determine the alcohol concentration in his blood. Therefore, in Example 7.2 it is lawful to obtain a urinalysis. It is suggested, however, that a nurse first obtain a physician's order before obtaining the specimen. The physician's order should comply with hospital policy.

Example 7.3: An unconscious patient was brought into the emergency room via an ambulance stretcher. The patient was involved in a traffic accident while he was driving his car on a public road. The patient smells strongly of alcohol, and the emergency medical technician states that the inside of the patient's car had many open beer cans. The accompanying police officer asks that a blood specimen be taken to determine the patient's blood-alcohol level. Is the request authorized by Texas law?

Answer: Yes.

Whether arrested or not, any person who is dead, unconscious, or otherwise in a condition rendering the person incapable of refusing shall not be deemed as having withdrawn his implied consent to have his blood or breath tested for drugs or alcohol. Therefore, in Example 7.3 the blood specimen can be drawn by a nurse pursuant to a physician's order and hospital policy. The nurse, however, should document in the medical chart the patient's unconscious status at the time of drawing the specimen.

Example 7.4: The physician orders the nurse to draw a blood specimen because of the police officer's request. The nurse is busy and needs to delegate the task. Whom can she ask to draw the blood?

Answer: The nurse can delegate the task to a qualified technician, chemist, or licensed vocational nurse but not to an emergency medical technician.

Only a physician, qualified technician, chemist, registered professional nurse, or licensed vocational nurse may draw a blood specimen for the purpose of determining alcohol concentration or the presence of a controlled substance or drug. A qualified technician does not include emergency medical services personnel. If the person is dead, however, the specimen may be drawn by the county medical examiner or, if there is no county medical examiner, a licensed mortician.

A breath specimen can be obtained only by a person certified by the Texas Department of Public Safety to obtain it. This person most likely will not be a nurse.

A person who gives a specimen of breath, blood, urine, or other bodily substance may, upon request and within a reasonable time not to exceed two hours after the arrest, have a physician, qualified technician, chemist, or registered professional nurse of his own choosing draw a specimen and have an analysis made of his blood. Also, upon the patient's request, full information concerning the analytical results of the test or tests must be made available to him or his attorney.

The nurse who draws a blood specimen at the request or order of a peace officer will not be held liable for damages arising from the request or order except for negligence if the specimen is not drawn according to recognized medical procedures. Therefore, if a nurse must draw a blood specimen on an unwilling patient, the nurse should ensure the patient's safety during the procedure; hospital policy should be followed.

If a nurse obtains specimens for drug or alcohol analysis, a properly written doctor's order should delegate the task to the nurse. In following the doctor's order, the nurse should implement relevant hospital policy.

Sexual Assault

A victim of sexual assault, aggravated sexual assault, or indecency with a child by sexual contact can ask the court to test the alleged perpetrator for sexually transmitted diseases, AIDS, or human immunodeficiency virus (HIV) infection.[3] The alleged perpetrator must have been indicted for the crime or have waived indictment for the crime, however; that is, a grand jury must have brought charges against the perpetrator. If the accused individual refuses to submit voluntarily to the test or procedure, the court may require the person to submit.

The person performing the procedure or test must make the test results available to the local health authority, which shall be required to make the notification of the test results to the victim of the alleged offense and to the defendant.

Testing must be conducted in accordance with written Texas Board of Health protocols[4] that respect the rights of the victim and the rights of the person accused. According to these protocols, the court, in consultation with the local health authority, shall use or arrange the use of a pseudonym for the person on all requests and reports; the pseudonym shall be known only to the physician, the local health authority, the person being tested, and the court. The person performing the procedure or test shall make the results available directly to the local health authority.

The local health authority shall meet with the alleged victim of the offense and disclose the results of the medical procedure or test. No other person shall be present during the notification unless permitted by the victim. The victim shall be advised of the medical implications of the test results, whether or not the test results are positive or negative. The victim will be instructed to receive further medical intervention by the victim's personal medical doctor. If the victim resides outside Texas, notification may be made by telephone.

If the results of the tests are positive for a communicable disease, the local health authority shall instruct the alleged perpetrator as required by the Communicable Disease Prevention and Control Act.

Disclosure of the test results to any person other than the victim or the accused without the person's legal consent is prohibited.

Religious Grounds

Except during an emergency, the Communicable Disease Prevention and Control Act neither authorizes nor requires the medical treatment of an individual with a communicable disease who chooses treatment by prayer or spiritual means as part of the tenets and practices of a recognized church of which the individual is an adherent or member. The individual, however, may be isolated or quarantined in an appropriate facility and must obey the rules, orders, and instructions of the department or health authority while in isolation or quarantine.[5]

A court order should be sought to provide medical treatment for (1) a pregnant woman or an adult with minor children who refuses treatment necessary to preserve life because of tenets or practices of the adult's religion and (2) a child when a parent refuses the necessary blood transfusion or other medical treatment for the child on religious grounds. Consent will be implied, however, during an emergency.[6]

Minors Generally

Generally, a child[7] does not have the capacity to consent to medical treatment for himself, and any consent that he attempts to give is invalid.[8] To avoid committing a battery, a health care provider must obtain consent for medical care on behalf of the child from one of the following individuals:

1. the natural mother,
2. a legitimate child's father,
3. an adoptive mother or father,
4. a parent who is appointed managing conservator of the child,
5. another person who is not a parent and who is appointed managing conservator of the child, or
6. a possessory conservator who has been granted specifically the power to consent to nonemergency medical treatment by a court.[9]

Except when immunizing a child, if the adult having the power to consent cannot be contacted and has not given actual notice that he does not consent, the health care provider should look to one of the following persons or institutions to obtain consent:

> (1) a grandparent;
> (2) an adult brother or sister;
> (3) an adult aunt or uncle;
> (4) an educational institution in which the minor is enrolled that has received written authorization to consent from the person having the power to consent . . . ;
> (5) any adult who has care and control of the minor and has written authorization to consent from the person having the power to consent . . . ;
> (6) any court having jurisdiction of the child; or
> (7) any adult responsible for the care and control of a minor under the jurisdiction of a juvenile court or committed by a juvenile court to the care of an agency of the state or county, if the adult has reasonable grounds to believe the minor is in need of immediate medical treatment.[10]

If consent is given by any of the above individuals or institutions, consent must (1) be in writing; (2) be signed by the person giving consent; (3) contain the name of the child; (4) contain the name of one or both parents if known and the name of the managing conservator or guardian of the person, if either has been appointed; (5) contain the name of the person giving consent and his relation to the minor child; and

(6) contain a statement of the nature of treatment and the date when it will begin.[11]

A ABORTIONS. A minor under eighteen years of age may not consent to an abortion without parental consent.[12] A physician, hospital, or medical facility, however, may rely on the written statement of the minor containing the grounds on which the minor has capacity to consent to his own medical treatment.[13]

B CONTRACEPTIVES. Minors do not have the ability to consent to contraceptive medical treatment without parental consent.[14] A physician, hospital, or medical facility, however, may rely on the written statement of the minor containing the grounds on which the minor has capacity to consent to his own medical treatment.[15]

C STERILIZATION. A therapeutic sterilization may be performed on a minor if a parent consents. The medical necessity for the surgery, however, should be fully documented. Nontherapeutic sterilization, however, *should not* be performed without a court order *even* if the parents consent.[16]

Immunization of Minors

If a parent, managing conservator, or guardian of a minor or other person who may consent legally for a minor cannot be contacted[17] and has not expressly refused consent to immunization, any of the following individuals or institutions may consent to the immunization of a minor:

1. a grandparent;
2. an adult brother or sister;
3. an adult aunt or uncle;
4. a stepparent;
5. the educational institution in which the minor is enrolled and that has written authorization to consent for the minor from a person with the authority to consent;
6. another adult who has care and control of the minor and has written authorization to consent from the person with the power to consent;
7. a court having jurisdiction of a suit affecting the parent-child relationship of which the minor is the subject;
8. an adult responsible for the care and control of the minor under the jurisdiction of a juvenile court or by commitment by a juvenile

court to the care of a state or county agency, if the adult reasonably believes the minor needs immunization;

9. an adult, as the primary caregiver, having care and control of the minor, if the adult is granted the right to consent to immunization of the minor by order of a district court; or
10. the Texas Youth Commission if the minor is committed to it and the person with the power to consent has been contacted and refuses to consent or delegate consent but does not expressly deny the commission the authority to consent for the minor.[18]

The person who has authority to consent to the immunization of a minor has the responsibility of ensuring that consent, if given, is informed consent. The health care provider must provide the same information to the person consenting to immunization of a child as would be provided to a parent. The information must include the procedure to recover unreimbursed expenses for certain injuries arising from certain immunizations.[19]

The person who may consent to the immunization of a minor may delegate the authority to consent in writing to any of the following individuals: (1) a grandparent, (2) an adult brother or sister, (3) an adult aunt or uncle, (4) a stepparent, or (5) another adult who has care and control of the minor.[20] Any individual listed in (1)–(4) who is the primary caregiver and who has been delegated authority to consent to the immunization of a minor may delegate this authority in the same manner permitted to any other person listed in (1)–(4).[21]

Consent Exceptions for Minors

Consent is needed neither before a minor is treated and examined in an emergency nor when child abuse is suspected.

Generally, a physician having reasonable grounds to believe that a child's physical or mental condition has been affected adversely by abuse or neglect can examine a child without the consent of the child, the child's parents, or any other person authorized to consent for the child or his parents. The examination can include xrays and blood tests. A child sixteen years of age or older can refuse consent to such an examination as can a court on behalf of the child.[22]

Generally, a licensed physician, psychologist, counselor, or social worker having reasonable grounds to believe that a child has been sexually or physically abused; is contemplating suicide; or is involved in chemical addiction, dependency, or abuse may counsel the child without the consent of the parents, managing conservator, or guardian.[23]

A minor can consent to medical treatment if the minor:

1. is on active duty with the armed forces of the United States;
2. is sixteen years of age or older, resides separately and apart from his parents, managing conservator, or guardian and manages his own financial affairs, regardless of the source of income;
3. consents to the diagnosis and treatment of any infectious, contagious, or communicable disease that is required by law to be reported to a health officer;
4. is unmarried and pregnant and consents to hospital, medical, or surgical treatment, *other than abortion*, related to her pregnancy;
5. consents to examination and treatment for drug addiction, drug dependency, or any other condition directly related to chemical use; or
6. consents to counseling or counseling in conjunction with treatment by a physician, psychologist, counselor, or social worker if the treatment or counseling is for sexual abuse; physical abuse; suicide prevention; or chemical addiction, dependency, or abuse.[24]

Incompetent Adults

In Texas, the husband-wife relationship in itself does not make one spouse the agent of the other.[25] Therefore, if either the husband or wife becomes mentally incompetent, the other spouse does not have legal authority to make medical decisions for the incompetent partner absent some other valid legal document, court order, or legal authority.

Authority for spouses to make medical decisions for the other may take many forms. First, a court can order a legal guardian for an incompetent adult; the guardian can then make health care decisions for the incompetent adult. Second, an individual can designate an agent through a living will (see Appendix B to Chapter 13) to make a treatment decision to withhold or withdraw medical treatment if the individual becomes terminally ill and incompetent. Third, an individual can appoint a guardian through a durable power of attorney for health care (see Appendix C to Chapter 13) if the individual later becomes incompetent or in need of a guardian; generally the power of attorney must state that "this power of attorney shall not terminate on disability of the principal" or else it will become invalid if the patient becomes incompetent. Finally, a surrogate decision maker may be authorized if prerequisites of the Texas Consent to Medical Treatment Act (the Act) are met.[26]

Under the Act, an adult[27] surrogate from the following list, in order of priority, who has decision-making capacity may consent to medical treatment on behalf of an adult patient in a hospital or nursing home who is comatose, incapacitated,[28] or otherwise mentally or physically incapable of communication:

1. the patient's spouse,
2. an adult child of the patient who has the waiver and consent of all other qualified adult children of the patient to act as the sole decision maker,
3. a majority of the patient's reasonably available adult children,
4. the patient's parents, or
5. the individual clearly identified to act for the patient by the patient before the patient became incapacitated, the patient's nearest relative, or a member of the clergy.

The surrogate decision maker's authority to consent to medical treatment is not unlimited, however. First, any consent to medical treatment must be based on knowledge of what the patient would desire, if known. Second, a surrogate decision maker may not consent to (1) voluntary inpatient mental health services, (2) electroconvulsive treatment, or (3) the appointment of another surrogate decision maker. Finally, the Act does not apply to the withholding or withdrawing of life-sustaining treatment pursuant to living wills, health care decisions made under a durable power of attorney for health care, consent to medical treatment of minors, consent to emergency care, hospital patient transfers, and the law regarding a patient's legal guardian.

An attending physician, hospital, or nursing home or a person acting as an agent for or under the control of the physician, hospital, or nursing home is not subject to criminal or civil liability and has not engaged in unprofessional conduct if the medical treatment consented to under the Act (1) is done in good faith under the consent to medical treatment and (2) does not constitute a failure to exercise due care in the provision of the medical treatment.

Health care professionals must ensure that prerequisites for consent are satisfied before relying on the limitation of liability. First, if an adult patient in a hospital or nursing home is comatose, incapacitated, or otherwise mentally or physically incapable of communication and, according to reasonable medical judgment, is in need of medical treatment, the attending physician must describe (1) the patient's comatose state, incapacity, or other mental or physical inability to communicate in the patient's medical record and (2) the proposed medical treatment in the patient's medical record.

Second, the attending physician must make a reasonably diligent effort to contact or cause to be contacted the persons eligible to serve as surrogate decision makers. Efforts to contact those persons must be recorded in detail in the patient's medical record.

Third, if a surrogate decision maker consents to medical treatment on behalf of the patient, the attending physician must record the date and time of the consent and sign the patient's medical record. The surrogate decision maker must countersign the patient's medical record or execute an informed-consent form.

Last, a surrogate decision maker's consent to medical treatment that is not made in person must be reduced to writing in the patient's medical record, signed by the hospital or nursing home staff member receiving the consent, and countersigned in the patient's medical record or on an informed-consent form by the surrogate decision maker as soon as possible.

8

Informed Consent

The legal basis for informed consent stems from the right of privacy guaranteed by the United States Constitution.[1] Justice Cardozo of the New York Court of Appeals, in describing this right, stated most eloquently that "[e]very human being of adult years and sound mind has a right to determine what shall be done with his own body."[2] The patient's right to accept or reject medical treatment forms the basis of the requirement that medical practitioners obtain their patients' informed consent before administering treatment.[3] For consent to be informed, a patient must be advised of the probable results if the patient gets treated or remains untreated, alternative treatments, and risks and hazards inherent in the procedure or treatment that could influence a reasonable person in deciding whether or not to consent.

RISKS AND HAZARDS TO BE EXPLAINED

Considering the vast number of medical procedures, how can a health care provider protect himself from liability by fully informing his patient of all the risks and hazards inherent in a medical procedure? In 1977 the Medical Liability and Insurance Improvement Act of Texas[4] was passed to improve and modify the health care liability system. This act created the Texas Medical Disclosure Panel (the Panel), whose job is to determine which risks and hazards must be disclosed by health care providers to their patients and to establish the general form and substance of such disclosure.

The Panel met and created two lists. List A contains all procedures that require disclosure (see Table 8-1). List B contains all procedures that require no disclosure (see Table 8-2). For procedures on List A, informed consent is effective if the risks and hazards identified by the Panel are in writing to the form and degree required by the Panel and if the consent form is signed by the patient and a competent witness. The Panel meets periodically to revise its findings and publishes them in the

Table 8-1 *List A—Procedures Requiring Full Disclosure*

- Anesthesia
  - Epidural
- Digestive system
  - Cholecystectomy
- Ear
  - Stapedectomy
  - Ear auricle reconstruction
  - Tympanoplasty with mastoidectomy
- Endocrine system
  - Thyroidectomy
- Eye
  - Eye muscle surgery
  - Cataract surgery
  - Retinal or vitreous surgery
  - Eye and eye region reconstruction/plastic surgery
  - Photocoagulation/cryotherapy
  - Corneal surgery
  - Glaucoma surgery
  - Enucleation/evisceration
  - Surgery for penetrating ocular injury
- Female genital system
  - Abdominal hysterectomy
  - Vaginal hysterectomy
  - Fallopian tube/ovarian surgery
  - Abdominal endoscopy
  - Fibroid removal
  - Uterine suspension
  - Presacral neurectomy
  - Cervix removal
  - Vaginal hernia repair
  - Abdominal bladder suspension
  - Cervix conization
  - Diagnostic uterus dilation/curettage
  - Obstetrical uterus dilation/curettage
- Hematic/lymphatic system
  - Blood component transfusion
- Integumentary system
  - Radical/modified radical mastectomy
  - Face/neck reconstruction/plastic surgery
- Male genital system
  - Orchidopexy
  - Orchidotomy
  - Vasectomy
- Maternity
  - Vaginal delivery
  - Cesarean section

Table 8-1 *Continued*

Musculoskeletal system
Arthroplasty of all joints with mechanical device
Mechanical internal prosthetic device
Open reduction with internal fixation
Osteotomy
Ligamentous joint reconstruction
Children's orthopedics
Nervous system
Craniotomy for excision of brain tissue/tumor/vascular malformation/ cerebral revascularization
Craniotomy for cranial nerve operation
Spine operation
Peripheral nerve operation
Cranial deformity correction
Pituitary gland operation
Cerebral spinal fluid shunting or revision
Radiology
Angiography, aortography, arteriography
Myelography
Therapeutic angiography with occlusion techniques
Angioplasty
Splenoportography
Respiratory system
Rhinoplasty
Nasal septum/nasal septoplasty submucus resection
Urinary system
Partial nephrectomy
Radical nephrectomy
Nephrectomy
Nephrolithotomy and pyelolithotomy
Pyeloureteroplasty
Kidney exploration for perinephric mass
Ureteroplasty
Ureterolithotomy
Ureterectomy
Ureterolysis
Ureteral reimplantation
Prostatectomy
Total/partial cystectomy
Urinary diversion
Ureterosigmoidostomy
Urethroplasty
Psychiatric
Electroconvulsive therapy
Radiation therapy

Source: Texas Department of Health (originally published in the *Texas Register*).

Table 8-2 *List B—Procedures Requiring No Disclosure*

Anesthesia
- Local/regional anesthesia

Cardiovascular system
- Varicose leg vein excision/ligation

Digestive system
- Appendectomy
- Hemorrhoidectomy
- Perirectal tissue incision/excision
- Anal/rectum lesion local excision/destruction
- Cleft palate corrections
- Inguinal hernia repair
- Anus/rectum repair/plastic operations
- Segmental colon resection
- Tonsillectomy

Ear
- Myringotomy
- Ear auricle reconstruction for skin cancer
- Tympanoplasty without mastoidectomy

Eye
- Topical, parenteral, or oral drug administration, including but not limited to fluorescein angiography, orbital injection, or periocular injections
- Extraocular foreign body removal
- Chalazion excision

Hematic and lymphatic system
- Lymph node biopsy

Integumentary system
- Breast biopsy
- Cutting/preparation of skin grafts/pedicle flaps
- Local skin or subcutaneous lesion removal/treatment
- Pilonidal sinus or cyst excision
- Skin suture
- Skin lesion wide or radical excision with or without graft
- Z plasty without excision
- Skin or mucus membrane biopsy
- Skin/mucus membrane lesion incision/drainage
- Skin ulceration debridement

Male genital system
- Testicle biopsy
- Testicular prosthesis placement
- Hydrocelectomy
- Circumcision
- Cystoscopy

Musculoskeletal system
- Arthrotomy
- Closed reduction without internal fixation

Table 8-2 *Continued*

- Lesion, muscle, tendon, fascia, bone excision
- Knee-joint semilunar cartilage excision
- Bone-marrow needle biopsy or aspiration
- Partial bone excision
- Internal fixation device removal
- Traction or fixation without manipulation for reduction

Nervous system

- Cranioplasty
- Lumbar puncture
- Meningomyelocele closure
- Ventriculostomy
- Diagnostic cysternal puncture
- Craniectomy or craniotomy for intracranial hematoma, abscess or penetrating injury
- Stereotaxic surgery for dystonia
- Skeletal tong insertion
- Intravenous cut-down
- Depressed skull fracture elevation
- Diagnostic cervical 1–2 puncture

Radiology

- Injection of contrast media or imaging media into spinal canal for diagnostic encephalography/cisternography
- Therapeutic intravascular infusion
- Lymphangiography
- Percutaneous transhepatic catheter placement
- Discography
- Venography with contrast media (Venogram)
- Cholangiography with contrast media
- Urography with contrast media (IVP)
- Digital subtraction angiography with contrast media
- Radionuclide scans/blood flow studies
- Gastrointestinal tract radiography and fluoroscopy
- Oral cholecystography
- Fistula or sinus tract injection
- Sialography
- Dachrocystography
- Cystography and cystourethrography
- Retrograde and antegrade urography
- Larynogography and bronchography
- Hysterosalpingography
- Endoscopic retrograde cholangio pancreatography
- Galactography
- T-tube cholangiography

Continued

Table 8-2 *Continued*

Skeletal radiography and fluoroscopy
Foreign body radiography and fluoroscopy
Chest and abdomen radiography and fluoroscopy
Portable radiography/fluoroscopy
Pelvimetry and fetogram
Computer tomography scan
Ultrasound and Doppler studies
Laminography, polytomography
Soft-tissue radiography
Kidney or bile-duct stone manipulation through percutaneous tube or tube tract
Pacemaker lead placement
Arthrography
Percutaneous nephrostogram/internal stent or external kidney drainage
Percutaneous transhepatic cholangiogram/internal stint or external liver drainage
Percutaneous abscess drainage
Respiratory system
Bronchus aspiration
Larynx, trachea, bronchus, or esophagus lesion biopsy
Lung biopsy
Lung needle biopsy
Lung segmental resection
Thoracotomy
Thoracotomy with drainage
Nasal fracture reduction
Tracheostomy
Urinary system
Nephrostomy
Prostate, bladder, or urethra biopsy
Cystolithotomy
Cystolitholopaxy
Cystostomy
Urethrotomy
Bladder diverticulectomy
Urethra diverticulectomy

Source: Texas Department of Health (originally published in the *Texas Register*).

Texas Register. Updated lists and forms can be obtained from the Texas Department of Health.[5]

What if a patient subsequently sues a health care provider and claims he was not adequately informed? If a health care provider followed the Panel's requirements for List A or if the procedure fell under List B, then this fact is admissible in evidence and creates a rebuttable presumption that the health care provider was not negligent. Consequently, absent other evidence, the health care provider would win.

If, on the other hand, a procedure fell under List A and inadequate disclosure was made, then this fact would be admissible in evidence and will create a rebuttable presumption of negligence. Thus, the patient would win absent some evidence offered by the health care provider that informed consent was obtained or that an emergency or some other situation made it infeasible to make disclosure. Thus, it is best for the health care provider to follow the Panel's guidelines to avoid a lawsuit based on informed consent.

What should a health care provider do if the procedure falls outside Lists A and B? If the procedure is absent from the lists, then the health care provider must disclose all inherent risks or hazards that could influence a reasonable person in making a decision to consent to the procedure.[6]

WHOSE DUTY IS IT TO INFORM PATIENTS OF RISKS AND HAZARDS?

In Texas, if a patient sues a health care provider for inadequately disclosing the risks and hazards inherent in a procedure, the only theory of recovery is negligence.[7] For the patient to win, he must prove that the health care provider owed him a duty to disclose the inherent risks and hazards of the procedure.[8]

Whose duty is it to inform the patient of the risks and hazards of a medical procedure in Texas? It is quite clear that it is the treating health care provider's responsibility to obtain informed consent.[9] Considering the proscriptions of the Medical Practice Act, it is most often the physician's responsibility to obtain informed consent.

> *Example 8.1: A general practitioner refers his patient to a surgeon. The surgeon determines that surgery is required and orders the nurse to have the patient sign the hospital's consent form before surgery. The nurse complies with the order. The patient has a bad outcome and sues the referring general practitioner, the surgeon, and the hospital under the legal theory of informed consent. Ignoring the merits of the lawsuit, which defendants have been sued properly?*

Table 8-3 *Disclosure of Risks and Hazards for Informed Consent at Childbirth*

	Information to be Disclosed
Vaginal delivery	1. Injury to bladder and/or rectum, including a fistula between bladder and vagina and/or rectum and vagina 2. Hemorrhage possibly requiring blood administration and/or hysterectomy and/or artery ligation to control 3. Sterility 4. Brain damage, injury, or even death occurring to the fetus before or during labor and/or vaginal delivery whether or not the cause is known
Cesarean section	1. Injury to bowel and/or bladder 2. Sterility 3. Injury to ureter between kidney and bladder 4. Brain damage, injury, or even death occurring to the fetus before or during labor and/or cesarean delivery whether or not the cause is known 5. Uterine disease or injury requiring hysterectomy

Answer: Only the surgeon has been sued properly.

It is neither the referring physician's nor the hospital's duty to obtain informed consent. The hospital does not assume the duty of obtaining informed consent from the patient just because the nurse, who is an employee of the hospital, gets the patient to sign the surgical consent form.[10]

Example 8.2: A nurse practitioner, unassisted by a physician, will be responsible for the vaginal delivery of a baby. Who should obtain informed consent?

Answer: The nurse practitioner should obtain informed consent and the appropriate documentation.

It is the treating health care provider's responsibility to obtain informed consent. The Medical Liability and Insurance Improvement Act's definition of "health care provider" includes registered nurses. Texas civil statutes proscribe when a registered nurse can treat patients. Under certain circumstances a registered nurse practitioner can deliver a baby vaginally. The Panel has decided that certain risks of a vaginal delivery must be explained to the patient (see Table 8-3). Consequently, the nurse practitioner would be responsible for obtaining informed consent and the appropriate documentation above in Example 8.2.

PHYSICIAN'S AUTHORITY TO DELEGATE DUTY OF INFORMED CONSENT

Generally, a physician can delegate a medical act to any qualified and properly trained person acting under the physician's supervision if the act can be properly and safely performed in its customary manner.[11] The Texas State Board of Medical Examiners, not the Texas State Board of Nurse Examiners, has the authority to determine whether any medical act may or may not be properly delegated by physicians to nurses.[12]

If the physician properly delegates a medical act to a nurse, she is not guilty of practicing medicine without a license unless the person acts with knowledge that the delegation and action violate the Medical Practice Act.[13] If, however, a physician improperly delegates a medical act to a nurse, she violates neither the Nursing Practice Act nor the Medical Practice Act if she *acts in good faith,* believing that the medical act was properly delegated.[14] In this situation, however, the nurse would be placed in the unenviable position of proving lack of knowledge.

Example 8.3: A surgeon writes in the doctor's orders: "I have informed patient of risks of procedure, expected results, and treatment alternatives. Please get consent form signed." Should the nurse institute the order?

Answer: First, the nurse should determine whether the doctor's order would violate the written policy of the institution where the nurse works; some institutions require that doctors get the patient's signature on consent forms witnessed. If the order does not violate the institution's policy, the nurse should next determine whether there is a reasonable belief that the patient was adequately informed by the physician. If the nurse is satisfied that the patient was adequately informed, it should be proper for him to witness the patient's signature on the consent form, although it is not the best situation for a nurse to be in.

A federal court applying Texas law stated that a doctor may delegate the duty of informed consent.[15] Thus, it would seem appropriate for the nurse to obtain the patient's signature in the scenario depicted in Example 8.3. It would, however, be dangerous to apply this statement to every situation likely to confront a nurse.

In the federal case mentioned above, a cardiologist did not personally tell the patient about the risks of a stress test. Instead he told the laboratory technician to review a consent form with the patient and have him sign it; the form was presumably already prepared. The consent form listed "death" as a risk of the test. The laboratory technician followed the doctor's orders. During the first stage of the stress test the patient experienced chest pain; he died the following day. The patient's family sued the cardiologist under the theory of informed consent. In this case a technician merely went over a prepared consent form with the patient before the patient signed it; the technician did not determine himself what risks the patient should be told. Therefore, the nurse is probably safe in instituting the doctor's order in Example 8.3. There are many situations, however, that confront nurses daily in which this case holding would not provide protection from liability.

Example 8.4: A surgeon writes in the doctor's orders: "Please explain risks of surgery to patient and then have him sign a consent form." No prepared consent form exists, and the doctor tells the nurse to prepare one herself. Should the nurse institute the order?

Answer: If the nurse institutes the surgeon's order, she is subjecting herself unnecessarily to liability.

It is true that a physician can delegate the task of obtaining informed consent to a qualified and properly trained nurse if the nurse obtains it properly and safely in its customary manner while acting under the physician's supervision. Is a nurse qualified to discuss with a patient treatment alternatives, the probable results if a patient gets treated or remains untreated, and the risks and hazards inherent in the procedure or treatment that could influence a reasonable person in deciding whether or not to consent? Probably not; this task may conflict with the Medical Practice Act.

A physician who delegates the task of obtaining informed consent to a nurse remains responsible for the nurse's performance.[16] This fact does not preclude the possibility, however, that a nurse could be held jointly responsible with the physician. Remember that a nurse is shielded from liability only if she did not know that she was not qualified and trained to properly and safely obtain informed consent in its customary manner. There is no case in Texas that has tested the liability of a nurse in these circumstances, yet. The groundwork for liability exists in the law, however. Therefore, a nurse may avoid liability in the situation depicted in Example 8.4 by refusing to institute the order and by informing the surgeon and the nurse supervisor of the nurse's decision immediately.

In Example 8.4 there is a broader principle by which a nurse should refuse to institute the surgeon's order. Informed consent is an educational process between a physician and his patient by which a patient is able to make an informed choice about what medical treatment he should accept. The consent form is only an efficient way to document consistently communications that have already occurred between a physician and his patient in order to protect the physician from legal liability.

The educational process between patient and physician should not be separated artificially from the signing of the consent form. Informed consent should not be reduced to getting a piece of paper signed. If it is and nurses become involved in the informed-consent process, nurses will find themselves in the future subject to legal liabilities that at one time did not exist.[17]

Example 8.5: A hospital policy states that it is the physician's responsibility to ensure that informed consent is obtained. A nurse is about to premedicate a patient for surgery. Should he investigate whether informed consent was given by the patient before he premedicates her for surgery?

Answer: First, if a written hospital policy states that the nurse must ensure that the patient has given informed consent before releasing the patient for surgery, then the nurse must investigate whether informed consent was given before he premedicates her for surgery. If the hospital has no such policy, the nurse should still investigate whether informed consent was given.

A hospital in Texas had a policy that specifically defined the tasks of surgical nurses when they were counting sponges. The court held that counting sponges was an administrative function to be carried out by nurses. Consequently, since the surgeon did not control these activities, he could not be held liable for a miscount. Instead, the hospital was liable for the acts of the nurses during this administrative task.[18] Ensuring that a consent form is signed or that informed consent was given could be labeled an administrative task by a Texas court. Consequently, a nurse should avoid liability for herself and the hospital by following a hospital policy that directs her to ensure that informed consent is obtained before a patient undergoes a procedure.

A case decided in North Carolina, if followed in Texas, could impose on nurses the duty to ensure that informed consent is given before a procedure begins despite the absence of a hospital policy. In this case the parents of a child sued the obstetrician and the hospital because their baby suffered brain damage during a breech delivery when the umbilical cord became wrapped around the infant's legs, causing severe asphyxia. The nurse noticed signs of distress several hours before delivery. When the physician ignored her concerns, she did not report her findings to her supervisor.[19]

The North Carolina court held that the hospital had a general obligation to make a reasonable effort to ensure that the patient's informed consent was obtained before the delivery. In reaching this conclusion, the court not only relied on a 1979 hospital policy that required delivery nurses to get the signatures of the parents on a hospital consent form but also relied on the testimony of a perinatal nurse expert, who stated that "[e]xplaining the risk of alternative procedures would be the responsibility of the physician[;] [a]ssuring that the patient has had an explanation would be the responsibility of the nurse."[20]

This question has not been tested in a Texas court, yet. It is foreseeable, however, that if the question is ever raised, a Texas court could follow the reasoning of the North Carolina court. Therefore, Texas nurses may wish to ensure that informed consent has been obtained before a procedure to avoid liability. Although by nurses' following this advice a standard of practice for nurses could be created that would subject a nurse to liability for not ensuring that informed consent has been obtained, this practice serves the patient's best interest.

OTHER INFORMED-CONSENT ISSUES

Example 8.6: A patient suffering from an abdominal gunshot wound is brought to the emergency room. The physician determines that the patient is hemorrhaging and emergency surgery is required. Is informed consent required?

Answer: Informed consent is not required.

Informed consent is required neither when there is an emergency nor if it is not medically feasible to obtain it.[21]

Example 8.7: A psychiatrist diagnoses a patient as schizophrenic. The patient has no legal guardian. The psychiatrist orders a nurse in writing to give the patient an appropriate dose of a neuroleptic drug. A side effect of the drug is tardive dyskinesia. Should the nurse give the drug?

Answer: The nurse should not give the drug to the patient until she has a reasonable belief that the patient has given informed consent.

The Supreme Court of Texas held that a mentally ill patient does not lose automatically his constitutional right to make his own medical decisions.[22] It is not medically infeasible to inform a patient of the risks of taking a medication just because a psychiatrist is afraid that a patient will refuse a medication if he knows about the possible side effects of the drug. It does not matter if the patient does not have the reactions of a reasonable person. The patient is entitled to know about material side effects of a drug that could influence a reasonable person in his decision of whether or not to take the drug. In determining whether a risk is material, the following factors are considered: (1) how the condition manifests itself, (2) the permanency of the condition caused by the risk, (3) the known cures for the condition, (4) the seriousness of the condition, and (5) the overall effect of the condition on the body.

The Supreme Court of Texas did not hold that tardive dyskinesia is a material risk of a neuroleptic drug. Instead the court sent the case back to the trial court so that a jury could decide if tardive dyskinesia is a material risk. Additionally, neuroleptic drug therapy is neither on List A nor on List B. To avoid litigation, in Example 8.7 it would be wise for the nurse to ensure that the patient has given informed consent before the nurse gives the medication.

Example 8.8: A patient is about to undergo brain surgery for a brain tumor. His brain tumor is causing mental confusion. The surgeon asks a nurse to get his consent form signed. Should the nurse have the confused patient sign the consent form? Should the nurse have the patient's spouse sign the consent form?

Answer: The confused patient should not sign the consent form. The patient's spouse should not sign the consent form unless the spouse has legal capacity to do so. The nurse should immediately tell the surgeon and the nurse supervisor about the situation.

When witnessing a consent form, a nurse attests to (1) authenticity, (2) voluntariness, and (3) capacity.[23] Authenticity means that the signature belongs to the patient. Voluntariness means that the patient was neither forced nor coerced into signing the consent form. Capacity means that the patient understood the physician's explanation of the nature of the procedure and its risks and alternatives, read the consent form, understood it, and agreed to submit to the proposed procedure.[24]

Arguably the patient in Example 8.8 does not have the capacity to sign the consent form since he is in a confused state of mind. Can the spouse sign the consent form for the patient? In Texas, the husband-wife relationship in itself does not make one spouse the agent of the other.[25] Therefore, in Example 8.8 the wife could not sign the consent form for her husband. If, however, a court of competent jurisdiction declared the wife the legal guardian of the husband, the wife could sign the consent form on behalf of her husband.[26] A properly executed durable power of attorney may satisfy this requirement, also. For these reasons a nurse faced with this situation should inform the surgeon and the nurse supervisor immediately about this situation.

It should be remembered, however, that if the brain surgery is an emergency, then no informed consent is required.

Example 8.9: A nurse who is about to have a patient sign his consent form realizes that he is illiterate. What should the nurse do?

Answer: The nurse must ensure that the patient has the capacity for understanding what he is signing. The nurse should read the consent form aloud verbatim and ask the patient whether his doctor has talked to him about the procedure, its risks and alternatives, and whether he understands the doctor's instruction and the consent form. If he answers yes, then she should have him place an X for his signature. Also, the nurse should document her actions in the nursing progress notes.[27]

Example 8.10: A nurse must get a patient to sign a consent form for surgery, but the patient speaks only Spanish and the consent form is written in English. What should the nurse do?

Answer: The nurse must locate an interpreter, either one provided by the institution or a family member of the patient's. First it should be determined whether the patient was informed by her doctor of the nature of the procedure, its risks and benefits, and alternative treatments. If the answer is yes, then the interpreter should read the consent form aloud to the patient in Spanish. Next the patient should be asked whether she understands the doctor's instruction and the consent form. If the answer is yes, then the patient can sign the consent form. Also, the nurse should document in the nursing progress notes the actions he took and the name of the interpreter.[28]

A nurse should not have the patient sign the consent form and should immediately inform the treating physician and the nurse supervisor if the nurse ever reasonably believes that

1. the doctor did not instruct the patient about the nature of the proposed procedure, its risks and benefits, the likely outcome if the patient remains untreated, and the alternative treatments;
2. the patient does not understand either the above instruction or the consent form;
3. the patient has decided not to undergo the procedure;
4. the nurse believes the patient is being forced or coerced into the treatment;
5. the nurse reasonably believes that the patient is without capacity to understand what is happening; or
6. the patient is not who he says he is.

Example 8.11: A newborn patient is scheduled for heart surgery. Who should sign the consent form, and whom should the physician counsel about the procedure?

Answer: Both parents of the child should be counseled by the physician, and both parents should sign the consent form.

The parents of a child have the right and duty to provide their child with medical care. A "child" is defined generally as any unmarried person under the age of eighteen years. A Fort Worth court answered the question posed in Example 8.11 when it held that an infant's parents are entitled to informed-consent instruction because a newborn infant is incapable of evaluating information about its medical condition or consenting to further diagnosis or treatment.[29]

Special care should be taken when a child's parents are divorced.[30] Informed consent should be obtained at least from the parent who is the managing conservator, that is, the parent who has the primary responsibility for the child. If the parents share the managing conservatorship, then both parents should sign the consent form. If it is unclear who the managing conservator is, in a nonemergency situation the parents could be asked by the physician or nurse supervisor to present a copy of the latest child-support order.

PRACTICE SUGGESTIONS

1. Health care professionals who treat patients should document informed consent in the manner dictated by the Panel to afford maximum legal protection.
2. Health care providers should not delegate their responsibility of obtaining informed consent from patients being treated.
3. A nurse should be reasonably assured that a patient has received adequate informed-consent instruction before she either premedicates him for a procedure or, if no premedication is required, releases him for a procedure.
4. If a nurse is involved in getting a consent form signed, it is best to have a patient's family member witness the signature.[31]
5. A nurse who witnesses a patient's signature should first be reasonably assured of authenticity, voluntariness, and capacity.

9

Drug Therapy

A nurse who violates state or federal drug laws may face jail time, the loss of her nursing license, and a possible nursing negligence lawsuit filed by a patient. Consequently, nurses have an incentive to know relevant drug laws.

DRUG CLASSIFICATIONS

Controlled Substances

Controlled substances[1] are drugs with a potential for abuse that may lead to physical or psychological dependence. They are categorized as either Schedule I, II, III, IV, or V. The categories reflect a continuum in the likelihood of creating dependence. Schedule I has the highest likelihood of producing dependence, with Schedule V having the lowest. In deciding how to categorize the drugs, the Texas commissioner of health weighs the potential for abuse versus its medical use. Both federal and state laws classify controlled substances in basically the same way. Lists of controlled substances by category can be obtained from the supplying pharmacy or a state poison control center. See the list of centers under "Poison Control Centers" later in this chapter.

Advanced nurse practitioners *may not* prescribe controlled substances. Additionally, Schedule I drugs generally may neither be administered nor dispensed; they have a high potential for abuse, have no accepted medical use in treatment in the United States, and lack accepted safety for use under medical supervision. Schedule I drugs include heroin, LSD, marijuana, mescaline, methaqualone, PCP, and peyote.[2]

Penalty Groups

Texas law categorizes controlled substances into what are called "penalty groups" to establish criminal penalties for violations of Texas drug laws.

Dangerous Drugs

Dangerous drugs[3] are any drugs that are not controlled substances and that cannot be purchased over the counter. These drugs must be labeled "Caution: Federal law prohibits dispensing without prescription."

DRUG-LAW VIOLATIONS

Controlled Substances

The following are proscriptions regarding controlled substances:

1. Unlawful possession, manufacture, or delivery of a controlled substance or of a simulated controlled substance
2. Manufacture, delivery, or possession of substances in a penalty group
3. Possession or delivery of marijuana
4. Delivery of a controlled substance or marijuana to a minor
5. Illegal investment of funds intended to further commission of offenses under the Texas Controlled Substances Act
6. Unlawful possession or delivery of drug paraphernalia
7. Refusal or failure to make, keep, or furnish required records
8. Unauthorized printing, manufacturing, possession, or production of triplicate prescription forms
9. Delivery or possession of counterfeit triplicate prescriptions
10. Use of registration number that is fictitious or has been suspended or revoked
11. Unauthorized use of another person's registration number or triplicate prescription forms
12. Providing of false or fraudulent information in or omission of material information from any application, report, records, or other document required to be kept under the law
13. Delivery of prescription for other than valid medical purpose
14. Falsification of drug-test results by use of substance designed to falsify drug-test results
15. Manufacture of substance designed to falsify drug-test results
16. Refusal of entry into premise for an authorized inspection

If a nurse violates a drug law, the crime he will be charged with and the resulting criminal penalty will depend on the controlled substance involved, the amount of the drug involved, and the presence of prior drug convictions.

A patient may not possess a controlled substance upon his release from the hospital unless (1) the drug was dispensed under a medication order while the patient was admitted to the hospital, (2) the substance is in a properly labeled container, and (3) the supply is for not more than seven days.

Dangerous Drugs

The following acts are violations of the dangerous drug laws: (1) illegal[4] possession of dangerous drugs, (2) illegal delivery of or offer to deliver dangerous drugs, (3) unauthorized manufacture of dangerous drugs, and (4) any other violation of the Texas Dangerous Drug Act, such as forging or altering prescriptions.

Texas Food, Drug, and Cosmetic Act

Under the Texas Food, Drug, and Cosmetic Act,[5] the following acts are examples of drug violations regarding any drug: (1) misbranding or adulterating any drug or device, (2) dispensing a different drug in place of the drug ordered or prescribed without the express permission of the person ordering or prescribing, (3) giving false guaranty when dispensing drug or device, and (4) accepting unused prescription or drug in whole or in part after it has been originally dispensed or sold for the purpose of resale to any person.

SPECIFIC DRUGS

Alcohol

Texas law allows a physician to prescribe liquor for medicinal purposes for a patient if the physician has a permit to do so.[6] Before he prescribes liquor, however, the physician must perform a physical examination to diagnose the disease or ailment afflicting the patient. The physician cannot do the following acts: (1) prescribe more than one pint of liquor for a person in any one day, (2) prescribe for any person showing evidence of intoxication, (3) prescribe for any minor unless the physician has the written consent of the minor's parent or guardian, and (4) issue more than one hundred prescriptions in any ninety-day period. Distilled spirits, wine, and beer are not scheduled drugs.

Anabolic Steroids

Anabolic steroids and human growth hormones that are listed as Schedule IV drugs may be prescribed and dispensed for a *valid medical purpose* in the course of professional practice. *Valid medical purpose* does not include bodybuilding, muscle enhancement, or increasing of muscle bulk or strength by a person who is in good health.[7] It is a violation of federal law to distribute or possess anabolic steroids or human growth hormone for a reason other than to treat a disease.[8]

Dimethyl Sulfoxide

A licensed physician can prescribe and administer dimethyl sulfoxide (DMSO). If the prescribed formulation, however, is not approved by the Food and Drug Administration (FDA), the physician must (1) provide a written statement to the patient informing him that the formulation has not been so approved and (2) inform the patient of alternative methods of treatment for the patient's disorder and the potential of alternative methods for cure.

Hospitals and health care facilities may not forbid or restrict the use of DMSO that is prescribed or administered by licensed physicians having staff privileges at their hospitals unless the hospital or facility (1) makes a formal finding that the drug will be harmful to the patient as it is prescribed or administered or (2) determines that the prescription or administration creates an immediate danger to the public.

It is a class B misdemeanor for a person to knowingly or intentionally represent DMSO as a cure for any human disease, ailment, or disorder when advertising or promoting its sale.[9]

Experimental Drugs

A nurse may not administer an experimental drug to a patient unless the physician has filed a completed and signed "Notice of Claimed Investigational Exemption for a New Drug" with the FDA. The drug must be labeled plainly in compliance with the federal Food, Drug, and Cosmetic Act.[10]

Drugs for Intractable Pain

"Intractable pain" is defined by Texas law as a pain state in which the cause of the pain cannot be removed or otherwise treated and in which, in the generally accepted course of medical practice, no relief or cure of the cause of the pain is possible or none has been found after reasonable efforts. Physicians can prescribe or administer dangerous drugs or controlled substances to a person for intractable pain.

No hospital or health care facility may forbid or restrict the use of dangerous drugs or controlled substances when prescribed or administered by a physician having staff privileges at the hospital and treating a patient diagnosed as having intractable pain. The Texas statute does not give physicians the authority to prescribe these drugs for a patient the physician knows or should know is using drugs for nontherapeutic purposes.[11]

Intravenous Conscious Sedation

The Texas Board of Nurse Examiners has determined that it is within the scope of practice of a registered nurse (RN) who is not a certified registered nurse anesthetist (CRNA) to administer intravenous (IV) conscious sedation, although optimal anesthesia care is best provided by qualified anesthesiologists and CRNAs.[12] Physicians can delegate the medical act of administering drugs to induce conscious sedation through properly written patient-specific orders to any *qualified and properly trained nurse* acting under the physician's supervision if, in the physician's opinion, the act can be *properly and safely performed* in its *customary manner*.[13] The American Nurses Association (ANA) and the American Association of Nurse Anesthetists (AANA)[14] have published position statements that serve as excellent guidelines in determining what skills an RN must possess before she is qualified and properly trained to properly and safely administer medications in the customary manner to induce conscious sedation.

According to the AANA, to be qualified, the RN must be able to

1. demonstrate the acquired knowledge of anatomy, physiology, pharmacology, cardiac arrhythmia recognition, and complications related to IV conscious sedation and medications.
2. assess the total patient-care requirement during IV conscious sedation. Physiologic measurements should include, but not be limited to, respiratory rate, oxygen saturation, blood pressure, cardiac rate and rhythm, and the patient's level of consciousness. Documentation intervals should be dictated by the patient's condition; however, vital signs should be recorded at least every five minutes.
3. understand the principles of oxygen delivery, transport and uptake, and respiratory physiology and understand and be able to use oxygen delivery devices.
4. anticipate and recognize potential complications of IV conscious sedation in relation to the type of medication being administered.
5. possess the requisite knowledge and skills to assess, diagnose, and intervene in the event of complications or undesired outcomes and to institute appropriate nursing interventions in compliance with orders (including standing orders) or institutional protocols or guidelines.
6. demonstrate skill in airway management and resuscitation.
7. have a thorough understanding and recognition of the legal ramifi-

cations of providing this care, especially of the RN's responsibility and liability in the event of an untoward reaction or life-threatening complication.

When an RN manages IV conscious sedation, it is the AANA's position that the following criteria be met:

1. Guidelines for patient monitoring, drug administration, and protocols for dealing with potential complications or emergency situations are available and have been developed in accordance with accepted standards of anesthesia practice.
2. The RN managing the care of the patient receiving IV conscious sedation shall have no other responsibilities during the procedure and may not leave the patient unattended or engage in tasks that would compromise continuous monitoring.
3. A qualified professional capable of managing complications that might arise should remain on site until the patient is stable.
4. A qualified professional authorized to discharge a patient under institutional guidelines should remain on site to discharge the patient in accordance with established criteria of the facility.

Further, it is the AANA's position that each institution or practice setting must have in place an educational and credentialing mechanism whereby evaluation and documentation of competence occurs on a periodic basis.

Finally, each of the following procedural guidelines should be incorporated into the facility's policies and procedures:

1. All patients having local anesthesia with IV conscious sedation will have a continuous IV line in place.
2. All patients receiving IV conscious sedation will be continuously monitored throughout the procedure as well as the recovery phase by electrocardiogram, pulse oximetry, and blood-pressure monitors.
3. Supplemental oxygen will be provided to all patients receiving IV conscious sedation per order (including standing orders).
4. An emergency cart must be immediately accessible to every location where IV conscious sedation is administered. This cart must include at least the following: emergency and resuscitative drugs, airway and ventilatory adjunct equipment, defibrillator, and a source for administration of 100 percent oxygen. A positive pressure breathing device, oxygen, and appropriate airways must be in each room where IV conscious sedation is administered.
5. Provisions must be in place for backup personnel who are expert in airway management, emergency intubation, and advanced cardiopulmonary resuscitation if complications arise.
6. An RN who is not a credentialed anesthesia provider should not ad-

minister drugs classified as anesthetics, including but not limited to ketamine, sodium thiopental, methohexital, propofol, etomidate, and nitrous oxide.[15]

Laetrile

Texas law authorizes a licensed physician to prescribe or administer laetrile for cancer treatment. The drug, however, cannot be administered to a patient who is known to be a habitual user of narcotic or dangerous drugs unless the physician first notifies the Texas Board of Medical Examiners in writing of the name and address of the patient being treated.

A hospital or other health care facility may neither forbid nor restrict the use of laetrile when it is requested by a patient and prescribed or administered by a physician unless the Texas Board of Medical Examiners finds the substance harmful as prescribed or administered.[16]

Marijuana

Marijuana is a Schedule I drug. It cannot be prescribed by a physician unless the patient is participating in a therapeutic research program that is supervised by either the Texas Board of Health review board or the United States Attorney General's office. Generally, only patients with glaucoma or cancer can participate. Additionally, the patients must not be responding to conventional treatment and must be experiencing severe side effects from the treatment, and those side effects may be alleviated by marijuana. A participant cannot be prosecuted for possessing, distributing, or dispensing a controlled substance or drug paraphernalia to the extent that he uses it per protocol.

PRESCRIPTIONS

Controlled Substances

Generally, controlled substances must be prescribed on triplicate forms that are serially numbered except when medication orders are written and filled for patients in the hospital.

Refills

Prescriptions for Schedule II drugs *may not* be refilled. Additionally, a Schedule II prescription cannot be filled after the end of the seventh day after it was issued. Schedule II drugs include amobarbital, amphetamine, cocaine, codeine, fentanyl, methadone, morphine, opium, pentobarbital, secobarbital, and sufentanyl.[17]

Schedule III and IV drugs cannot be filled or refilled more than six months from the date of issuance. Dangerous drugs can be refilled only if the practitioner so designates on the prescription. A prescription may not authorize more than five refills.

Oral Prescriptions

Except in hospitals, in an emergency, or when dispensed directly by the practitioner to the patient, no Schedule II drug may be dispensed or administered without a written prescription by a practitioner on a triplicate prescription form.

An emergency means that the immediate administration of the drug is necessary if (1) the drug is used to properly treat the patient; (2) no appropriate alternative treatment is available, including the administration of a drug that is not a Schedule II drug; and (3) it is not reasonably possible for the prescribing practitioner to provide a written prescription to be presented to the person dispensing the substance before the dispensing. An individual may administer or dispense a Schedule II drug during an emergency after the prescription has been communicated, either orally or over the telephone, by a practitioner. The person who administers or dispenses the drug must promptly write the communicated prescription on a triplicate prescription form (unless dispensed in a hospital) and shall include the following information in the written record: (1) the name, address, and federal Drug Enforcement Administration number of the prescribing practitioner; (2) the date of the prescription; (3) the drug prescribed, quantity, instructions for use; and (4) the name, address, and age of the patient. The person must send a copy of the written record to the Department of Public Safety no later than the thirtieth day after the date the prescription is filled. The physician, within seventy-two hours after authorizing the prescription, must, in person or through the mail, give the dispensing pharmacy a written prescription.

Schedule III and IV drugs may be prescribed orally or over the telephone.

Inspections

An inspector from the Texas Department of Public Safety or from the United States Attorney General's office can enter the site where controlled substances and dangerous drugs are dispensed at any reasonable time to inspect, copy, and verify the correctness of records that must be kept. Before he enters the premises, the inspector must state the purpose of the entry and present to the owner, operator, or agent in charge of the premises appropriate credentials and a written notice of inspection authority. Before a nurse gives an inspector access to medications or her work station, she should ask to see the inspector's credentials and a written notice of his inspection authority.

An inspector can examine the following things: (1) within reasonable limits and in a reasonable manner the records, the controlled premises, and all pertinent equipment, drugs, containers, and labels; (2) inventory stock of a controlled substance; and (3) material to be used or that is capable of or is being used to dilute or adulterate a controlled substance. Additionally, an inspector can obtain a sample of a controlled substance but must leave a receipt.

Advanced Nurse Practitioners' Prescriptions

Advanced nurse practitioners (ANPs) practicing in medically underserved populations can prescribe dangerous drugs for medication through presigned prescription drug orders. The ANP should be familiar with the material in this chapter and should refer also to Chapter 4, "Advanced Nurse Practitioners," especially the material included under "Medically Underserved Populations."

Dispensing of Medication in Rural Areas

A licensed physician who practices in a *rural area* in which there is no pharmacy may maintain a supply of dangerous drugs in his office to be dispensed in the course of treating his patients and may be reimbursed for the cost of supplying those drugs without obtaining a license under the Texas Pharmacy Act. A *rural area* is an area in which there is no pharmacy within a fifteen-mile radius of the doctor's office and is within a county with a total population of five thousand or fewer or is within a city or town with a population of fewer than twenty-five hundred. It should not include, however, a city or town whose boundaries are adjacent to an incorporated city or town with an equal or greater population.

A physician dispensing dangerous drugs in a rural area must comply with all appropriate labeling rules and oversee compliance with packaging and recordkeeping.[18]

POISON CONTROL CENTERS

In Texas there are six regional centers for poison control and drug information services, which serve both the public and health professionals:

1. University of Texas Medical Branch at Galveston;
2. Dallas County Hospital District/North Texas Poison Center;
3. University of Texas Health Science Center at San Antonio;
4. R.E. Thomason General Hospital, El Paso County Hospital District;

5. Northwest Texas Hospital, Amarillo Hospital District; and
6. Scott and White Memorial Hospital, Temple, Texas.

The Texas Board of Health may vote to designate a seventh regional or satellite poison control center in Harris County.

Each center ensures that treatment facilities and services are available within the region and that they identify and make available to the public and to appropriate health professionals information concerning analytical toxicology, emergency and critical care, and extracorporeal capabilities within the region.

The poison control centers employ physicians, pharmacists, nurses, and support personnel who are trained in various aspects of toxicology and poison control and prevention. Their job is to provide the following services:

1. community education programs on poison prevention methods to inform the public, such as presentations to persons attending a primary or secondary school, a parent-teacher association meeting, an employee safety meeting at an industrial company, or other interested groups;
2. information and education to health professionals involved in the management of poison and overdose victims, including information regarding appropriate therapeutic use of medications, their compatibility and stability, and adverse drug reactions and interactions;
3. professional and technical assistance to state agencies requesting toxicologic assistance; and
4. consultation services concerning medical toxicology, for which a fee may be charged in an amount set by the institution in which the center is located to cover the costs of the service.[19]

Information on poison is available twenty-four hours a day. At the time this book was written, a commission was developing the telephone service routing system. It was tentatively planned that calls would be routed to regional poison control centers through the 911 service rather than through toll-free telephone referrals for each regional center.

PEER ASSISTANCE

In Texas, persons or institutions who are required by law to report an impaired (chemically dependent or mentally ill) RN or licensed vocational nurse (LVN) to the nurse's licensing board satisfy that duty if the nurse is reported to the Texas Peer Assistance Program for Nurses (TPAPN) instead.[20]

The purpose of the TPAPN is to identify and assist RNs and LVNs whose abilities to provide nursing services have been impaired by mental illness or dependency on drugs so that they can return to competent practice. Emphasis of the program is on education, advocacy, and opportunity as opposed to punitive action against the nurse. The philosophy of the TPAPN is that nurses should not lose their jobs or licenses because of chemical dependency or mental illness without first being offered the opportunity for education, treatment, and recovery. Furthermore, the TPAPN believes that nurses whose impairment prevents them from practicing at an acceptable professional level should not be allowed to practice. The TPAPN helps provide assessment, referral, support, and monitoring services to nurses whose abilities to practice nursing have been impaired by chemical dependency or mental illness. The TPAPN works with employers of nurses to help ensure appropriate referral, treatment, a return to work, and monitoring for nurses in need.[21]

Nurses can refer themselves to the TPAPN, or others can report the nurse directly to the TPAPN by calling 1-800-288-5528. A case manager is on call twenty-four hours a day for emergencies. Most referrals are made to the TPAPN by nurse employers. The TPAPN is independent of the Texas Board of Nurse Examiners and the Texas Board of Vocational Nurse Examiners and operates as a program of the Texas Nurses Foundation. Participation in the TPAPN is voluntary, but nurses who refuse assistance and continue to practice, thereby endangering patients and others, will be reported to the nurse's licensing board when appropriate. Nurses who refer themselves to the TPAPN will not be reported to the nurse's licensing board normally unless it is determined that the nurse is an immediate danger to patients or others. The TPAPN adheres to the philosophy of total abstinence from all mood-altering drugs (including alcohol) as being essential to the nurse's successful chemical dependency recovery. The TPAPN, however, views relapse as a normal part of the recovery/disease process. With the licensing board's approval, a nurse who relapses and is willing to continue the treatment program may be allowed to remain in the TPAPN.[22]

When an employer reports a nurse to the TPAPN, the following process occurs, generally:

1. An employer identifies a nurse as impaired.
2. The employer calls the TPAPN.
3. The employer confers with a case manager.
4. If appropriate, a case number is assigned.
5. An approved provider is contacted by the TPAPN. A case number is given.
6. An approved provider contacts the employer. Intervention and evaluation are set.
7. A volunteer advocate is contacted by the TPAPN.

8. The advocate contacts the employer and/or nurse. The advocate remains available as a resource and as support.
9. An approved provider communicates the outcome to the TPAPN.

Nurses who suspect that drugs or alcohol or mental illness are affecting their practice should consider referring themselves to the TPAPN immediately. Seeking treatment not only protects the patient from harm but also affords greater job and license protection. Some employers will have employee assistance programs to assist nurses in the recovery process so that recovering nurses can reenter the workplace.[23]

Employers and nurses with impairment questions, such as how to identify impaired nurses, how to intervene on behalf of nurses, or how they can sign up to become volunteer advocates, should contact the TPAPN for information.

10

Documentation

CHARTING

The medical record serves many functions: it enhances communication between health care professionals, serves as a tool for planning and evaluating patient care, is a source of clinical data for research, provides proof for reimbursement, and is a legal document. This section will concentrate on the function of the medical record as a legal document.

The first commandment is that the medical record should not raise suspicions by what it says or by what it does not say. When a plaintiff's attorney evaluates a patient's potential nursing negligence claim, the attorney has two sources of information, generally: the recollection of the patient or of the patient's family and the medical record. A medical record that reconstructs the hospitalization and clearly shows the plan of care may prevent a lawsuit from being filed, because bad results are not actionable in Texas. Consequently, if the record documents the assessment of a problem, the plan, and the implementation and evaluation, it is unlikely that a lawsuit will be filed. If, however, the record is incomplete by the omission of one of these steps or contains hints of trouble, a suit may be filed. Additionally, a suit may be filed if there is no hint of a problem in the medical record and the patient or his family relates a cover-up by the health professionals. If a suit is filed, the medical record also serves as the single most important piece of evidence concerning whether negligence occurred. Nursing negligence suits come to trial generally at least two years after they are filed. Because memories fail and witnesses cannot be found, the medical record becomes the material piece of evidence on the care a patient received. Following a few guidelines can make the medical record the nurse's best defense to a suit.

Legibility

The medical record should be legible. Illegible records can raise a jury's suspicions. Every person who makes an entry in the chart should clearly sign the entry and include his position or title.[1] Only abbreviations accepted by the hospital should be used. The nurse should follow his institution's policy regarding changing medical record errors. Generally, nurses can correct minor transcription errors by crossing out the incorrect entry with a single line, entering the correct information, initialing the change, and entering the date and time. The incorrect information should never be erased or obliterated by whiting out or blacking out the information.[2] An empty space should be crossed out with a single line to prevent others from altering the record.

Completeness

The medical record should be complete. It is complete if it documents the nursing process: assessment, plan, implementation, and evaluation (which includes the patient's response). The record should reflect changes in the nursing-care plan. If a routine procedure is not given, the chart should reflect why. A complete record is important for a nurse's defense because if a hospital can demonstrate that complete records are kept, the patient's statement that his complaints were not attended to can be rebutted when the record is silent. For an incomplete record, however, the jury can infer that care was not given if the record is silent about observations.[3]

Paul Greve alerts nurses to three common situations in which charting gaps occur: (1) when vital signs are abnormal, (2) when a patient code occurs, and (3) when a patient is transferred. Greve suggests the following prevention measures.

ABNORMAL VITAL SIGNS. Any significant deviation from normal vital signs demands a notation that shows what is being done. If a physician is notified, the nurse should chart the time of the call, the physician's response, and whether the nurse carried out the order. If the physician cannot be reached, the nurse should note the time the physician returned the nurse's call, subsequent attempts to contact the physician, or when the physician was contacted. If the nurse's response to abnormal findings is to monitor the patient more closely, this fact should be noted in the chart together with whether the patient's condition improves or deteriorates. The nurse should note how often a change occurs.

PATIENT CODES. It is crucial for documentation to be completed after a code to deflect patient complaints that monitoring was inadequate and intervention was too late. The completion of code sheets by an assigned member of the code team is an effective way of generating a complete record. Documentation should be reviewed for completeness once the code is over. If feasible, the nurse should follow the patient to the intensive care unit (ICU) to ensure a complete record.

PATIENT TRANSFERS. A patient's condition must be assessed before the patient is transferred to another floor or to another institution. Documentation of the patient's condition before and after a transfer is required.[4]

Timeliness and Accuracy

The medical record should be completed timely. Notations made weeks after the fact or made after a complaint is lodged are not as credible as notations made at the time of the event.

The medical record should never be falsified. Falsifying medical records can result in an indefensible lawsuit, the loss of a job, the loss of a nursing license, and jail time.

Generally only the person who writes the notation should change the notation. Suppose, however, that a nurse from a prior shift calls another nurse and asks her to chart some relevant information that the nurse from the prior shift forgot to chart. The nurse should chart the information but only in a way that does not imply that the transcribing nurse carried out the procedure or was there when it was performed. Stephen Bergerson suggests using the following notation form: "At 3:25 P.M., Mary Jackson called and reported that at 8:25 this morning, she . . ."[5]

If a nurse realizes that she omitted important information regarding a patient a day or so later, she should chart it at the next available space in the record. The nurse should entitle the note, "Addendum to Nurse's Note of [month, date, time]."[6]

The nurse should use special caution when involved in the situations discussed below.

HOSTILE PATIENTS. The behavior of a patient who the nurse perceives as hostile should be described clinically if clinically significant. The description should be accurate and objective. For example, a patient should be quoted rather than only labeled as abusive or noncompliant. Derogatory statements about the patient should not be charted. To do so will raise the question whether the nurse's personal feelings about the patient interfered with nursing care. Additionally, such notations may contribute to the inability of others to care for the patient.[7]

While health care institutions should have policies securing medical records, this concern is especially acute with hostile patients who may be tempted to alter medical records to bolster a negligence cause of action. An institution's policy should forbid that original medical records leave the premises except pursuant to legal process and should forbid patients or their representatives to examine their records while patients are alone.[8]

NONCOMPLIANT PATIENTS. Patients have the right to refuse medical treatment. When a patient refuses to comply, the behavior should be described. A patient should be quoted if feasible.[9] The nurse should describe the behavior objectively, refraining from charting judgmental or opinionated statements especially relating to motive or character.[10] Recording noncompliant behavior and nursing instructions regarding probable results if the treatment is foregone will go a long way in either preventing a suit if an injury occurs or in minimizing damages because of a patient's involvement in the injury.

AGAINST-MEDICAL-ADVICE DISCHARGE. Mentally competent adult patients cannot be forced to stay in the hospital. Patricia Iyer has outlined the steps a nurse should take if a patient wants to leave a health care institution against medical advice. The nurse should find out why the patient wants to leave and notify the nurse supervisor and the attending physician. The physician should inform the patient of the risks associated with refusing treatment and ask him to sign an against-medical-advice (AMA) form. Additionally, the nurse should document the conversation with the patient, any statements or actions reflecting on the patient's mental state, and any refusal by the patient to sign an AMA form. An incident report should be filled out if required by hospital policy. See the discussion below under "Incident Reports." Documentation should adhere to the following checklist:

- Record the risks and consequences of the AMA discharge as explained to the patient.
- Note any instructions regarding alternative sources of follow-up care given to the patient.
- Name relatives or friends who accompanied the patient at discharge and any instructions given to them.
- Document any drugs or prescriptions given to the patient.
- Note the patient's stated destination.[11]

Verbal Orders and Telephonic Communications

Physician's verbal orders should be limited as much as possible to telephone orders and in all cases must be transcribed in the medical record and signed by the physician within twenty-four hours.[12]

Ann Bailey-Allen offers information on how to deal with telephone orders.[13] A common problem with telephone orders is that physicians and nurses can differ over what information was exchanged over the telephone. One way to possibly avoid this problem is for the nurse to read back the order once the nurse transcribes the order in the record. The nurse should seek clarification of the appropriateness of orders. The telephone cannot be used as a substitute for the physician's actual examination of the patient. The nurse should document the nursing observations that were reported to the physician and the orders that were carried out. Life-threatening laboratory results that are communicated via the telephone should be verified and documented, along with resulting action. The nurse should follow up on whether the physician signs the telephone order.[14]

Telephone consultations with patients should also be recorded, including canceled appointments.[15]

Charting Wars and Objectivity

It is controversial whether disagreements among professional staff should be recorded. If a nurse follows hospital policy by documenting her objections to improper orders and her efforts to obtain responsible intervention in settling a professional disagreement, the nurse must create a medical record that is sufficiently objective and factual to preclude its use as evidence against the other professional in a suit. The notation should be objective, concise, and completely factual but not judgmental, vindictive, or full of groundless opinion.[16] The bottom line is that the record should not be a place to settle the dispute or to assign blame. The notation should merely document objectively the actions taken by the nurse and resulting interventions.

Incident Reports

An incident is defined as "any happening which is not consistent with the routine operation of the hospital or the routine care of a particular patient. It may be an accident or a situation which might result in an accident."[17] Hospital policy will dictate when and how an incident report must be made out. In preparing an incident report, the nurse should assume the report is discoverable and admissible in a court of law. With this assumption, the nurse should be mindful of suggestions proposed by William Roach, Jr., et al.:

- Treat the report as a confidential document and clearly mark it as such.
- Strictly limit the number of copies made and the distribution of the reports in the institution.
- Do not place a copy in the medical record or in a file in the patient-care unit.

- Limit the content of the report to facts rather than conclusions or assignments of blame. Place an analysis of the cause of the incident in a separate document.
- Address the report and any separate analysis of the incident to the hospital attorney or claims manager by name.
- Train hospital personnel to complete the form with the same care as used in completing a medical record.
- Generally treat the report as a quality assurance record and subject it to the same stringent policies as are applied to other quality assurance records.[18]

Countersigning Notations

Stephen Bergerson has addressed countersigning notations. Signing off on someone else's entry (countersigning), while not implying that the nurse performed the procedure, represents that the nurse reviewed the entry and approved the care given. A nurse should be wary if hospital policy dictates that a nurse must countersign a subordinate's entries. The nurse should review each entry and make sure it identifies clearly whoever did the procedure. A nurse who negligently overlooks a problem that the entry raises could share liability for any resulting patient injury.[19]

Discharge Planning

Paul Greve has commented on discharge planning. He notes that legal experts foresee that as hospital stays get shorter, more suits claiming premature discharge will be filed. To defend against such a claim, the nurse should ensure that the record demonstrate not only that a patient was well enough to be discharged but also that the patient and his family were given adequate preparation. The nurse should follow these guidelines:

- Note any handouts or written instructions the patient received.
- Chart any restrictions in activity, functional deficits, and conditions that warrant a call to the physician.
- Include information about any scheduled visits.[20]

CONFIDENTIALITY

The nurse has a duty to protect confidential patient communications. Texas law defines the physician-patient relationship as privileged and dictates that nurses who receive information from a confidential communication or records and who are acting on a patient's behalf may not disclose the information unless an exception exists in the law. Confidential communications include all communications and records between a physician and patient relative to or in connection with any professional services provided.[21]

> A communication is confidential if it is not intended to be disclosed to third persons other than those present to further the interest of the patient in the consultation, examination or interview or with persons reasonably necessary for the transmission of the communication or who are participating in the diagnosis and treatment under the doctor's supervision including members of the patient's family.[22]

If an exception applies, the communication is not privileged or confidential and can be disclosed without a patient's written authorization for release of the information.[23] There are several exceptions to confidentiality that may be relevant to a nurse's practice:

1. criminal proceedings;
2. certain court or administrative proceedings in which
   a) the patient brings the complaint before an administrative agency or files a lawsuit complaining against a physician;
   b) the communication is relevant to any physical, mental, or emotional condition of the patient that any party relies on as a claim or defense;
   c) the communication is relative to collection of a fee for medical services;
   d) a disciplinary proceeding has been filed against a nurse;
   e) a suit involves a parent-child relationship;
   f) involuntary commitment proceedings have been instituted;
   g) any proceeding involves abuse or neglect of an "institutionalized individual";
3. qualified personnel for management of audits, financial audits, and program evaluations or research, provided patients' identities are protected;
4. communications to justify and collect fees for medical services; and
5. other physicians or personnel who are participating in the diagnosis, evaluation, or treatment of the patient.[24]

Nurses who disclose confidential communications can be sued by their patients for breach of confidentiality. Nurses should follow institutional policies regarding the disclosure of confidential communications. If questions still arise, legal advice should be sought before the information is released. Vicki Brann suggests some commonsense rules for nurses to follow to avoid revealing patient confidentiality:

1. Keep professional discussions professional.
2. Confine professional discussions to professional areas of the facility and avoid discussing patients in common areas, such as elevators, the cafeteria, and hallways.
3. Protect the medical record from casual access by visitors.
4. Keep red flags in professional areas and inside records.
5. Avoid "cocktail party" discussions of patient cases on or off duty.
6. Know whom the patient defines as family members to be included in professional discussions.
7. Know who is asking for patient information.
8. Intervene early in problems of communication breakdown with patients and families.
9. Treat all patient communications with care.
10. Ask for written authorization from the patient before discussing anything with a nonhealth care professional.[25]
11. Do not record test results on a telephone answering machine without the patient's written authorization to do so, even if a test result is negative. A nurse could be held legally liable if a patient's wife discovers that her husband had an affair when the nurse leaves the result of the patient's negative chlamydia test result on the telephone answering machine.[26]

Before releasing a confidential communication, the patient or the patient's legal guardian must sign a written release that specifies (1) the information or medical records to be covered by the release, (2) the reasons or purposes for the release, and (3) the name of the person to whom the information is to be released.[27]

PHYSICIANS' ORDERS

Generally, physicians can delegate medical acts to any qualified and properly trained person acting under the physician's supervision if the act can be properly and safely performed in its customary manner.[28] The Texas Board of Medical Examiners (TBME), rather than the Texas Board of Nurse Examiners, has the authority to determine when and how physicians may delegate medical acts to nurses. Generally, physicians delegate medical acts to nurses through physician's orders, standing delegation orders, and standing medical orders.

Standing Delegation Orders

Pursuant to its authority, the TBME has established rules regarding how and under what circumstances medical acts may be delegated to nurses through standing delegation orders. These rules, however, do not apply to several situations in which

1. a patient is institutionalized and the care is to be delivered in the hospital, nursing home, or other institution that has an organized medical staff with authorized or approved standing delegation orders or standing medical orders;
2. care is rendered in an emergency;
3. care is rendered as a part of disaster relief and charges for the services are not made;
4. the Good Samaritan law applies;
5. first-aid care is provided at the site of an injury or as an interim measure before transfer of the patient to a medical facility where medical services are available;
6. care rendered is provided by a nurse when she is acting within the scope of the Nursing Practice Act; and
7. care is delivered as authorized by the Medical Practice Act.

Standing delegation orders[29] are written instructions, orders, rules, regulations, or procedures that are prepared by a physician to provide authority for acts and duties to be used *before* the patient is examined by a physician. Standing delegation orders do not require the exercise of independent medical judgment. The plan of care established by these orders is written not for a specific patient but for patients with specific diseases, disorders, health problems, or sets of symptoms. The orders must delineate under what set of conditions and circumstances action should be taken.

Standing delegation orders at a minimum, must

1. include a written description of the method used in developing and approving them and any revision thereof;
2. be in writing, dated, and signed by the delegating physician;
3. specify which acts require a particular level of training or licensure and under what circumstances they are to be performed;
4. state specific requirements to be followed by persons acting under the requirements in performing particular functions;
5. specify any experience, training, and educational requirements for those persons who shall carry out the orders;
6. establish a method for initial and continuing evaluation of the competence of those persons authorized to perform the acts;
7. provide for a method of maintaining a written record of those persons authorized to perform the acts;
8. specify the scope of supervision required for persons to perform the acts, for example, immediate supervision by a physician;
9. set forth any specialized circumstances under which a person per-

forming the acts is to immediately communicate with the patient's physician concerning the patient's condition;

10. state limitations on setting, if any, in which the plan is to be carried out;
11. specify patient record-keeping requirements that shall, at a minimum, provide for accurate and detailed information regarding each patient visit; personnel involved in treatment and evaluation on each visit; drugs or medications administered, prescribed, or provided; and other information that is routinely noted on patient charts and files by physicians in their offices; and
12. provide for a method of periodic review, which shall be at least annually, of the plan, including the effective date of termination of the plan after which date the physician shall issue a new plan.

Except when a physician delegates medical acts to advanced nurse practitioners in medically underserved populations, the scope of standing delegation orders is limited to the following acts:

1. The taking of personal and medical history.
2. The performance of the appropriate physical examination and the recording of physical findings.
3. The ordering of tests appropriate to the services provided under such orders, such as tuberculin tests, skin tests, venereal disease tests, venereal disease research laboratory tests, gram stains, pap smears, and serological tests.
4. The administration or providing of drugs ordered by direct personal or voice communication by the authorizing physician, who shall assume responsibility for the patient's welfare and shall comply with other state or federal laws. Presigned prescriptions shall be utilized only

   a) for the following class or type of drugs: oral contraceptives, diaphragms and contraceptive creams and jellies, topical anti-infectives for vaginal use, oral antiparasitic drugs for treatment of pinworms, topical antiparasitic drugs, or antibiotic drugs for treatment of venereal disease;
   b) if the drugs are in compliance with the Texas Pharmacy Act and the rules adopted by the Texas State Board of Pharmacy; and
   c) if the prescriptions are not issued for any controlled substance.

5. The administration of immunization vaccines if the recipient is free of any condition for which the immunization is contraindicated.
6. The providing of information regarding hygiene and the administration or providing of medications for health problems resulting from a lack of hygiene, including the institution of treatment for conditions such as scabies, ringworm, pinworm, head lice, diaper

rash, and other minor skin disorders, if the administration or providing of drugs adheres to (4) above.

7. The providing of services and the administration of therapy by public health departments as officially prescribed by the Texas Department of Health for the prevention or treatment of specific communicable diseases or health conditions for which the Texas Department of Health is responsible for control under state law.
8. The issuance of medications that do not require a prescription (over-the-counter medications) for the symptomatic relief of minor illnesses if the medications are packaged and labeled in compliance with state and federal laws and regulations.

Standing Medical Orders

Standing medical orders are orders, rules, regulations, or procedures that have been prepared by a physician or approved by a physician or the medical staff of an institution for patients who have been examined or evaluated by a physician and that are used as guides to prepare for and carry out medical or surgical procedures or both. These orders give authority and direction to authorized persons to perform certain prescribed acts for patients as distinguished from specific orders written for a particular patient.[30]

"No Code" Orders

A "No Code" or "Code Blue" order is an order by a patient's attending physician that cardiopulmonary resuscitation should be withheld if the patient has a cardiac or respiratory arrest. Because such an order involves withholding a life-sustaining procedure, it should comply with the Natural Death Act or law regarding the durable power of attorney, if applicable; see Chapter 13, "Ethical Issues." A multidisciplinarian consultation regarding this decision is suggested.

Verbal Orders

Nurses should follow their institution's policies regarding verbal orders. Medical acts orally delegated to nurses should be limited as much as possible to telephone orders and should be transcribed in the medical record and signed by the delegating physician within twenty-four hours. This practice will protect nurses from being accused of performing a medical act without proper authority and will alert health care professionals to any discrepancies about what was ordered.

11

AIDS and Hepatitis B

A quagmire of federal and state laws exists relating to the transmission of blood-borne pathogens in the health care setting. The most prominent laws include federal regulations enforced by the Occupational Safety and Health Administration (OSHA),[1] federal regulations developed by the Centers for Disease Control and Prevention (CDC), and state laws codified in the Texas Health and Safety Code.[2] The purpose of this chapter is to harmonize laws that concern blood-borne pathogens (such as AIDS and hepatitis B) relevant to Texas nurses.

NURSE AS CARRIER

Voluntary Testing

The Texas Health and Safety Code does not mandate the testing of health care workers. It does state, however, that health care workers who perform exposure-prone procedures *should* know their human immunodeficiency virus (HIV) antibody status. Additionally, health care workers who perform exposure-prone procedures and who do not have serological evidence of immunity to the hepatitis B virus (HBV) from vaccination or from previous infection should know their hepatitis B surface antigen (HBsAg) status; if that is positive, they should also know their hepatitis B e antigen (HBeAg) status.

"Exposure-prone procedure" means a specific *invasive procedure* that poses a direct and significant risk of transmission of HIV or HBV. Invasive procedures include

1. a surgical entry into tissues, cavities, or organs, or
2. repair of major traumatic injuries associated with any of the following settings or procedures:
    a) an operating or delivery room, emergency department, or outpatient setting, including a physician's or dentist's office;
    b) cardiac catheterization or angiographic procedure;

c) a vaginal or cesarean delivery or other invasive obstetric procedure during which bleeding may occur; or
d) the manipulation, cutting, or removal of any oral or perioral tissues, including tooth structure, during which bleeding occurs or the potential for bleeding exists.

The CDC defines characteristics of exposure-prone procedures as

> digital palpation of a needle tip in a body cavity or the simultaneous presence of the health care worker's fingers and a needle or other sharp instrument or objects in a poorly visualized or highly confined anatomic site. Performance of exposure-prone procedures presents recognized risks of percutaneous injury to the health care worker and, if such an injury occurs, the health care worker's blood is likely to contact the patient's body cavity, subcutaneous tissues and/or mucous membranes.[3]

Health professional associations and health facilities are supposed to take the guesswork out of this process by identifying which procedures are exposure prone. "Health professional associations" and "health facilities" are not defined but will likely include hospitals and state/local professional associations; what other institutions will likely be included within these definitions are not known.[4]

There are two situations in which a nurse may be requested to have her blood tested for HIV or HBV. The first situation is an accidental exposure to blood or other body fluids: if the patient was exposed to the nurse's blood or if the nurse was exposed to the patient's blood.

There are rules that must be followed to protect the nurse's rights, however. First, the blood test must be conducted under written infectious disease control protocols that have been adopted by the health care agency or facility. Second, these protocols must respect the rights of the person with the alleged infection and the person who may have been exposed to the infection. If the nurse was exposed to the patient's blood, she *will not* be required to be tested; she will have to be tested within ten days of the exposure to protect her right to workers' compensation benefits, however, if she later tests positive for HIV and she wants to make a claim for occupational exposure. Last, the confidentiality of the person with the possible infection must be protected.

The second situation in which a nurse may be asked to have her blood tested for HIV is if the employer claims the test is necessary as a bona fide occupational qualification and there is not a less-discriminatory means of satisfying the occupational qualification. In reality, nurses may rarely be asked by an employer to have their blood tested for this reason; the employer has the burden of proving this allegation, and if the employer is wrong in his assertion, he will commit a class A misdemeanor, which carries a possible jail term. Additionally, the Americans with Disabilities Act of 1990 requires that the testing be justified on one of the following grounds:

1. a preemployment examination that focuses on the ability to perform essential job functions instead of the disabilities of the employee or the applicant;
2. an employment entrance examination uniformly required of all employees that produces information maintained in confidence to inform supervisors, first-aid and safety personnel, and governmental enforcement personnel about the implications of disabilities; or
3. another type of medical examination or inquiry that is part of a voluntary employee wellness program or is aimed solely at determining ability to perform job related functions and can be shown to be job related and consistent with business necessity.[5]

In conclusion, there is no mandatory testing of nurses for HIV or HBV in Texas. Nurses who perform exposure-prone invasive procedures, however, are asked to know voluntarily their HIV and HBV status. A nurse can be asked by her employer to be tested for HIV or HBV according to infectious disease control protocols if there has been an accidental exposure to blood or other body fluids. If the nurse is exposed to the patient's blood, she can refuse to have her blood tested, although she should have it tested within ten days of exposure to protect her workers' compensation benefits if she later has seroconversion. Additionally, an employer may ask a nurse to be tested for HIV or HBV if the employer determines it is necessary as a work qualification; this request can be challenged, however.

Practice Restrictions

A nurse who tests positive for HIV or HBV will not lose his nursing license if he follows the guidelines regarding practice restrictions. It may also be comforting to know that the Texas Health and Safety Code encourages employers of nurses to provide infected nurses with opportunities to continue patient-care activities if practicable and to give them career counseling and job retraining to promote their talents, knowledge, and skills. A nurse infected with HIV or HBV will not have his nursing practice restricted if he adheres to universal precautions and if his practice involves only (1) noninvasive procedures, (2) invasive procedures that are not identified as exposure prone, (3) emergency situations, and (4) services provided to persons infected with HIV including exposure-prone procedures. "Universal precautions" means those procedures defined by the CDC to disinfect and sterilize reusable medical devices and the appropriate use of infection control, including hand washing, the use of protective barriers, and care in the use and disposal of sharp instruments and needles. Additionally, if the nurse has exudative lesions or weeping dermatitis, he must refrain from all direct patient-care and from handling patient-care equipment and devices used in performing invasive procedures until the condition resolves.

Generally, the practice of a nurse who is infected may be restricted if the nurse performs exposure-prone procedures. A nurse infected with HIV or HBV can perform exposure-prone procedures only after he has consulted an expert review panel; the panel will advise him under what circumstances, if any, he may continue to perform exposure-prone procedures. The expert review panel is to make a case-by-case determination after considering the following factors:

1. a physical or mental condition that may interfere with the worker's ability to perform assigned tasks or regular duties;
2. the presence of exudative or weeping lesions, particularly on exposed areas such as the hands or forearms;
3. lack of compliance with established guidelines to prevent the transmission of disease or documentation or evidence of previous exposure incidents that had the potential to transmit HIV and HBV; and
4. the appropriateness of techniques as related to performance procedures.[6]

The nurse's employing institution should develop guidelines for the expert review panels and identify exposure-prone procedures. Expert review panels, however, should consist of the nurse's personal physician and experts with knowledge of infectious diseases, infection control, the epidemiology of HIV and HBV, and procedures performed by nurses. No guidance is given to a nurse who has no access to an expert review panel.[7]

If the expert review panel allows a nurse to continue performing exposure-prone procedures, he must first notify a prospective patient of his seropositive status and obtain the patient's consent before the patient undergoes the procedure. No consent is required if the patient is unable to consent. The Texas Health and Safety Code, however, does not specify that consent can be obtained alternatively from the patient's legally responsible person.[8]

Protection against Employment Discrimination

There are state and federal statutes that may protect the nurse with an HIV or HBV infection from employment discrimination, depending on who her employer is. The nurse facing this problem should seek legal advice immediately since there are short statute-of-limitations periods associated with these statutes. It may be comforting to know, also, that a nurse's attorney's fees may be taxed against the employer if the problem is ultimately resolved in the nurse's favor in a court of law.

The Americans with Disabilities Act of 1990[9] should ensure that a nurse who is HIV positive is not excluded from a job opportunity unless she is actually unable to do the job. This act applies to any employer of twenty-five or more employees[10] and basically requires three things. First, an employer may not disqualify a nurse for a job because of her inability to perform marginal or nonessential job functions. Second, an employer must demonstrate the job relatedness and business necessity of selection criteria that tend to screen out HIV-positive applicants. Third, an employer must make reasonable accommodation to help HIV-positive nurses meet legitimate criteria. Consequently, an HIV-positive nurse should have job protection during the job application procedure and in job training, hiring, advancement, and firing, with other terms, conditions, and privileges of employment.

The prevailing view is that the Rehabilitation Act of 1973[11] protects persons with HIV infection from employment discrimination, also. Under this act, employers may not exclude from participation, deny benefits to, or otherwise subject to discrimination employees solely by reason of their HIV infection. Many health care institutions fall within the reach of the Rehabilitation Act through their participation in the Medicare program.

The Texas Commission on Human Rights Act[12] will protect a nurse with HIV infection from employment discrimination unless she constitutes a direct threat to the health or safety of other persons or, because of the disease, is unable to perform the duties of her employment. Under this state act, an employer may not fail or refuse to hire and may not discharge an HIV-positive nurse or otherwise discriminate against her with respect to compensation or the terms, conditions, or privileges of employment because of her infection. Additionally, the employer may not limit, segregate, or classify employees or applicants for employment in a way that would deprive or tend to deprive them of employment opportunities or otherwise adversely affect their employment status because of the infection.

Under the Texas Commission on Human Rights Act, an aggrieved nurse can file a sworn, written complaint with the Texas Commission on Human Rights (the Commission). The complaint, however, must be filed within 180 days after the alleged unlawful employment practice occurred. If the Commission dismisses the complaint or if within 180 days after the filing of the complaint the Commission has not filed its own civil suit against the employer or has not negotiated a conciliation agreement, the Commission must notify the nurse by certified mail. The nurse must then request in writing from the Commission permission to individually sue the employer. An expedited permission can be obtained if the nurse certifies in writing from a medical doctor that she has a life-threatening illness. Within 60 days after the notice of permission to sue, the nurse can file a civil action. The suit, however, must be filed within one year from the date the original complaint was filed with the Commission.

Confidentiality

All proceedings and communications of the expert review panel, which decides if an HIV-positive nurse can perform exposure-prone procedures, are confidential. Any release of information relating to a nurse's HIV status must comply with strict rules. Under these rules, a panel member should be allowed to reveal the nurse's HIV status only to the following persons: (1) a physician, nurse, and other health care personnel who have a legitimate need to know the test results in order to provide for their protection and to provide for the patient's health and welfare and (2) an employee of a health care facility whose job requires the employee to deal with permanent medical records and who may view test results in performing the employee's duties under reasonable practices of the health care facility. Any panel member who violates this rule and with criminal negligence releases or discloses a test result or other information or allows a test result or other information to become known will be subject to prosecution for a class A misdemeanor.

Additionally, any medical information that an employer possesses about an employee must be placed in an individual employee medical file and *not* in the personnel file.[13] This requirement will prevent other employees from learning about a nurse's HIV status.

PATIENT AS CARRIER

Testing Patients

There are two situations, other than for diagnosing a patient's condition, in which a patient may be asked to take an AIDS test. First, a patient may be asked to take an AIDS test if he is about to undergo a medical procedure that could expose health care personnel to HIV and there is sufficient time to receive the test result before the procedure is conducted. An elective orthopedic surgical procedure would most likely fall under this category.

Second, a patient may be required to take an AIDS test to manage accidental exposure to blood or other body fluids if the test is conducted under written protocols for infectious disease control adopted by the health care agency or facility. For instance, written protocols for hospital infectious disease control may request that a patient be tested for AIDS if the nurse is exposed to the patient's blood after an accidental needle stick. The protocols, however, must establish clearly procedural guidelines with criteria for testing that respect the rights of the patient and the nurse and ensure the confidentiality of the patient.

Hospital protocol concerning consent and informed consent should be followed when patients are tested for HIV.[14] If a nurse is accidentally exposed to a patient's blood but the patient refuses to have his blood tested for HIV, the nurse must be evaluated clinically and by antibody testing as soon as possible and will be advised to seek medical evaluation of any acute febrile illness occurring within twelve weeks after exposure. If the nurse tests negative for HIV, she must be retested at six weeks, twelve weeks, and six months after exposure.

If either the nurse or patient test positive for HIV, they cannot be told until individual face-to-face posttest counseling is available. Posttest counseling must include

1. the meaning of the test result;
2. the possible need for additional testing;
3. measures to prevent the transmission of HIV;
4. the availability of appropriate health care services, including mental health care, and appropriate social and support services in the geographical area of the person's residence;
5. the benefits of partner notification; and
6. the availability of partner notification programs.

Any nurse who has a percutaneous or mucous membrane exposure to body fluid or a cutaneous exposure when her skin is abraded or chapped must protect her future right to seek workers' compensation coverage for work-related exposure to HIV or any reportable disease by being tested for the disease within ten days of exposure. To qualify for workers' compensation or any other similar benefits for compensation for work-related exposure to HIV or any reportable disease, the nurse must provide the employer with a sworn affidavit of the date and circumstances of exposure and documentation that not later than the tenth day after the date of exposure, the employee had a test result that indicated an absence of a reportable disease.

PREVENTING TRANSMISSION IN THE WORKPLACE

The Risk

As of July 1991, there were 186,895 cases of AIDS reported to the CDC. Of these cases, at least thirty were health care workers who were infected through occupational exposure; five exposures occurred outside the United States.[15]

Although it does not get as much attention as exposure to AIDS, exposure to hepatitis B is a bigger threat to nurses. The CDC estimates that 8,700 health care workers are infected with HBV every year through occupational exposure to blood. These infections cause over 2,100 cases of clinical acute hepatitis, 400 to 440 hospitalizations, and two hundred deaths per year.[16]

Occupational Exposure Plan

In recognition of the significant health risk of contracting HIV or HBV from occupational exposure to blood or other potentially infectious materials, OSHA passed the "Occupational Exposure to Bloodborne Pathogens" rules (the BBP rules). The reader can request a copy of the rules from OSHA.[17]

According to the BBP rules, every employer whose employees have a reasonably anticipated skin, eye, mucous membrane, or parenteral contact with blood or other potentially infectious material must establish a written "Exposure Control Plan" (the Plan) that is designed to eliminate or minimize exposure. Consequently, the BBP rules would apply to most employers of nurses, including hospitals and clinics, or to any other health care employer such as professional associations.[18] The Plan must be accessible to the employees and must be reviewed and updated at least annually.

The Plan must devise an infectious disease program that institutes procedures for universal precautions whereby certain body fluids of all patients are presumed infectious: the presumed infectious body fluids are blood; semen; vaginal secretions; cerebral spinal fluid; and synovial, pleural, peritoneal, pericardial, and amniotic fluid.[19] Sharps disposal containers, self-sheathing needles, and personal protective equipment must be maintained, repaired, and provided free of charge to employees to institute procedures for universal precautions. Additionally, the BBP rules require that employers provide the HBV vaccination series free of charge within ten working days of initial assignment to nurses who may have an occupational exposure to blood. The nurse will not have to take the vaccinations if she previously received a complete HBV vaccination series, an antibody test reveals immunity, or the vaccine is contraindicated for medical reasons. A declination statement must be signed by the nurse, however, if she turns down the vaccine.

Nurses must be trained about the Plan at no cost during working hours. Training must be given at the time of initial assignment and at least annually thereafter. The training program must cover the following items: precautionary measures, epidemiology, modes of transmission and prevention of HIV and HBV, possible risks to fetuses, the location and proper use of personal protective equipment, proper work practices, universal precautions, and the meaning of color-coded labels.

Postexposure Evaluation and Follow-up

If a nurse is exposed to a patient's body fluids despite these precautions, the employer must provide the nurse with confidential medical evaluation and follow-up.

The medical evaluation and follow-up must be free of charge, available at a reasonable time and place, and performed by and under the supervision of another licensed health care professional. Additionally, the evaluation and follow-up must document the route and circumstances of the exposure, identify and document the source individual, and test the blood of the source individual.[20] If the source individual's blood is tested, the nurse will be informed of the results. The nurse will also be asked to have his blood tested for HIV and HBV; the nurse must give informed consent.[21] It may be necessary for the employer to provide the following information for consent to be informed:

1. the purpose of the test;
2. relationship of HIV and development of AIDS;
3. the consequence of a positive test result, including changes in lifestyle;
4. risks if no test is conducted;
5. possibility of false positive and false negative test results;
6. necessity of reporting a positive test result to local health authority;
7. necessity of notifying partners of the patient; and
8. confidentiality of the test results.[22]

The nurse who desires can consent to having the blood drawn but not for it to be tested for HIV; the sample will be preserved for at least ninety days, during which time the nurse can elect to have the blood tested for HIV. The nurse should be reminded, however, that he must obtain a test for HIV within ten days of exposure to preserve his right to workers' compensation benefits if he later has seroconversion.

If a nurse's blood tests positive, he must be given immediate, individual face-to-face counseling when he is told. Counseling should include

1. the meaning of the test result;
2. the possible need for additional testing;
3. measures to prevent the transmission of HIV;

4. the availability of appropriate health care services, including mental health care, and appropriate social and support services in the geographic area of the person's residence;
5. the benefits of partner notification; and
6. the availability of partner notification programs.

The employer must provide the nurse with a copy of the evaluating health care professional's written opinion within fifteen days of the completed evaluation. The report may only contain whether the HBV vaccination is indicated, that the nurse has been informed of the evaluation's results, and that the nurse was told about any medical conditions resulting from exposure that require further evaluation or treatment. Any other findings or diagnosis must remain confidential and shall not be included in the written report. Any medical information about the nurse must be kept in an employee medical file and must not be kept in the personnel file.

The employer must establish and maintain an accurate record, which includes the following information:

1. the name and Social Security number of the nurse;
2. a copy of the nurse's hepatitis B vaccination status, including dates of all hepatitis B vaccinations and any medical records relative to an employee's ability to receive vaccinations;
3. a copy of all results of examinations, medical testing, and follow-up procedures;
4. the employer's copy of the health care professional's written opinion; and
5. a copy of the information provided to the health care professional.

These records must be kept confidential and may not be disclosed or reported without the nurse's express written consent to any person within or outside the workplace. The nurse's employer must maintain these records for at least the duration of employment plus thirty years.

12

Employment Issues

CREDIBILITY INVESTIGATIONS

Preemployment

A nurse's employer can be liable legally if a patient is injured by a nurse and the injury could have been prevented had the nurse's background been investigated before she was hired. Therefore, a nurse can expect to be investigated by her prospective employer before she is hired: character and expertise may be investigated by checking personal and work references; the Texas Board of Nurse Examiners (TBNE) or the Texas Board of Vocational Nurse Examiners (TBVNE) may be consulted to determine the status of the nurse's license; the employer may institute a criminal-conviction investigation.

Drug and Alcohol Testing

Mandatory drug testing of all nurses is not required. The rules regarding whether employers can test for drugs or alcohol are different depending on whether the nurse is an at-will or contract employee and whether the nurse works in the private or public sector.

PRIVATE SECTOR. Private Texas employers are relatively free to impose drug or alcohol testing on applicants and employees. Private-sector (civilian) nurses who are employed for an indefinite period (the at-will form of employment) may be required to be tested for drugs as a condition of their employment or continued employment, which is true even if the drug-testing policy is enacted after the nurse is employed, because the at-will employment arrangement can be modified by the employer; the employee can reject the modification by quitting or accept the modification by continuing to work. The nurse who refuses to submit to drug testing under the employer's established drug-testing program and either quits or is discharged may be denied the benefit of unemployment compensation for misconduct.

A private-sector nurse may be in a better position to refuse drug testing if she has an employment contract that limits the employer's right to discharge her. This contract provision generally needs to be in writing. The protection this contract would afford is not complete, however, because an employer can terminate the nurse for an act that is detrimental to the business. Consequently, a nurse with a contract could still be fired if she is caught using, selling, or stealing drugs while on duty or if drugs are impairing the nurse's work performance.[1]

PUBLIC SECTOR. Public-sector nurses (who are employed by the federal or state government) can be drug tested if the government's interest in testing the nurse outweighs the nurse's individual privacy interest. Unless the nurse is involved in distributing scheduled drugs, it is unlikely that random or across-the-board drug testing will be tolerated. Instead only those nurses suspected of drug abuse will be tested. What is not clear is whether it is constitutional to test public-employee job applicants.[2]

FALSIFYING DRUG-TEST RESULTS. Nurses who participate in a drug-testing program at work should not use or attempt to use any substance or device to falsify the drug-test result, because the nurse would commit a misdemeanor offense punishable by a jail sentence.[3]

Polygraph Tests

Whether a nurse can be asked by her employer to submit to a polygraph test (lie-detector test) depends on who her employer is and the employer's justification for the test. According to a federal statute[4] that will apply to most large institutions, polygraph tests cannot be used to test prospective employees. One exception to this prohibition that is most applicable to nursing is that a polygraph test can be used in a prehiring examination by an employer if, through her job, the nurse will have direct access to the manufacture, storage, distribution, or sale of any controlled substance.

Additionally, under this federal act, a polygraph test cannot be administered once the nurse is hired unless the nurse is suspected of some wrongdoing. The employer can test the nurse only if the employer experiences a theft, loss, or damage to property; if there is some evidence to suspect the nurse of the wrongdoing; and if the nurse had access to the property.

If a nurse consents to a polygraph examination, the federal act does provide some protection against abuses. First, throughout all phases of the test, the nurse shall be permitted to terminate the test at any time.

Additionally, she can neither be asked questions in a manner designated to degrade or needlessly intrude on her nor be asked any questions touching on the following subjects: (1) religious beliefs or affiliations; (2) beliefs or opinions regarding racial matters and political beliefs or affiliations; (3) sexual behavior or beliefs; or (4) affiliations, opinions, or lawful activities regarding unions or labor organizations.

Before the test begins, the nurse must be given written notice of her right to obtain and consult with legal counsel or an employee representative. The written notice must also inform the nurse whether she will be tested before a two-way mirror, camera, or recording equipment. Additionally, the nurse must sign a notice acknowledging that she cannot be required to take the test as a condition of employment and that any statement she makes during the test may constitute additional evidence supporting an adverse employment action.

During the test, the polygraph examiner cannot ask any relevant question that was not presented in writing for the nurse's review before the test.

If the employer takes any adverse employment action against the nurse after the test, he must further interview her on the basis of the test results, must provide her with a written copy of any opinion or conclusion that was rendered as a result of the test, and must give her a copy of the questions that were asked during the test along with the corresponding charted responses.

Whether or not the nurse's employer falls under the federal act, the examiner must be licensed to perform polygraph tests by the state of Texas.

If a nurse's employer does not fall within the reach of the federal act, it is likely that under Texas law the nurse can be tested only when there is a reasonable suspicion of wrongdoing if she is a public employee.[5]

If a nurse is asked to take a polygraph test as a condition of employment, it may be wise to consult a labor law attorney before she takes the examination or denies consent to the examination.

EMPLOYMENT CONTRACTS

Generally

Employment is a contractual relationship: a nurse performs a service and is therefore paid money by his employer. The employment agreement itself can be either oral or written. The following scenario is one way that an oral employment contract is created. At the completion of an interview, the hospital's personnel manager states to the nurse that the hospital would like to hire him as a staff nurse for the general medicine ward of 3B. The nurse will be paid $20 per hour (with a 5 percent pay increase when working the night shift) and will join the hospital's medical insurance plan. Work will begin two weeks from the date of the interview. The nurse will benefit from a two-week orientation and then will work according to the floor's work schedule. An oral employment contract is created when the nurse either accepts the offer or begins to work. Most nurses will have oral employment agreements.

In Texas, employment for an indefinite period or for a term that is left to the discretion of either party creates an *at-will* employment situation. The at-will doctrine allows a nurse to quit his job for any reason at any time but also permits the employer to fire the nurse, with or without notice, for a good reason, a bad reason, or no reason at all. Most employment arrangements for nurses fall under this category.

Because of the at-will employment doctrine and the statute of frauds, it can be said generally that in Texas most employment agreements are prospectively unenforceable unless they are in writing for a definite term or unless the employment relationship was understood expressly to be of no more than one year's duration.[6] Prospectively enforceable employment agreements can be terminated only for good cause.[7]

The at-will employment agreement favors the employer. Generally, a nurse has no legal recourse for an unfair discharge. There are many exceptions, however, when a nurse can attack his termination indirectly. Some exceptions will be discussed.

Job Protection—Judicial and Statutory

First, an employer may not discharge a nurse for the sole reason that the nurse refused to perform an illegal act that would subject her to a criminal penalty.[8] For instance, an advanced nurse practitioner (ANP) would be subject to a criminal penalty if she prescribed a controlled substance. Consequently, an ANP's employer could not fire her solely for the reason that she refused to follow a physician's order to prescribe a controlled substance. Second, the nurse cannot be fired for a reason prohibited by statute (whistle-blower protection).

There are statutory protections against retaliatory discharges in some situations in which a nurse reports a violation of a particular law. These statutes are sometimes referred to as whistle-blower protections. There are four relevant areas of protection.

FILING WORKERS' COMPENSATION CLAIM. A nurse cannot be fired or in any manner discriminated against if the nurse (1) has in good faith filed a workers' compensation claim, (2) hired a lawyer to represent the nurse in the claim, (3) instituted or caused to be instituted in good faith any proceeding under the Workers' Compensation Act, or (4) has testified or is about to testify in such a proceeding.[9]

REPORTING PATIENT ABUSE. A nurse who has cause to believe that an inpatient at a convalescent or nursing home has or may suffer physical or mental abuse or neglect must report the abuse to the Texas Department of Health or a local or state law enforcement agency.[10] The nurse must make an oral report immediately upon learning about the abuse and then must make a written report to the same agency not later than the fifth day after the oral report is made. The report must contain the name and address of the resident and of the person responsible for the resident's care and any other relevant information. Anonymous reports will be accepted, although they are not encouraged. The agency receiving the complaint will investigate the charge, which may include visiting the institution and interviewing the resident.

The nurse who reports the abuse is immune from civil and criminal liability unless the nurse makes a report in bad faith or with malice. If a nurse is subsequently suspended, fired, or is otherwise discriminated against for reporting the abuse, she has a cause of action against the institution, the owner, or any relevant employee of the institution. The cause of action has a short statute of limitations, however; the nurse must bring suit or notify the Texas Employment Commission of her intent to sue under this statute no later than the ninetieth day after the suspension or termination. Each nurse must sign a statement as a condition of employment that she realizes she may be criminally liable for failing to report these abuses (she will be punished for a class A misdemeanor). If the institution did not require the nurse to read and sign the statement, then the nurse has two years from the day of suspension or termination to bring suit.

A nurse who is successful in her lawsuit may recover (1) the greater of $1,000 or actual damages (including mental anguish), (2) exemplary damages, (3) court costs, (4) attorney's fees, and (5) reinstatement to former position.

REPORTING VIOLATIONS OF LAW—PUBLIC EMPLOYEES. A nurse who works for the state of Texas or for a local government cannot be fired, suspended, or otherwise discriminated against if she reports in good faith a violation of law to an appropriate law enforcement authority.[11] If a nurse does experience any retaliatory action, she must sue within ninety days after the alleged violation occurred or was discovered by her through the use of reasonable diligence.

Before a nurse sues, however, she must exhaust any applicable grievance or appeal procedures adopted by the employing local governmental body. Additionally, the nurse must invoke these procedures before the ninetieth day after the violation. This statute's limitations period is a little complicated, so if a nurse thinks she has a cause of action, she should immediately contact an attorney, preferably one with labor law experience.

If a nurse is successful in her lawsuit, she may recover (1) actual and exemplary damages, (2) costs of court, (3) attorney's fees, (4) reinstatement to former position, (5) compensation for wages lost during the period of suspension or termination, (6) reinstatement of any fringe benefits or seniority rights that were lost because of suspension or termination, and (7) injunctive relief.

Each state or local governmental body must notify its employees of these rights by posting a sign in a prominent location in the workplace.

The three statutory protections against retaliatory discharge that were just discussed are defined narrowly. For instance, a nurse can be fired if she reports *suspected* illegal activity[12] or if she refuses to carry out an employer's order that will result in only a *civil* penalty.[13] Whether a nurse can be fired or not, she must also guard against carrying out an employer's order that could result in a disciplinary action by the entity—TBNE or TBVNE—that regulates the nurse's practice. Additionally, the whistle-blower protections have a very short statute-of-limitations period. If a nurse is caught in a situation in which she feels she must decide whether to risk losing her job versus losing her nursing license or causing harm to the patient, she should consult an attorney before making her choice if possible.

FILING COMPLAINTS UNDER OSHA REGULATIONS. The Occupational Safety and Health Administration (OSHA) enforces work safety standards that every employer must follow. A nurse cannot be discharged or discriminated against for filing a complaint with OSHA against her employer for a safety violation.[14] If an employee is discriminated against after filing a complaint, she must file a complaint with the secretary of the Department of Labor within thirty days after the violation. The secretary of labor will investigate the complaint and will file a lawsuit against the aggriever in United States district court if the secretary feels there was a violation of the statute. The nurse will be informed about the secretary of labor's decision within ninety days of receipt of her complaint.

STAFFING

Nurse-Patient Relationship

A contract between the patient and a nurse employed by a health care institution has not been recognized. Instead, the nurse's duties extend from his contractual relationship with his employer and those imposed on him by membership in the nursing profession.

Health care institution staff nurses generally assume responsibility for a designated group of patients during a specified period, usually for eight to twelve hours. The nurse must continuously care for and monitor the patients during the shift. For example, the nurse may be liable legally if he takes a break or leaves the unit at a time when he should know that he is needed on the unit.

Nurses who practice independently have a nurse-patient relationship that is more akin to the physician-patient relationship. The nurse has a contractual relationship with the patient to provide episodic health care when it is required.

Staffing Shortages

Health care institutions have a duty to staff their nursing units at levels sufficient to give patients safe and competent nursing care. For whatever reason, health care institutions sometimes struggle with this duty. Perhaps the following scenario sounds familiar to the reader. A nurse has just completed a grueling eight-hour shift. The nurse took no lunch break. The nurse's supervisor approaches the nurse and informs her that she is needed to cover the evening shift. Considering how hungry and tired she is, the nurse has doubts about the kind of care she can give the patients during the evening shift. What should the nurse do?

Unfortunately, this scenario is more common than nurses prefer. It places the nurse in a situation of conflicting interests. The nurse knows that if she works the extended shift, the patients may receive suboptimal care because of her fatigue and hypoglycemia, although any nurse is better than no nurse. If the patient receives suboptimal care, the nurse could be subject to discipline by the TBNE or TBVNE and subject to a nursing negligence lawsuit. If the nurse refuses to continue working, however, will she have a job tomorrow?

There is no one answer to the nurse's dilemma. Each nurse will have to analyze and weigh the following factors for herself before choosing how to react. First, the health care institution as an employer of nurses retains authority over all details of the work; no matter how foolish, it is the hospital's prerogative to understaff their nursing units. If the nurse is employed at will, she does not have much bargaining power in deciding not to work an extended shift; it is likely that if the nurse refuses to work the additional shift, she will be discharged without legal recourse.

Second, Texas courts have recognized that the nurse's first duty is to the patient. If a patient is injured, a Texas court may not be terribly sympathetic as to her workload when the accident happened; the court will be more concerned with the fact that the patient was injured rather than why he was injured. The nurse could argue that considering her dilemma, it was better for the patient to have a tired, hungry attending nurse than no nurse at all. Again, the court may not give much credence to this view.

Third, if the nurse refuses to work an extended shift, she may be liable legally for abandoning the patient if the patient is injured by the nurse's not being on duty.

Fourth, the nurse may be subject to discipline by her licensing board if the patient is injured when either the nurse works an extended shift or if the nurse abandons the patient.

The reader is probably asking by now whether the nurse has any choices. If she does not work the extended shift, she may lose her job without legal recourse. If she agrees to work the extended shift despite her misgivings, then she will be legally and professionally responsible if any patient is injured while under her care. But if she refuses to work the extended shift, she can be legally and professionally responsible if any patient is injured because she was not on duty. It sounds, looks, and feels like an unacceptable catch-22. The nurse who has these thoughts understands perfectly.

There are some real-life factors that may help ameliorate the risk to nurses and their patients. First, most health care institutions take their duty of adequately staffing nursing units seriously and will institute measures to avoid the problem. Hospitals will be liable legally if a patient is injured because of a staffing shortage, also. Second, nurses who help employers avoid a staffing-shortage problem are in a position to ask for concessions. In the previous example, the nurse is in a position to ask for a break to rest and eat before the next shift begins. Additionally, the nurse could ask the supervisor to have the night-shift nurse split the additional shift. Third, it is surprising how many accidents do not happen even when nurses are tired. Finally, even if a mistake happens, not all result in lawsuits.

Staffing shortages are no-win situations. There are some measures that nurses can take to try to avoid them. First, nurses should investigate the health care institution's staffing practices before accepting employment. The nurse should talk to nurses on the floor to determine (1) whether the floor is adequately staffed, (2) what institutional policies are in place to avoid staffing shortages, (3) whether nurses are on call, (4) whether nurses are offered a certain number of days off for "stress relief" to avoid nurses calling in sick when they really are well, and (5) what the hospital's call-in policy is when nurses are sick. If the employer will agree, the nurse should have a written employment contract that defines whether and under what circumstances the nurse will work with staffing shortages. Under a properly drafted contract, a nurse cannot be fired if she refuses to work in situations defined in the contract. Nurses who are confronted with a staffing-shortage problem can express objections to the assignment in writing before starting work. The nurse should retain a copy of the written objection and submit a copy to the nurse supervisor. Expressing dissatisfaction in writing sends a powerful message to the employer and should be used sparingly and wisely.

PEER REVIEW

In 1987 the Texas legislature enacted a mandatory peer review[15] and reporting statute of registered nurses (RNs) in response to the public's skepticism of health professionals' ability to self-regulate.[16]

Peer Review Defined

"Peer review" means the evaluation of professional nursing services, qualifications of professional nurses, quality of patient care rendered by professional nurses, merits of complaints concerning professional nurses and professional nursing care, and determinations or recommendations regarding complaints, including

1. accuracy of nursing assessments and observations;
2. appropriateness and quality of care rendered by a professional nurse;
3. reports made to a professional nursing peer review committee concerning activities under the committee's review authority;
4. reports by a professional nursing peer review committee to other committees or to the TBNE as permitted or required by law; and
5. implementation of the duties of a professional nursing peer review committee by its members, agents, or employees.

Professional Nursing Peer Review Committees Defined

Professional nursing peer review committees are established to conduct peer review. Peer review committees are established under the authority of the governing body of a national, state, or local professional nursing association; a school of professional nursing; the nursing staff of a hospital or health science center; nursing home; home health agency; temporary nursing service; other health care facility; or state agency or political subdivision for the purpose of conducting peer review. Three-fourths of the membership of the peer review committee must be composed of RNs with only RNs as voting members, and, to the extent feasible, be composed of at least one RN who has a working familiarity with the area of nursing in which the nurse being reviewed practices.

Confidential Nature of Proceedings

Except as provided in "Disclosure of Information" below, all proceedings of a professional nursing peer review committee are confidential and all communications made to a professional nursing peer review committee are privileged, which means that a member, agent, or employee of a professional nursing peer review committee or a participant in any proceeding before the committee may not disclose or be required to disclose a communication made to the committee or a record or proceeding of the committee. Additionally, a person who attends a proceeding of a professional nursing peer review committee may not disclose or be required to disclose any information acquired in connection with or during the proceeding or disclose any opinion, recommendation, or evaluation of the committee or of any member of the committee. The members of the committee and the persons who provide information to the committee may not be questioned about their testimony before the committee or about opinions formed as a result of the committee proceedings.

Generally, all confidential peer review information is not subject to subpoena or discovery in any civil matter, is not admissible as evidence in any judicial or administrative proceeding, and may not be introduced into evidence in a professional nursing liability suit arising out of the provision of or a failure to provide professional nursing services.

Disclosure of Information

Upon request, a professional nursing peer review committee *must* disclose written or oral communications made to the committee and committee records and proceedings to the state board of registration or licensure of any state (including the TBNE) or to a law enforcement authority investigating a criminal matter.

A professional nursing peer review committee *may* disclose written or oral communications made to the committee and the records and proceedings of the committee to

1. the state board of registration or licensure of any state;
2. a law enforcement authority investigating a criminal matter;
3. the association, school, agency, facility, or other organization under whose authority the committee is established;
4. another professional nursing peer review committee;
5. a peer assistance program approved by the TBNE under chapter 467 of the Texas Health and Safety Code;
6. appropriate state or federal agencies or accrediting organizations that accredit health care facilities or schools of nursing or that survey facilities for quality of care; or

7. persons engaged in bona fide research, if all individual-identifying information is deleted.

If a committee discloses information pursuant to the above provisions, the committee has not waived the privilege of nondisclosure of committee information and proceedings.

The peer review committee disclosing the information and the person receiving such disclosed information must protect, to the extent possible, the identities of patients.

Retaliatory Actions

A legal cause of action does not accrue against any member of a peer review committee, the committee's sponsoring institution, or against any person who furnishes records, information, or assistance to the committee if the individual or institution *acts without malice*. If any person or institution is named as a defendant in a civil suit or is subjected to other retaliatory action as a result of the participation, a counterclaim can be filed to recover any defense costs (including court costs and reasonable attorney's fees) and actual and punitive damages if the suit or retaliatory action is determined to be frivolous, unreasonable, without foundation, or taken in bad faith. A committee member or person participating in peer review who is named as a defendant as a consequence of the person's participation in peer review may use information that is confidential in defense of the civil action. This use of confidential information will not waive the privilege of nondisclosure of all other privileged information.

The Reviewed Nurse's Rights

The nurse being reviewed by a peer review committee is entitled to minimum due process, including notice and opportunity for hearing. The peer review committee must provide the nurse with a detailed summary of information disclosed or the basis of its action or recommendation. The nurse is entitled to offer rebuttal information and to file a rebuttal statement of reasonable length if the committee discloses information pursuant to the provisions discussed in "Disclosure of Information" above when such disclosure could result in the reprimand, suspension, termination, or other disciplinary action or if the committee itself recommends or takes such action. The nurse's rebuttal statement must be included with the disclosed information.

Beyond these details, the peer review statute does not specify what due process rights the nurse enjoys. Typically, due process envelopes the right to receive fair notice and an opportunity to be heard before a person is stripped of property rights.

Historically, Texas nurses have not always been afforded minimum due process during the peer review process.[17] Despite changes in the law, abuses still occur. Even though there is disagreement concerning the nurse's right to legal counsel during peer review hearings, nurses who are being reviewed by a peer review committee may wish to hire an attorney to represent the nurse's interests. The findings of the committee may affect adversely the nurse's employment status and the nurse's standing with the licensing board. Additionally, with some situations such as drug diversions, a nurse could be the subject of a criminal investigation. Consequently, it is better generally for a nurse to have legal representation as soon as the nurse is informed that she is being reviewed. In choosing an attorney, the nurse may wish to find an attorney with knowledge of nursing practice. The Texas chapter of the American Association of Nurse Attorneys is an excellent resource for finding such an attorney.

PROTECTION BEYOND EMPLOYMENT CONTRACT

Other laws may provide further protection for nurses depending on the public or private status of the employer.

Wage and Hour Laws

According to federal law, most nurses must be paid at least time and a half for working overtime, even if they are salaried employees.[18] Before the nurse starts to work, if she is paid at an hourly rate and works for an inpatient health care institution, the employer can define overtime as working more than eighty hours in a fourteen-day period pursuant to an agreement or understanding. Otherwise, overtime will be defined as working more than forty hours in a seven-day period.

The Texas wage and hour laws[19] also set standards that employers must follow. Most nurses must be paid semimonthly. If a nurse is discharged from employment, she must be paid in full for services already rendered not later than the sixth day after she was discharged. If she leaves her employer for any reason other than discharge, she must be paid in full not later than the next regularly scheduled payday. An employer can designate which days are paydays. If payday is not designated, then the first and fifteenth day of each month will be paydays. A nurse who is absent on payday or for any reason is not paid on that day must be paid on a regular business day at her request.

Health and Safety

The Occupational Safety and Health Act[20] was passed to ensure safe and healthful working conditions. Under the act the secretary of the Department of Labor develops standards relating to the workplace that employers must follow. The Occupational Safety and Health Administration (OSHA) enforces these standards through its compliance officers.

A nurse can ask OSHA to inspect his workplace if he feels there is a safety violation that threatens physical harm. The request must be in writing, allege that a violation exists at the workplace, set forth with reasonable particularity the grounds on which it is based, and be signed by the nurse (although he can request that his name be withheld from the employer). The complaint must be submitted to either the area OSHA director or a compliance officer.

After the nurse lodges his complaint, an OSHA compliance officer will inspect the workplace. If the compliance officer determines that a safety standard has been or is being violated, the compliance officer can either fine the employer or enjoin the employer from continuing business until the dangerous working condition is corrected.

This federal act contains retaliatory discharge provisions protecting nurses who file a complaint or who testify about safety violations from being discharged or discriminated against.

All employers must post an official OSHA poster in a place conspicuous throughout the work site that informs employees of their rights and tells them they may contact their employer or OSHA for information and copies of the act and safety standards.

The Occupational Safety and Health Administration currently does not regulate the smoking of tobacco products in the workplace. In Texas, however, it is a class C misdemeanor to carry or smoke a burning tobacco product in a hospital.[21] Local ordinances may further apply restrictions that limit smoking at the work site.

Employment Discrimination

It is unlawful for an employer to refuse to hire, to discharge, or to otherwise discriminate against any individual because of race, color, religion, sex, age, national origin, disability, or pregnancy.[22] An employer must reasonably accommodate an employee on the basis of these characteristics unless doing so would create undue hardship for the employer.

Freedom from discrimination on the basis of pregnancy means that the employer must treat women who are affected by pregnancy, childbirth, or related medical conditions the same for all employment-related purposes, including offering benefits under fringe-benefit programs, as the employer treats other persons who are not so affected but who are similar in their ability or inability to work. An employer, however, is not required to pay for health insurance benefits for abortion except when the life of the mother would be endangered if the fetus were carried to term or when medical complications have arisen from an abortion. This provision, however, does not prevent an employer from offering abortion benefits.

If a nurse believes that she has been illegally discriminated against, she can file a complaint with either the Texas Commission on Human Rights (TCHR) or the Equal Employment Opportunity Commission (EEOC). She does not need an attorney to file a complaint, but she may want to contact one anyway to avoid missing the filing deadline and to discuss other complexities of her case.

The statute of limitations for filing a complaint with either agency is extremely short. A complaint must be filed with either the TCHR or the EEOC within 180 days of the alleged violation. If the nurse chooses to file with the TCHR first, she will have an additional 120 days to file her complaint with the EEOC.

After the nurse files her complaint, she must wait for the agency to investigate and correct the problem before she files a lawsuit. If the agency cannot reach an agreement with the employer, the agency will then give the nurse the right to file a lawsuit against her employer.

Abortion

Under Texas law, a nurse may not be required to perform or participate either directly or indirectly in an abortion procedure if she objects to participating.[23] It follows that the hospital or health care facility may not discriminate in any manner against a nurse or an applicant who refuses to perform or participate in an abortion procedure. Similarly, a hospital or health care facility may not discriminate against a nurse for the nurse's willingness to participate in an abortion procedure at other facilities.

Nursing schools may not discriminate against an applicant for admission because of the applicant's attitudes concerning abortion.

If a nurse is discriminated against in any of the ways listed above, the nurse can sue the hospital, health care facility, or educational institution and enjoin the institution from discriminatory practices or may get relief whereby the nurse is granted admission or reinstated with back pay plus 10 percent or any other appropriate relief.

Tort Law

A nurse may have a tortious defamation claim against her employer (including perhaps nurse supervisors) if the employer publishes defamatory, false statements about the nurse's character or professional ability, thereby injuring the nurse's reputation. This cause of action is likely to arise when the employer is asked to serve as a reference for the nurse's next job, during performance evaluations, during disciplinary actions, while investigating employee misconduct, and when explaining reasons for termination.[24]

An intentional infliction of emotional distress cause of action may also be available to a nurse if the nurse's employer intentionally or recklessly causes severe emotional distress through extreme and outrageous behavior. This cause of action has been applied to sexual harassment. The nurse through this cause of action does not claim that emotional distress resulted from an unjust termination but instead challenges behavior that caused emotional distress during the employment.

Unions

Nurses in Texas have not unionized even though changes in the law make it easier for them to do so. Forming a union is a way for nurses to acquire better conditions of employment. The idea, however, is controversial; some individuals think that forming a nurses' union would reflect poorly on the professionalism of nurses.

Unemployment Compensation

Unemployed nurses may apply for unemployment compensation through the Texas Employment Commission (TEC).[25] A nurse will be granted benefits if certain eligibility requirements are met. Benefits will be denied for a certain period if the nurse (1) was fired for misconduct; (2) quit a job without good cause; (3) failed to apply for or to accept available, suitable work without good cause; (4) stopped work because of a labor dispute; or (5) quit a job to attend school.

After a nurse makes a claim for unemployment compensation, the employer has twelve days to tell the TEC facts that may preclude the nurse's eligibility to receive benefits. The nurse's employer has an incentive to protest the nurse's claim because unemployment compensation benefits are financed by taxes paid by the employer. If the nurse's claim worsens the employer's experience rating, the employer could be charged directly for the nurse's unemployment benefits rather than the benefits being paid by the general fund.

If the nurse is denied unemployment compensation benefits, the nurse can request a redetermination of or appeal the decision within fourteen days of the denial according to TEC rules. The appeal will be heard by an appeals referee in an informal hearing. If the nurse is dissatisfied with the appeals referee's decision, she can request review by the TEC within ten days of the referee's decision.

The nurse does not need a lawyer for these initial appeals. If the nurse has an interest in exhausting the available appeals process by eventually filing a lawsuit, it would be advantageous to have legal representation at the beginning of the appeals process; statements made by the nurse at the hearings may be admissible in court.

In addition to unemployment compensation, the nurse may want to explore eligibility for general welfare, financial assistance for parents of dependent children, or food stamps, also.

Disability

A nurse can apply for Social Security disability benefits if he will be unemployable competitively for one year or more because of physical or mental impairment. The nurse can apply for benefits through any Social Security office. During the eligibility interview, the nurse's work and medical history will be reviewed.

If the nurse is denied benefits, he may file a request for reconsideration at the Social Security office within ten days unless good cause can be shown for any delay. If the claim is rejected again, the nurse may file for a hearing before an administrative law judge or a Social Security appeals council or he can file a suit in federal court.

If disability benefits are granted, the nurse must serve a waiting period of five months from the date of onset before payment begins. This provision is onerous if the nurse is without private disability insurance or sick leave.

Workers' Compensation

Texas employers are not required to obtain workers' compensation insurance,[26] although there are incentives for them to do so. If an employer does elect coverage, then all of his employees are covered. Under this insurance, an employee will receive financial benefits for work-related illnesses, disabilities, and fatalities whether or not the injury was caused by the negligence of the employee himself or another employee. Financial benefits may include the following: income benefits for injuries lasting more than one week, death benefits, burial benefits, and medical benefits.

When a nurse is hired, the employer must tell the nurse whether the employer has workers' compensation insurance coverage. Additionally, the employer must post a conspicuous, up-to-date notice in the place of business that indicates whether the employer is covered. If the employer has coverage, the employee cannot sue the employer over work-related injuries although the nurse would still have a cause of action against a third party. For example, a nurse who receives a work-related injury from an electrical shock from a patient's equipment would have no cause of action against the employer for injuries since the employer is covered by workers' compensation insurance; a nurse may, however, have a products liability cause of action against the manufacturer of the equipment that shocked her.

A nurse can elect not to waive her right to sue her employer for work-related injuries by rejecting benefits under her employer's workers' compensation policy. To do so, the nurse must notify the employer in writing within five days after her employment begins or within five days of receiving written notice from the employer that coverage has been obtained. Generally, it is not a good idea for nurses to exercise this election. Injured workers receive benefits under their employer's workers' compensation policy relatively quickly without having to prove fault. Additionally, attorney's fees are not deducted from the nurse's benefits but instead are paid by the insurance company. If the nurse rejects benefits under the policy and elects to sue the employer, it will be several years before the nurse can hope to receive any money, the nurse must prove fault on the part of the employer and minimize the appearance of her own fault, and attorney's fees will be deducted from the award if one is ever obtained.

The nurse's employer must notify employees within fifteen days if workers' compensation insurance is purchased or if present insurance coverage is terminated or canceled.

A nurse who is covered by a workers' compensation policy must give the employer notice of any injury within thirty days of the injury. Notice is adequate if it is given to any employee who has a supervisory or management position in the employer's business. If the nurse is claiming an occupational disease, she must give the employer notice within thirty days after the date on which the nurse knew or should have known the injury may be work related. If, however, the nurse is claiming exposure to human immunodeficiency virus at work, she must have documentation that she got tested for the virus within ten days of exposure and that the result was negative. The nurse must provide the employer with a sworn affidavit of the date and circumstances of the exposure.

The nurse must file a claim with the Texas Workers Compensation Commission within one year of the injury. If she is claiming an occupational disease, she must file the claim not later than one year after the date on which she knew or should have known that the disease was related to employment.

A nurse will be denied workers' compensation benefits in the following situations:

1. injury occurred while the employee was intoxicated;
2. injury was caused by the employee's willful intention and attempt to injure herself or unlawfully injure another person;
3. employee's horseplay was the producing cause of the injury;
4. injury arose out of an act of a third person who intended to injure the employee for personal reasons and was not directed at the employee as an employee or because of employment;
5. injury arose out of the employee's voluntary participation in off-duty recreation, social, or athletic activity not constituting part of the employee's work-related duties except when the activities are the reasonable expectancy of or are expressly or impliedly required by employment; or
6. injury arose out of an act of God, unless employment exposes the employee to a greater risk of injury from an act of God than ordinarily is applied to the general public.

These provisions will not apply to employees of the federal government, who are covered by federal workers' compensation.

A nurse who has a work-related injury or illness should hire an attorney, preferably one with workers' compensation experience, to handle the case as soon as possible. The attorney will be paid by the insurance company once the claim is processed and benefits are received.

Retirement Plans and Medical Insurance

Employers are not required to offer their employees retirement benefits or medical insurance, presently. If, however, a private employer provides benefit plans, there are federal standards regarding the plans that the employer must follow.[27] These standards apply to benefit plans such as pensions, medical care, accident insurance, death and disability plans, and unemployment insurance. The rules are too complicated to be covered in this book, but it is good to know that certain protections exist considering past abuses and mismanagement.

Group health insurance plans are further regulated if an employer employs more than nineteen individuals and offers the benefit.[28] Generally, all employees are eligible to continue coverage under their employer's health insurance plan after their employment is terminated, after they terminate employment, and when they are fired (unless they are fired for gross misconduct). The insurance plan's administrator is responsible for notifying the employee of this right to continue coverage.

The nurse must choose within sixty days of the termination of employment whether to continue under the plan. The nurse will have to pay the premium, but the plan can be offered to her at no greater than 102 percent of the original plan's cost. The nurse will not be able to continue the coverage if she will be covered by another group health policy unless she has a preexisting condition that would not be covered under the new policy. Additionally, the nurse will not be allowed to continue the policy if the employer terminates all group health insurance. The nurse will have to start paying her own premiums within forty-five days of making the decision to continue under the plan.

13

Ethical Issues

ARTIFICIAL INSEMINATION

Example 13.1: An infertile couple wants to undergo artificial insemination. The husband's low sperm count necessitates insemination by a sperm donor. If the procedure is successful, who will be the father of the child—the sperm donor or the husband of the child's mother?

Answer: The husband of the child's mother is the father if he consents to the artificial insemination in an acknowledged writing.

In Texas, a child resulting from artificial insemination is not the child of the sperm donor unless the sperm donor is the husband of the child's mother. Therefore, the sperm donor in Example 13.1 will not be the legal father of the child since the sperm donor is not the husband of the child's mother. If a husband consents to the artificial insemination of his wife in an acknowledged writing, then any resulting child is the child of both of them.[1]

IN VITRO FERTILIZATION

The only law in Texas regarding in vitro fertilization concerns insurance coverage, that is, under what circumstances an insurance company must offer coverage. Readers interested in this area should consult the American College of Obstetricians and Gynecologists guidelines or the American Fertility Society minimum standards.

ABORTION

In Texas, abortions are permissible during the first and second trimesters of pregnancy. Abortions of a *viable* unborn child during the third trimester are prohibited unless (1) the abortion is necessary to prevent the death or a substantial risk of serious impairment to the physical or mental health of the woman or (2) the fetus has a severe and irreversible abnormality, as identified through reliable diagnostic procedures. "Viable" means the stage of fetal development when, in the medical judgment of the attending physician based on the particular facts of the case, an unborn child possesses the capacity to live outside its mother's womb after its premature birth resulting from any cause. The term, however, does not apply to a fetus whose biparietal diameter is less than sixty millimeters.[2]

LIFE-SAVING MEDICAL TREATMENT

The American Hospital Association estimates that 70 percent of the 1.3 million people who die in American hospitals each year die after a decision to forgo life-saving medical treatment (LSMT) has been made.[3] Until the well-known case of Karen Ann Quinlan in 1976, a decision regarding LSMT was within the exclusive control of the patient, the patient's family and friends, and the treating physician.

Because of publicity surrounding LSMT cases, it may appear deceivingly that courts have become the exclusive LSMT decision makers. In reality, from the 1976 *Quinlan* decision[4] until May 1992, there were only 114 *published* final judicial LSMT opinions in the entire United States. In fact, courts that have issued LSMT opinions have taken great pains to limit the role of the judiciary in making LSMT decisions. Generally, these courts have felt that these decisions are inherently private medical decisions that are best resolved through discussions between the patient, his family and friends, and the treating physician. Typically, these courts consider judicial intervention appropriate only as a matter of last resort when irreconcilable differences exist between decision makers.[5]

Cases involving LSMT will only likely go to court when (1) parties seek clarification of the law, (2) parties disagree over appropriate future action, or (3) parties seek approval of the court even though there is no disagreement over the law or future actions. Otherwise, when the law has not specified procedures and standards to be used in making LSMT decisions, relevant parties typically forge ahead on their own, attempting to do the right thing while recognizing that litigation may result to review the process. Because LSMT decisions present broad social, moral, and medical issues, a multidisciplinarian approach to decision making seems appropriate.

A multidisciplinarian approach to LSMT decisions should consider many factors. First, the patient's right to die is based primarily on informed-consent doctrine.[6] The LSMT decision, therefore, should embrace the patient's bill of rights. See Appendix A at the end of this chapter for the American Hospital Association's patient's bill of rights. The patient's family and friends should be made part of the decision-making process when possible, also. Second, while a patient generally has the right to refuse medical treatment,[7] the multidisciplinarian team may wish to balance the patient's desire against countervailing societal issues that have been enumerated by courts of various jurisdictions. Such societal issues include (1) the preservation of life, (2) the prevention of suicide, (3) the safeguarding of the medical profession's integrity, (4) the protection of innocent third parties, and (5) the encouragement of charitable and humane care of afflicted persons.[8]

In most states, legal issues associated with forgoing LSMT are unresolved and the procedural route by which these matters should be settled has not been established. The Texas legislature has defined this process partly through its recognition of the living will and health care durable power-of-attorney provisions. Tough legal questions remain when the patient is incompetent and has not made his wishes known through either instrument or when the patient's wishes have never been known, such as with infants or persons who were never competent.

The following discussion will explore the established procedural guidelines in Texas for patients to express their desires concerning LSMT.

Living Wills

Living wills are valid in Texas if they fulfill the requirements of the Natural Death Act (the Act).[9] Through a living will, a competent[10] adult can instruct his physician to withhold or withdraw life-sustaining procedures if the patient is in a terminal condition.[11] The Texas legislature has published in the Act a sample form for a living will that may be used (see Appendix B at the end of this chapter).

MAKING AND REVOKING A LIVING WILL.

Example 13.2: A man who is about to have his tonsils excised tells his surgeon, in private with no witnesses, that he does not have a written living will. Still, he wants the surgeon to know that if anything goes wrong during surgery, he does not want a respirator. The patient has an allergic reaction to his anesthesia and is comatose. He cannot maintain spontaneous respirations temporarily. According to reasonable medical judgment, the apnea is reversible and will not cause brain damage. Is the patient's nonwritten living will valid?

Answer: No.

A competent adult may at any time execute a written living will. An oral living will, however, is valid only when it is issued by a competent patient with a *terminal* condition.

In Example 13.2, the tonsillectomy patient was not terminally ill when he told the surgeon not to put him on a respirator. Therefore, according to the Act, the patient's oral living will was not valid.

Example 13.3: The surgeon put the tonsillectomy patient on a respirator. When he told the patient's family about the surgical outcome, the family demanded that he take the patient off the respirator. Their rationale was that he never wanted to be put on a respirator under any circumstances. Does the surgeon have authority pursuant to the Act to take the patient off the respirator?

Answer: No.

For reasons stated above, the tonsillectomy patient has neither a valid oral nor a valid written living will. Under these circumstances, when the adult patient is comatose, incompetent, or otherwise mentally or physically incapable of communication, the attending physician and the patient's legal guardian may make a treatment decision that may include a decision to withhold or withdraw life-sustaining procedures from the patient. The patient, however, must have a terminal condition. The tonsillectomy patient's condition is not terminal, because it is temporary and reversible. Therefore, the surgeon has no authority under the Act to disconnect the patient from the respirator.

Example 13.4: The surgeon keeps the patient on a respirator. While rummaging through the patient's papers at home, the family finds a written living will that the patient apparently forgot about. The living will instructs that he should never be put on a respirator even for reversible conditions. Does the patient or his family have a legal cause of action against the surgeon because the patient was put on a respirator?

Answer: No.

Assuming the living will was valid, the surgeon could not be sued since he did not know the living will existed. It is the patient's duty to notify the attending physician of the existence of the living will. In example 13.4, the patient told the surgeon that he did not have a living will. A physician, health care facility, or health care professional who has no knowledge of a living will is not civilly or criminally liable for failing to act in accordance with the living will. Thus, the surgeon cannot be sued since the patient told him that he did not have a living will.

In Example 13.4, if the patient had given the surgeon his written living will, the attending surgeon would have had a duty to make it a part of the patient's medical record.[12]

Example 13.5: A pediatric patient is five years old. He has leukemia and has exhausted all known treatment for his illness. He was admitted with the medical diagnosis of disseminated intravascular coagulation. In front of his parents the patient tells the nurse that he does not want any more needles and that he wants to die. Has the child made a valid oral living will?

Answer: No. The nurse, however, can try to implement the child's wishes by coordinating the execution of a written living will through an attorney.

A person who is younger than eighteen years of age cannot issue an oral living will. A terminally ill patient who is younger than eighteen years of age can have a living will executed on his behalf by either (1) the patient's spouse if the spouse is an adult, (2) the patient's parents, or (3) the patient's legal guardian. Thus, the nurse in Example 13.5 could talk to the child and his parents to see if the parents are willing to execute a living will on behalf of their son through an attorney.

Assuming there is no hospital policy against the nurse's approaching the patient and his family about a living will, there is nothing illegal about the nurse's action. In fact, a federal law requires hospitals, nursing homes, home health care agencies, and health maintenance organizations that are Medicare providers to inform their patients about their rights to execute living wills.[13]

Example 13.6: A pediatric nurse was auditing patient charts during the night shift. The nurse read the living will that the parents executed on behalf of their son. The living will was signed by both parents on behalf of their son and was witnessed by the day-shift pediatric nurse and a hospital volunteer who answers the telephone at the patient-location desk. Is the living will valid?

Answer: No. The day-shift pediatric nurse was an improper witness.

The parents' signatures were adequate since both parents can execute a living will on behalf of their minor son. The parents had to sign the living will in the presence of two witnesses, and the two witnesses had to sign the living will.

The witnesses to any living-will execution, however, may not be (1) related to the declarant by blood or marriage, (2) entitled to any part of the declarant's estate after the declarant's death under a will or codicil executed by the declarant or by operation of law, (3) the attending physician, (4) an employee of the attending physician, (5) an employee of a health care facility in which the declarant is a patient if the employee is providing direct patient care to the declarant or is directly involved in the financial affairs of the facility, (6) a patient in a health care facility in which the declarant is a patient, or (7) a person who, at the time the directive is executed, has a claim against any part of the declarant's estate after the declarant's death.

The day-shift pediatric nurse was an improper witness because she, as an employee of the hospital, was providing direct patient care to the boy. The hospital volunteer who worked at the patient-location desk is an adequate witness, however, because even if a volunteer is considered an employee because of the control the hospital exerts over her, she is involved neither in direct patient care nor in the financial affairs of the facility.

Example 13.7: Because of the astuteness of the nurse in Example 13.6, the living will was properly executed the following day. The attending physician certifies the boy as terminal in the patient's chart. Some days later during morning rounds, the boy tells the nurse he had nightmares during the night about dying and that he wants to cancel his living will. After hearing their son say this, the parents agree and ask the nurse to get the living will from the chart and to tear it up. What should the nurse do?

Answer: The nurse should explain to the boy that she does not have the authority to tear up the living will. The nurse should (1) inform the boy's attending physician immediately that his living will has been revoked orally, and (2) ensure that the revocation is properly recorded in his medical chart.

A living will is effective until it is revoked properly. The patient can properly revoke a living will by (1) personally canceling, defacing, obliterating, burning, tearing, or otherwise destroying the document (or by directing someone else to do it in his presence); (2) signing and dating a written revocation that expresses his intention to revoke the living will; or (3) orally stating his intention to revoke the living will.

In Example 13.7, the parents executed the living will on behalf of their son. The Act seems to require that the parents revoke the living will since they executed it. Because the parents orally stated their intention to revoke the living will, the living will is revoked. A written or oral revocation, however, takes effect only when the attending physician is notified by the declarant (the parents in this instance) or by someone acting on their behalf. Therefore, the nurse should immediately inform the attending physician that the patient's living will has been revoked orally.

The revocation is not affected by the boy's fearful state of mind after his nightmares, because a patient can revoke a living will at any time without regard to his mental state or competency. In fact, the desires of either a competent adult or child who is terminally ill will always supersede the effect of a living will.

Once the attending physician is notified that the living will has been revoked either orally or in writing, he must record in the patient's medical record the time, date, and place of the revocation and, if different, the time, date, and place that the attending physician received notice of the revocation. Additionally, he must also enter the word *void* on each page of the copy of the living will in the patient's medical record. The attending physician can designate that someone else chart the above information.

Consequently, the nurse should inform the family that, although a living will can be revoked by tearing up the document, a different procedure will be used since the living will has already been made a part of the medical record. The provisions of the Act seem to recognize the general feeling that anything that goes in a patient's hospital chart is the property of the hospital and therefore should not be destroyed.

The patient and his parents can reexecute the living will in the future if they desire by following the proper procedure for executing a living will.

Example 13.8: A pregnant woman is brain dead after a car accident and cannot breathe spontaneously. A valid living will in her medical record states that she wants to be disconnected from a ventilator if she becomes brain dead. Should the ventilator be turned off?

Answer: The ventilator cannot be turned off under the authority of the Act.

A person may not withdraw or withhold life-sustaining procedures from a pregnant patient under the provisions of the Act. Under the Act the living will of a pregnant woman is probably not automatically revoked; instead the living will probably has no force or effect during pregnancy. Thus, the ventilator cannot be turned off under the authority of the Act as long as the patient is pregnant.

The Act applies to terminally ill Medicaid patients in nursing facilities.[14]

Example 13.9: An end-stage renal disease patient has been diagnosed and certified in writing as having a terminal condition by the attending physician and by one other physician who has personally examined the patient. During nursing rounds, the patient says in front of his wife and the priest from his parish that he wants all life-sustaining procedures withheld from him if they are needed in the future. Has the patient made an oral living will?

Answer: No.

A competent adult who has been certified in writing as having a terminal condition by his attending physician and by one other physician who has personally examined the patient may issue a living will orally. The patient, however, must issue the living will in the presence of the attending physician and two witnesses. The witnesses cannot fall under any category previously listed.

In Example 13.9, the parish priest is likely an adequate witness, but the spouse is not. Additionally, the attending physician was not present when the instruction to withhold treatment was made. Consequently, the oral living will was not valid. The nurse, however, can gather the attending physician and two appropriate witnesses at the bedside so that the oral living will can be executed properly. If the nurse is successful in bringing these parties together, after the patient issues his oral instruction to withhold/withdraw, the physician must make the patient's instruction a part of his medical record and the witnesses must sign the entry in the medical record.

ENFORCING THE LIVING WILL.

Example 13.10: A fifty-six-year-old competent lupus patient has been diagnosed as having multiple-system failure. A living will is part of his medical record. Can the physician terminate his renal dialysis according to the Act?

Answer: The physician must first determine that death is imminent, note this determination in the patient's medical record, and determine that the proposed steps are in compliance with the Act and the patient's existing desires.

Before an attending physician can withhold or withdraw life-sustaining procedures from a qualified patient,[15] the physician must (1) determine that the patient's death is imminent or will result within a relatively short time without the application of those procedures, (2) note that determination in the patient's medical record, and (3) determine that the steps proposed to be taken are in accord with the Act and the patient's existing desires. The nurse should remember that the desires of a competent, terminally ill patient, even when younger than eighteen years of age, will always supersede the effect of a living will.

Therefore, to be sure that the Act's provisions have been satisfied, the attending physician should ensure that the living will is a part of the record and that the living will has been properly executed. Additionally, the attending physician should check the medical record to ensure that he and another physician who has examined the patient have certified in writing that the patient is a "qualified patient," that is, a patient with a terminal condition.

Once the above steps have been fulfilled, the attending physician may also want to satisfy any hospital policy before withholding dialysis.

A health professional who acts under the direction of a physician and who participates in withholding or withdrawing life-sustaining procedures from a qualified patient in accordance with the Act is neither civilly nor criminally liable and is not guilty of unprofessional conduct as a result of that action unless the health professional was negligent. There is no case law or statutory provisions to determine what a nurse's duty is concerning the Act. To protect herself, it is probably prudent for a nurse to ensure that the Act's provisions have been satisfied before she participates in withholding or withdrawing medical treatment.

Example 13.11: The attending physician in Example 13.10 orders the dialysis nurse to discontinue the patient's treatment. The nurse, for religious reasons, does not want to discontinue dialysis. Can the nurse be sued civilly or criminally for failing to carry out the order?

Answer: The nurse is not civilly or criminally liable for failing to carry out a living will's instructions. However, the nurse could face retribution from the hospital or the Texas Board of Nurse Examiners (TBNE) or Texas Board of Medical Examiners (TBME), depending on how she deals with her dilemma. Therefore, she should immediately bring her dilemma to the attention of the nurse supervisor and work with the hospital and the attending physician on a solution.

A physician or a health professional acting under the direction of a physician is not civilly or criminally liable for failing to effectuate a qualified patient's living will. Because living wills can instruct the withdrawing of medical treatment as well as the withholding of medical treatment, a nurse should not reason that she has authority to provide medical care when the patient does not want it.

A nurse can execute only those medical acts that are delegated by physicians. If a physician does not authorize a treatment, the nurse in effect is practicing medicine without a license if she provides the medical treatment. Consequently, the nurse can have administrative actions brought against her by the TBNE or TBME. Also, a patient must consent to treatment. If a patient does not want the medical treatment and the nurse forces it on him, she is guilty of assault and battery no matter what the statute says. Consequently, the nurse could be subject to disciplinary proceedings by the TBNE for unprofessional conduct, sued by the patient for civil negligence, and prosecuted criminally by the state of Texas. Finally, the hospital would not be happy with a nurse who practices medicine without a license or assaults a patient. Consequently, the hospital may fire the nurse for good reason.

The best way for the nurse in Example 13.11 to deal appropriately with her legitimate moral dilemma is to tell her nurse supervisor immediately about her dilemma and work with the hospital and the attending physician toward a solution.

What the nurse should certainly not do is to intentionally conceal, cancel, deface, obliterate, or damage the patient's living will without his consent. Such an act constitutes a class A misdemeanor.

A nurse is guilty of criminal homicide if, with the intent to cause life-sustaining procedures to be withheld or withdrawn from a person contrary to that person's desires, she falsifies or forges a living will or intentionally conceals or withholds personal knowledge of a revocation and thereby directly causes life-sustaining procedures to be withheld or withdrawn from the person with the result that the person's death is hastened.

Example 13.12: A two-year-old child has been hospitalized since birth with a syndrome that causes hydrocephalus, pulmonary hypertension, and a heart defect. The child is mentally retarded with no hope of ever performing activities of daily living independently. The child had heart surgery one month ago and has been on a respirator since the surgery. The parents executed a living will on behalf of their child. In compliance with the parent's wishes, the physician orders the nurse to turn off the respirator. What should the nurse do?

Answer: The nurse should not turn off the respirator and should tell the nurse supervisor and the physician of her decision immediately.

A nurse can be held civilly and criminally liable and guilty of unprofessional conduct if he negligently follows a doctor's order to withhold or withdraw life-sustaining procedures from a terminally ill patient. Therefore, before effecting such an order, a nurse should first ensure that the provisions of the Act, any federal statutes, and the hospital's policies have been satisfied.

Parents can execute a directive on behalf of their terminally ill child. The Act does not require that the child be competent. Texas children's protective services rules, however, should cause a nurse to pause before turning off the child's respirator.

To get federal funding, the Texas children's protective services program must provide rules on what constitutes medical neglect.[16] The Texas rules must reflect the federal policy that nutrition, hydration, or medication may not be withheld or withdrawn from infants under one year of age unless (1) the infant is chronically ill and irreversibly comatose, (2) the treatment would merely prolong dying and would not be effective in ameliorating or correcting all the life-threatening conditions or otherwise would be futile in terms of survival, or (3) the treatment would be futile in terms of survival and the treatment under such circumstances would be inhumane.

The Texas standards must also apply to infants older than one year of age who have been continuously hospitalized since birth, who have been born extremely prematurely, or who have a long-term disability.[17] Consequently, the child in Example 13.12 would fall under this federal policy even though he is more than one year old, since he has been hospitalized continuously since birth.

In Texas, "child neglect" is defined as "the failure to seek, obtain, or follow through with medical care for the child, with the failure resulting in or presenting a substantial risk of death, disfigurement, or bodily injury or with the failure resulting in an observable and material impairment to the growth, development, or functioning of the child" or "the failure to provide the child with food, clothing, or shelter necessary to sustain the life or health of the child."[18]

Because of these laws, the decision to withhold or withdraw medical treatment from a child, especially when the child is younger than one year of age, should be a multidisciplinary approach, including at least the medical, nursing, legal, and administrative staffs and the social worker of an institution. In fact, it may be helpful for them to consult the local child protective services before proceeding.

What procedure should the attending physician follow when his adult patient, who has been properly diagnosed as terminally ill, is comatose, incompetent, or otherwise mentally or physically incapable of communication? If the patient designates a person in his living will to make a treatment decision for him if he is comatose, incompetent, or otherwise mentally or physically incapable of communication, then the attending physician and the designated person together may make the treatment decision of whether to withhold or withdraw life-sustaining procedures from the patient. If, however, the adult patient does not designate a person to make a treatment decision for him, then the attending physician shall comply with the living will unless the physician believes that the living will does not reflect the patient's present desires.

What procedure should the attending physician follow when his terminally ill adult patient has no living will and is incompetent? The attending physician and the patient's legal guardian can make a treatment decision to withhold or withdraw life-sustaining procedures from a terminally ill adult patient who is comatose, incompetent, or otherwise mentally or physically incapable of communication when there is no living will.

If the patient has no legal guardian, then the attending physician and at least two persons, if available, in the following categories and priority may make the decision: (1) the patient's spouse, (2) a majority of the patient's reasonably available adult children, (3) the patient's parents, or (4) the patient's nearest living relative. The treatment decision, however, must be made in the presence of at least two proper witnesses. Also, the treatment decision must be based on knowledge of what the patient would desire, if known. The fact that a terminally ill adult patient has not executed a living will does not create a presumption that the patient does not want a life-sustaining procedure withheld or withdrawn.

Durable Power of Attorney for Health Care

Since 1989 Texas has recognized a durable power of attorney for health care[19] whereby an adult can delegate to another adult the authority to make health care decisions for him when he is no longer capable of making them himself. The durable power of attorney must conform substantially to the form in Appendix C at the end of this chapter. Before this form is executed, the person must sign a document that he has received a disclosure statement and has read and understood its contents. The disclosure statement must be substantially the same form as the one in Appendix D. By reading these forms, the reader can gain much knowledge about the requirements and limitations of a durable power of attorney for health care. Some further points need to be made, however.

Before an agent may make decisions on behalf of the principal, the attending physician must certify in writing in the principal's medical record that the attending physician's reasonable medical judgment is that the principal lacks the capacity to make health care decisions.

> *Example 13.13: A patient executed a valid durable power of attorney for health care and named his wife as his agent. The patient was diagnosed with Alzheimer's disease. His attending physician has certified in writing in the patient's medical record that he lacks capacity to make health care decisions. The wife has given consent for nonemergency surgery. The patient is paranoid and thinks that his wife and his doctor are trying to kill him. Consequently, the nurse overhears the patient yelling at his doctor and his wife that he revokes his durable power of attorney for health care and that he refuses to undergo surgery. Should the nurse follow the physician's order to premedicate the patient for surgery?*
>
> *Answer: The nurse should not premedicate the patient for surgery and should inform her nurse supervisor and the attending physician immediately of her decision.*

Treatment may not be given to or withheld from the patient if the patient objects regardless of whether, at the time of the objection, a durable power of attorney for health care is in effect or the patient has the capacity to make health care decisions. Additionally, a patient may revoke a power of attorney either orally or by written notification at any time to the agent or a licensed or certified health or residential care provider or by any other act evidencing a specific intent to revoke the power, *regardless of the patient's mental state, competency, or capacity* to make health care decisions.

Consequently, the patient in example 13.13 revoked the durable power of attorney for health care orally to his wife (the agent) and his attending physician. Therefore, the wife no longer has the power to consent to medical treatment on behalf of her husband. Additionally, because the patient objects, the surgery may not be performed despite the patient's confusion and paranoia caused by his Alzheimer's disease. Therefore, the nurse should not premedicate the patient for surgery and should inform the attending physician and her nurse supervisor of her decision immediately. The physician or hospital could seek a court order that enables them to perform the surgery.

In addition to being barred from consenting to the procedures and treatments listed in Appendix D, an agent may not consent to the neglect of the patient through the omission of care primarily intended to provide for the comfort of the patient.

Example 13.14: A nurse is performing an admission assessment. The nurse's quadriplegic patient directs his mother to give the nurse his durable power of attorney for health care. The patient says his attorney's secretary signed the patient's name in his presence after he directed the attorney to sign on the patient's behalf. Is the durable power of attorney signature valid?

Answer: The signature is valid.

If a patient is physically unable to sign the durable power of attorney for health care, another person may sign it with the patient's name in the patient's presence at the patient's express direction.

Note that a health or residential care provider can neither refuse care to a person solely because he has executed a durable power of attorney for health care nor require a person to execute one before the provider admits the person to the institution or provides him with health care.

Example 13.15: The nurse notices that the durable power of attorney was executed in California. Is the document enforceable in Texas?

Answer: The durable power of attorney that was executed in California is enforceable in Texas if it complies with Texas law.

A durable power of attorney for health care is enforceable in Texas when it is executed in another state if it complies with Texas law. It would be wise to have legal counsel review the durable power of attorney for health care to determine its enforceability in Texas.

Example 13.16: An agent for the patient wants to get a second medical opinion before giving consent for a particular treatment. Therefore, the agent requests copies of the patient's medical and hospital records. Can the records be released to the patient's agent under the authority of a durable power of attorney for health care?

Answer: The medical and hospital records can be released to a patient's agent under a durable power of attorney for health care.

Subject to any limitations in the durable power of attorney for health care, an agent may, for the purpose of making a health care decision, do the following things: (1) request, review, and receive any information, oral or written, regarding the principal's physical or mental health, including medical and hospital records; (2) execute a release or other document required to obtain the information; and (3) consent to the disclosure of the information. Therefore, the agent in example 13.16 can obtain a release of the patient's hospital and medical records to get a second opinion.

Example 13.17: A terminally ill patient has both a living will and a durable power of attorney. The living will does not give the physician permission to withhold artificial nutrition, but the durable power of attorney gives the agent the authority to withhold artificial nutrition. Which document should be followed?

Answer: The document that was executed later in time controls.

To the extent that a durable power of attorney for health care conflicts with a living will, the instrument executed later in time controls. A physician who withholds or withdraws life-sustaining procedures from a patient with a terminal condition as required by an agent's command is not required to comply with the Act, which governs living wills. Therefore, in Example 13.17, the document that was executed later in time controls whether artificial nutrition can be withheld.

Example 13.18: A patient's durable power of attorney does not authorize his agent to withhold artificial nutrition. The physician, however, orders the withdrawal of artificial nutrition per request of the agent. Should the nurse follow the physician's order?

Answer: The nurse should bring the situation to the attention of his nurse supervisor.

The rules regarding the durable power of attorney for health care cannot be construed to require a nurse to act in a manner contrary to a physician's order. Therefore, even though the physician's order is contrary to the durable power of attorney, the nurse cannot institute artificial nutrition on his own since doing so constitutes a medical act.

The nurse has a duty to his patient regardless of hospital policy or a physician's duty. Therefore, the nurse has a duty to ensure that the will of the patient, as expressed through the durable power of attorney for health care, is realized by the nurse's informing the nurse supervisor, who can intercede on the nurse's behalf to resolve this conflict.

Example 13.19: A patient named his wife as his agent under a valid durable power of attorney for health care. The attending physician has certified the patient as incompetent. The wife as agent has given permission for a medical procedure in accordance with her authority as granted by the durable power of attorney. The patient's daughter by a previous marriage objects to the procedure and threatens to sue "everyone" if the procedure is done. Will the nurse be subject to legal liability if she assists the physician in performing the procedure?

Answer: No, the nurse will not be liable for assisting in the procedure if she exercises due care in providing her nursing services.

A nurse acting under a physician's control is subject to neither criminal nor civil liability and has not engaged in unprofessional conduct for an act or omission done in good faith under the terms of and according to the rules applying to a durable power of attorney for health care, and this act or omission does not constitute a failure to exercise due care in providing health care services.

Because the procedure in example 13.19 was consented to by the patient's agent under the authority of a valid durable power of attorney, the assisting nurse cannot be held liable as long as she provides her nursing services in accordance with established nursing practices. The feelings of the patient's daughter should be recognized, however, and perhaps dealt with as a multidisciplinarian team approach as soon as possible.

Additionally, a nurse has not engaged in unprofessional conduct for failing to act as required by a durable power of attorney for health care if the nurse was not provided with a copy of the document or had no knowledge that it existed. The same is true if the nurse acted in accordance with an expired or revoked durable power of attorney for health care if the nurse had no knowledge that it expired or was revoked.

"No Code" Orders

A "No Code" order is an order by a patient's attending physician that cardiopulmonary resuscitation should be withheld if the patient has a cardiac or respiratory arrest. Because such an order involves withholding a life-sustaining procedure,[20] it should comply with the Act or law regarding the durable power of attorney, if applicable, and result from a multidisciplinarian approach if appropriate.

Withholding Food

The Act is silent on whether nutrition and hydration constitute life-sustaining procedures that can be withheld or withdrawn pursuant to the Act's provisions. A patient can include presently in his living will instructions regarding nutrition and hydration; it is hoped the patient will have done so. If the patient fails to include such provisions in his living will, the procedure that should be followed has not been established by the Texas legislature or by Texas courts. The trend in the United States, however, is to allow the withholding or withdrawal of food.[21]

The ill-defined procedure if the Act does not apply raises exceptional problems when an incompetent adult patient's wishes have never been known, when a patient has never been competent, and when the patient is an infant or minor, especially if mentally or physically challenged. In these situations, the decision to withhold or withdraw food should incorporate a multidisciplinarian consultation that includes, when possible, the patient's family and friends; the medical, nursing, legal, and administrative staffs and a social worker of an institution; the local child protective services; and clergy, if appropriate.

ASSISTED SUICIDE

Aiding suicide is a crime in Texas. A person commits an offense if, with intent to promote or assist the commission of suicide by another, he aids or attempts to aid the other to commit or attempt to commit suicide. Aiding suicide is a class C misdemeanor unless the actor's conduct causes suicide or attempted suicide that results in serious bodily injury, in which event the offense is a felony of the third degree.[22] If the nurse follows the provisions of the Act, however, he does not commit the criminal offense of aiding suicide.[23]

MERCY KILLING

For present purposes, "mercy killing" is defined as the affirmative or deliberate act or omission to end another's life. The Act does not condone, authorize, or approve of mercy killing or permit an affirmative or deliberate act or omission to end life, except to permit the natural process of dying as provided by the Act.[24] Involvement in mercy killing could subject the nurse to prosecution as a murderer.

ORGAN DONATION—TEXAS ANATOMICAL GIFT ACT

Under the Texas Anatomical Gift Act,[25] each Texas hospital must develop a protocol for identifying potential organ and tissue donors for patients who die. Only appropriately trained persons from an organ or tissue procurement organization are to make donation inquiries. Additionally, the hospital protocol must (1) encourage sensitivity to families' beliefs and circumstances in all discussions relating to donations and (2) provide for documentation of the inquiry and of its disposition in the decedent's medical records.

PATIENT DUMPING

A practice developed in the United States whereby hospital emergency department personnel would transfer uninsured patients to other hospitals. This practice often resulted in further injury and sometimes death because emergency medical care was delayed. To stop this unethical practice, state[26] and federal[27] regulations were passed. These statutes are often referred to as "antidumping statutes."

Medical Screening

In a hospital with an emergency department (ED), if an individual or someone on his behalf asks for an examination or treatment for a medical condition, the ED must provide an appropriate medical screening examination within its capability (including ancillary services routinely available to the ED) to determine whether an *emergency medical condition* exists. "Emergency medical condition" means a medical condition manifesting itself by acute symptoms of sufficient severity (including severe pain) that in the absence of immediate medical attention could reasonably be expected to result in (1) placing the health of the individual (or, with respect to a pregnant woman, the health of the woman or her unborn child) in serious jeopardy; (2) serious impairment to bodily functions; or (3) serious dysfunction of any bodily organ. A pregnant woman who is having contractions has an emergency medical condition if (1) there is inadequate time to effect a safe transfer to another hospital before delivery, or (2) the transfer may pose a threat to the health or safety of the woman or the unborn child.

The hospital or an officer or employee of the hospital cannot delay screening the patient or providing further medical examination and treatment that is required in order to inquire about the patient's method of payment or insurance status or because of the patient's race, religion, or national ancestry.

Transfer after Condition Stabilizes

When the hospital determines that any patient has an emergency medical condition, the hospital must either treat the patient there until the medical condition is stabilized or transfer the patient to another medical facility after the patient's medical condition is *stabilized*. A medical condition is stabilized when no material deterioration of the condition is likely, within reasonable medical probability, to result from or occur during the transfer of the individual from a facility. If the patient is a pregnant women who is having contractions, her condition is stabilized when she has delivered the baby (and the placenta).

The hospital can only transfer an unstable patient to another hospital when (1) the patient (or a legally responsible person acting on his behalf), after being informed of the hospital's obligations under the federal statute and of the risk of transfer, in writing requests transfer to another medical facility; (2) a physician has signed a certification that, based on the information available at the time of the transfer, the medical benefits reasonably expected from the provision of the appropriate medical treatment at another medical facility outweigh the increased risks to the patient and, in the case of labor, to the unborn child from effecting the transfer; or (3) a physician is not physically present in the ED at the time a patient is transferred, a qualified medical person has signed a certification as in (2) after a physician, in consultation with the person, has made the determination described in (2) and subsequently countersigns the certification. Additionally, the transfer to the facility must be appropriate.

If the hospital chooses to treat the patient at its facility, after the patient is informed of the risks and benefits of the treatment, he may refuse treatment. The hospital, however, must take all reasonable steps to secure the patient's written informed consent to refuse further examination and treatment.

The patient may also refuse *an appropriate* transfer to another hospital once he is informed of the risks and benefits of the transfer. The hospital must take all reasonable steps to secure the patient's written informed consent to refuse the transfer.

Appropriate Transfer

There are five requirements to effect an appropriate transfer to another health care facility. First, the transferring hospital must provide medical treatment within its capacity that minimizes the risks to the patient's health and, in the case of a woman in labor, the health of the unborn child. Second, the receiving hospital must have available space, qualified personnel for the treatment of the patient, and must have agreed to accept the transfer of the patient and to provide appropriate medical treatment. Third, the transferring hospital must send to the receiving facility all medical records (or copies) related to the emergency condition available at the time of the transfer, including records related to the patient's emergency medical condition, observations of signs or symptoms, preliminary diagnosis, treatment provided, results of any tests, the informed written consent or certification, and the name and address of any on-call physician who has refused or failed to appear within a reasonable time to provide necessary stabilizing treatment. Fourth, the transfer must be effected through qualified personnel and transportation equipment as required, including the use of necessary and medically appropriate life-support measures during the transfer. Finally, the transfer must meet other requirements that the secretary of the Department of Health and Human Services finds necessary in the interest of the health and safety of the patient being transferred.

A hospital that has specialized capabilities or facilities (such as burn units, shock-trauma units, neonatal intensive care units, or regional referral centers) cannot refuse to accept an appropriate transfer of a patient who requires specialized capabilities or facilities if the hospital has the capacity to treat the patient.

Transfer Agreements

Hospitals can establish transfer agreements between themselves. The agreement, however, must be approved by the Texas Board of Health. Once approved, the agreement governs all patient transfers. If there is no approved agreement between hospitals, the transfer must follow Texas Board of Health rules regarding patient transfers.

Inspections

An officer, employee, or agent of the Texas Department of Health can enter and inspect a hospital at any reasonable time to ensure compliance with or prevent a violation of the Texas antidumping statute.

Penalties

Violators of the federal antidumping statute can face civil penalties. A participating hospital that negligently violates the statute can be fined not more than $50,000 per violation (not more than $25,000 per violation for hospitals with fewer than one hundred beds). Any physician who examines, treats, or transfers a patient, including an on-call physician, and who negligently violates the statute can be fined when he signs a certification for transfer and he knew or should have known that the benefits did not outweigh the risks or when he misrepresents the patient's condition or other information (including a hospital's obligations). He will be fined not more than $50,000 per violation. If the violation is gross and flagrant or is repeated, the physician can be excluded from participating in federal or state health care programs.

Additionally, a patient who is injured as a direct result of violations of the statute may sue the hospital within two years of the violation to obtain personal injury relief. Any hospital that suffers financial loss as a direct result of the participating hospital's violation may sue the transferring hospital for damages within two years of the violation.

An officer, employee, or medical staff member of a hospital who recklessly violates the Texas antidumping statute can be convicted of a class B misdemeanor. If, however, the violation results in permanent injury, permanent disability, or death, the individual can be convicted of a class A misdemeanor. If the individual intentionally or knowingly violates the Texas statute, he can be charged with a class A misdemeanor. That offense will be elevated to a third-degree felony if a person dies because he is denied emergency services.

Additionally, a hospital can have its license denied, suspended, or revoked for violations; be enjoined for violations; or have civil penalties imposed for violations of the Texas statute (up to $1,000 per day per each act of violation).

Whistle-Blower Protections

Hospitals are not authorized to penalize or take adverse action against a qualified medical person or physician who refuses to authorize the transfer of a patient with an emergency medical condition that has not been stabilized. Additionally, a hospital is not authorized to penalize or take adverse action against an employee who reports a violation of the federal antidumping statute.

REPORTING CHILD ABUSE

In Texas "[a] person having cause to believe that a child's physical or mental health or welfare has been or may be adversely affected by abuse or neglect by any person" must report in accordance with provisions found in the Texas Family Code.[28] A person who fails to report child abuse when required by Texas law commits a class B misdemeanor.[29] The language "by any person" means that abuse occurring outside the home must be reported.[30]

Abuse and Neglect Defined

The statutory definitions of abuse and neglect, as reprinted from the Texas Family Code, are found in Appendix E at the end of this chapter.

The Texas Department of Human Services provides its caseworkers with a manual entitled *Child Protective Services Handbook*, which includes additional definitions or interpretations of terminology used in the statutory definitions.[31] The 1988 manual (the manual) defines "substantial harm" as real and significant physical injury or damage to a child that includes but is not limited to bruises, cuts, welts, skull or other bone fractures, brain damage, subdural hematoma, internal injuries, burns, scalds, wounds, poisoning, human bites, concussions, dislocations and sprains, choking, suffocating, and shaking.[32]

The manual instructs the caseworkers to consider certain factors to determine if an injury is substantial: the location of the injury on the child's body, the child's age, the frequency and duration of similar incidents, and any previous history of abuse or neglect.[33]

"Accident" is defined by the manual as an unforeseen event that causes or threatens physical injury despite prudent efforts to avoid the risk of injury. "Genuine threat" means a verbal or behavioral expression of intent that appears true, likely, or believable; a realistic likelihood of harm based on past history or present circumstances; or a substantial risk. "Sexual assault" is defined as any sexually oriented act or practice that results in harm or in substantial risk of harm to a child's growth, development, or psychological functioning.[34]

As explained by the manual, "necessary to sustain the life or health of the child" is a condition of the statutory definition of "physical neglect." The condition is met if the failure to provide food, clothing, or shelter results in an observable and material impairment to the child's growth, development, or functioning or in a substantial risk of observable and material impairment in the foreseeable future.[35]

How to Report and to Whom

The Texas Family Code prescribes the procedure for reporting child abuse or neglect.

> Nonaccusatory reports reflecting the reporter's belief that a child has been or will be abused or neglected, or has died of abuse or neglect, has violated the compulsory school attendance laws on three or more occasions, or has, on three or more occasions, been voluntarily absent from his home without the consent of his parent or guardian for a substantial length of time or without the intent to return shall be made to:
>
> (1) any local or state law enforcement agency;
>
> (2) the [Department of Protective and Regulatory Services];
>
> (3) the state agency that operates, licenses, certifies, or registers the facility in which the alleged abuse or neglect occurred; or
>
> (4) the agency designated by the court to be responsible for the protection of children.[36]

An oral report must be made immediately upon learning of the abuse or neglect, or likelihood of abuse or neglect. If a professional[37] has cause to believe that a child has been or may be abused or neglected, the professional must make an oral report not later than the forty-eighth hour after the hour the professional first suspects that the child has been or may be abused or neglected. In all instances a written report must be made within five days to the same agency or department. Anonymous reports, while not encouraged, will be received and acted on as prescribed by law.

All reports must contain the name and address of the child, the name and address of the person responsible for the care of the child, if available, and any other pertinent information.

The Form

Reports of suspected child abuse may be made pursuant to a form promulgated by the Texas Department of Protective and Regulatory Services (the Department). Copies of the form are distributed to all licensed Texas hospitals and must be available for use without charge to all hospital employees, physicians, patients, and other persons. The form includes a statement that child-abuse reports are confidential and that information contained in the reports, including the name of the person making the report, may be used only for the purposes consistent with the investigation of child abuse. Additionally, the form will give the address of the Department. Hospital employees, physicians, patients, and other persons must complete the form and return it to the Department.

Immunity from Liability

Generally, a person reporting or assisting in the investigation of a report of child abuse is immune from both civil and criminal liability that might otherwise be incurred or imposed. Immunity extends to persons who participate in any judicial proceeding resulting from the report. Three exceptions exist, however: persons who report their own conduct, persons who report in bad faith or with malice, and persons who assist in the investigation of a report in bad faith or with malice are not immune from liability.[38]

If a person files suit against a reporter of suspected child abuse or a person who assists in the investigation of such a claim, a trial court will award the defendant reasonable attorney fees and other expenses related to the defense of the claim if the trial court finds the suit is frivolous, unreasonable, or is without foundation because the defendant is immune from liability, and if the suit is dismissed or judgment is entered on behalf of the defendant.[39] A person who knowingly or intentionally makes a false report of child abuse that the person knows lacks factual foundation commits a class B misdemeanor.[40]

REPORTING ELDER ABUSE

In Texas "a person having reasonable cause to believe that an elderly or disabled person is in the state of abuse, exploitation, or neglect shall report the information to the [Department of Human Services]."[41] A person who knowingly fails to report abuse of an elderly or disabled person when required by Texas law commits a class B misdemeanor.[42] The offense is a class A misdemeanor if abuse in a convalescent or nursing home is not reported. See the discussion under "Reporting Patient Abuse" in Chapter 12.

Abuse, Exploitation, and Neglect Defined

"Abuse" is defined as "the willful infliction of injury, unreasonable confinement, intimidation, or cruel punishment with resulting physical harm or pain or mental anguish or the willful deprivation by a caretaker or one's self of goods or services which are necessary to avoid physical harm, mental anguish, or mental illness."[43]

"Exploitation" means "the legal or improper act or process of a caretaker using the resources of an elderly or disabled person for monetary or personal benefit, profit, or gain."[44]

"Neglect" means "the failure to provide for one's self the goods or services which are necessary to avoid physical harm, mental anguish, or mental illness or the failure of a caretaker to provide such goods or services."[45]

How to Report and to Whom

Generally, the abuse, exploitation, or neglect of elderly or disabled persons must be made to the Department of Human Services. Several exceptions exist, however:

1. If the abuse occurs in a facility operated, licensed, certified, or registered by a state agency, the person must report the information to the state agency that operates, licenses, certifies, or registers the facility.
2. If the abuse occurs in the Texas School for the Deaf or the Texas School for the Blind and Visually Impaired, the person must report the information in the manner required for child abuse.
3. If the abuse occurs in a convalescent or nursing home or a related institution, the report should be made to the Texas Department of Health or a local or state law enforcement agency.[46]

The report must be made orally or in writing and must include the following information:

1. the name, age, and address of the elderly or disabled person;
2. the name and address of any person responsible for the elderly or disabled person's care;
3. the nature and extent of the elderly or disabled person's condition;
4. the basis of the reporter's knowledge; and
5. any other relevant information.[47]

Immunity from Liability

A person filing a report of abuse of an elderly or disabled person, participating in an investigation, or testifying or otherwise participating in any judicial proceeding arising from a petition, report, or investigation is immune from civil or criminal liability unless the person acted in bad faith or with a malicious purpose.[48]

APPENDIX A TO CHAPTER 13
AMERICAN HOSPITAL ASSOCIATION'S PATIENT'S BILL OF RIGHTS

Introduction

Effective health care requires collaboration between patients and physicians and other health care professionals. Open and honest communication, respect for personal and professional values, and sensitivity to differences are integral to optimal patient care. As the setting for the provision of health services, hospitals must provide a foundation for understanding and respecting the rights and responsibilities of patients, their families, physicians, and other caregivers. Hospitals must ensure a health care ethic that respects the role of patients in decision making about treatment choices and other aspects of their care. Hospitals must be sensitive to cultural, racial, linguistic, religious, age, gender, and other differences as well as the needs of persons with disabilities.

The American Hospital Association presents *A Patient's Bill of Rights* with the expectation that it will contribute to more effective patient care and be supported by the hospital on behalf of the institution, its medical staff, employees, and patients. The American Hospital Association encourages health care institutions to tailor this bill of rights to their patient community by translating and/or simplifying the language of this bill of rights as may be necessary to ensure that patients and their families understand their rights and responsibilities.

*Bill of Rights**

1. The patient has the right to considerate and respectful care.
2. The patient has the right to and is encouraged to obtain from physicians and other direct caregivers relevant, current, and understandable information concerning diagnosis, treatment, and prognosis.

   Except in emergencies when the patient lacks decision-making capacity and the need for treatment is urgent, the patient is entitled to the opportunity to discuss and request information related to the specific procedures and/or treatments, the risks involved, the possible length of recuperation, and the medically reasonable alternatives and their accompanying risks and benefits.

   Patients have the right to know the identity of physicians,

---

*These rights can be exercised on the patient's behalf by a designated surrogate or proxy decision maker if the patient lacks decision-making capacity, is legally incompetent, or is a minor.

Source: American Hospital Association. Reprinted with permission of the American Hospital Association, copyright 1992.

nurses, and others involved in their care, as well as when those involved are students, residents, or other trainees. The patient also has the right to know the immediate and long-term financial implications of treatment choices, insofar as they are known.

3. The patient has the right to make decisions about the plan of care prior to and during the course of treatment and to refuse a recommended treatment or plan of care to the extent permitted by law and hospital policy and to be informed of the medical consequences of this action. In case of such refusal, the patient is entitled to other appropriate care and services that the hospital provides or transfer to another hospital. The hospital should notify patients of any policy that might affect patient choice within the institution.
4. The patient has the right to have an advance directive (such as a living will, health care proxy, or durable power of attorney for health care) concerning treatment or designating a surrogate decision maker with the expectation that the hospital will honor the intent of that directive to the extent permitted by law and hospital policy.

   Health care institutions must advise patients of their rights under state law and hospital policy to make informed medical choices, ask if the patient has an advance directive, and include that information in patient records. The patient has the right to timely information about hospital policy that may limit its ability to implement fully a legally valid advance directive.
5. The patient has the right to every consideration of privacy. Case discussion, consultation, examination, and treatment should be conducted so as to protect each patient's privacy.
6. The patient has the right to expect that all communications and records pertaining to his/her care will be treated as confidential by the hospital, except in cases such as suspected abuse and public health hazards when reporting is permitted or required by law. The patient has the right to expect that the hospital will emphasize the confidentiality of this information when it releases it to any other parties entitled to review information in these records.
7. The patient has the right to review the records pertaining to his/her medical care and to have the information explained or interpreted as necessary, except when restricted by law.
8. The patient has the right to expect that, within its capacity and policies, a hospital will make reasonable response to the request of a patient for appropriate and medically indicated care and services. The hospital must provide evaluation, service, and/or referral as indicated by the urgency of the case. When medically appropriate and legally permissible, or when a patient has so requested, a patient may be transferred to another facility. The institution to

which the patient is to be transferred must first have accepted the patient for transfer. The patient must also have the benefit of complete information and explanation concerning the need for, risks, benefits, and alternatives to such a transfer.

9. The patient has the right to ask and be informed of the existence of business relationships among the hospital, educational institutions, other health care providers, or payers that may influence the patient's treatment and care.
10. The patient has the right to consent to or decline to participate in proposed research studies or human experimentation affecting care and treatment or requiring direct patient involvement, and to have those studies fully explained prior to consent. A patient who declines to participate in research or experimentation is entitled to the most effective care that the hospital can otherwise provide.
11. The patient has the right to expect reasonable continuity of care when appropriate and to be informed by physicians and other caregivers of available and realistic patient care options when hospital care is no longer appropriate.
12. The patient has the right to be informed of hospital policies and practices that relate to patient care, treatment, and responsibilities. The patient has the right to be informed of available resources for resolving disputes, grievances, and conflicts, such as ethics committees, patient representatives, or other mechanisms available in the institution. The patient has the right to be informed of the hospital's charges for services and available payment methods.

The collaborative nature of health care requires that patients, or their families/surrogates, participate in their care. The effectiveness of care and patient satisfaction with the course of treatment depend, in part, on the patient fulfilling certain responsibilities. Patients are responsible for providing information about past illnesses, hospitalizations, medications, and other matters related to health status. To participate effectively in decision making, patients must be encouraged to take responsibility for requesting additional information or clarification about their health status or treatment when they do not fully understand information and instructions. Patients are also responsible for ensuring that the health care institution has a copy of their written advance directive if they have one. Patients are responsible for informing their physicians and other caregivers if they anticipate problems in following prescribed treatment.

Patients should also be aware of the hospital's obligation to be reasonably efficient and equitable in providing care to other patients and the community. The hospital's rules and regulations are designed to help the hospital meet this obligation. Patients and their families are responsible for making reasonable accommodations to the needs of the hospital, other patients, medical staff, and hospital employees. Patients are responsible for providing necessary information for insurance claims and for working with the hospital to make payment arrangements, when necessary.

A person's health depends on much more than health care services. Patients are responsible for recognizing the impact of their life-style on their personal health.

Conclusion

Hospitals have many functions to perform, including the enhancement of health status, health promotion, and the prevention and treatment of injury and disease; the immediate and ongoing care and rehabilitation of patients; the education of health professionals, patients, and the community; and research. All these activities must be conducted with an overriding concern for the values and dignity of patients.

APPENDIX B TO CHAPTER 13
SAMPLE FORM FOR LIVING WILL

DIRECTIVE TO PHYSICIANS

Directive made this ________ day of ______________ (month, year).

I, ______________________________________, being of sound mind, willfully and voluntarily make known my desire that my life shall not be artificially prolonged under the circumstances set forth in this directive.

1. If at any time I should have an incurable or irreversible condition caused by injury, disease, or illness certified to be a terminal condition by two physicians, and if the application of life-sustaining procedures would serve only to artificially postpone the moment of my death, and if my attending physician determines that my death is imminent or will result within a relatively short time without the application of life-sustaining procedures, I direct that those procedures be withheld or withdrawn, and that I be permitted to die naturally.
2. In the absence of my ability to give directions regarding the use of those life-sustaining procedures, it is my intention that this directive be honored by my family and physicians as the final expression of my legal right to refuse medical or surgical treatment and accept the consequences from that refusal.
3. If I have been diagnosed as pregnant and that diagnosis is known to my physician, this directive has no effect during my pregnancy.
4. This directive is in effect until it is revoked.
5. I understand the full import of this directive and I am emotionally and mentally competent to make this directive.
6. I understand that I may revoke this directive at any time.

Signed ______________________________

(City, county, and state of residence)

I am not related to the declarant by blood or marriage. I would not be entitled to any portion of the declarant's estate on the declarant's death. I am not the attending physician of the declarant or an employee of the attending physician. I am not a patient in the health care facility in which the declarant is a patient. I have no claim against any portion of the declarant's estate on the declarant's death. Furthermore, if I am an employee of a health facility in which the declarant is a patient, I am not involved in providing direct patient care to the declarant and am not directly involved in the financial affairs of the health facility.

Witness ______________________________

Witness ______________________________

Source: Texas Health & Safety Code § § 672.001–.021.

APPENDIX C TO CHAPTER 13
FORM FOR DURABLE POWER OF ATTORNEY FOR HEALTH CARE

DESIGNATION OF HEALTH CARE AGENT.

I, ______________________________, appoint:

Name: ______________________________

Address: ______________________________

Phone: ______________________________

as my agent to make any and all health care decisions for me, except to the extent I state otherwise in this document. This durable power of attorney for health care takes effect if I become unable to make my own health care decisions and this fact is certified in writing by my physician.

LIMITATIONS ON THE DECISION-MAKING AUTHORITY OF MY AGENT ARE AS FOLLOWS: ______________________________
____

DESIGNATION OF ALTERNATE AGENT

(You are not required to designate an alternate agent but you may do so. An alternate agent may make the same health care decisions as the designated agent if the designated agent is unable or unwilling to act as your agent. If the agent designated is your spouse, the designation is automatically revoked by law if your marriage is dissolved.)

If the person designated as my agent is unable or unwilling to make health care decisions for me, I designate the following persons to serve as my agent to make health care decisions for me as authorized by this document, who serve in the following order:

A. First Alternate Agent

Name: ______________________________

Address: ______________________________

Phone: ______________________________

(Continued on next page)

Source: Texas Civil Practice & Remedies Code § 135.016.

B. Second Alternate Agent

Name: ______________________________

Address: ______________________________

Phone: ______________________________

The original of this document is kept at ______________________________

____

The following individuals or institutions have signed copies:

Name: ______________________________

Address: ______________________________

____

Name: ______________________________

Address: ______________________________

____

(Continued on next page)

DURATION.

I understand that this power of attorney exists indefinitely from the date I execute this document unless I establish a shorter time or revoke the power of attorney. If I am unable to make health care decisions for myself when this power of attorney expires, the authority I have granted my agent continues to exist until the time I become able to make health care decisions for myself.

(IF APPLICABLE) This power of attorney ends on the following

date: ____

PRIOR DESIGNATIONS REVOKED.

I revoke any prior durable power of attorney for health care.

ACKNOWLEDGMENT OF DISCLOSURE STATEMENT.

I have been provided with a disclosure statement explaining the effect of this document. I have read and understand that information contained in the disclosure statement.

(YOU MUST DATE AND SIGN THIS POWER OF ATTORNEY.)

I sign my name to this durable power of attorney for health care on

__________day of 19_____ at ______________________________
(City and State)

____
(Signature)

____
(Print Name)

(Continued on next page)

STATEMENT OF WITNESSES.

I declare under penalty of perjury that the principal has identified himself or herself to me, that the principal signed or acknowledged this durable power of attorney in my presence, that I believe the principal to be of sound mind, that the principal has affirmed that the principal is aware of the nature of the document and is signing it voluntarily and free from duress, that the principal requested that I serve as witness to the principal's execution of this document, that I am not the person appointed as agent by this document, and that I am not a provider of health or residential care, an employee of a provider of health or residential care, the operator of a community care facility, or an employee of an operator of a health care facility.

I declare that I am not related to the principal by blood, marriage, or adoption and that to the best of my knowledge I am not entitled to any part of the estate of the principal on the death of the principal under a will or by operation of law.

Witness Signature: ______________________________

Print Name: ______________________ Date: __________

Address: ______________________________________

Witness Signature: ______________________________

Print Name: ______________________ Date: __________

Address: ______________________________________

APPENDIX D TO CHAPTER 13
DISCLOSURE STATEMENT FOR DURABLE POWER OF ATTORNEY FOR HEALTH CARE

INFORMATION CONCERNING THE DURABLE POWER OF ATTORNEY FOR HEALTH CARE

THIS AN IMPORTANT LEGAL DOCUMENT. BEFORE SIGNING THIS DOCUMENT, YOU SHOULD KNOW THESE IMPORTANT FACTS:

Except to the extent you state otherwise, this document gives the person you name as your agent the authority to make any and all health care decisions for you in accordance with your wishes, including your religious and moral beliefs, when you are no longer capable of making them yourself. Because "health care" means any treatment, service, or procedure to maintain, diagnose, or treat your physical or mental condition, your agent has the power to make a broad range of health care decisions for you. Your agent may consent, refuse to consent, or withdraw consent to medical treatment and may make decisions about withdrawing or withholding life-sustaining treatment. Your agent may not consent to voluntary inpatient mental health services, convulsive treatment, psychosurgery, or abortion. A physician must comply with your agent's instructions or allow you to be transferred to another physician.

Your agent's authority begins when your doctor certifies that you lack the capacity to make health care decisions.

Your agent is obligated to follow your instructions when making decisions on your behalf. Unless you state otherwise, your agent has the same authority to make decisions about your health care as you would have had.

It is important that you discuss this document with your physician or other health care provider before you sign it to make sure that you understand the nature and range of decisions that may be made on your behalf. If you do not have a physician, you should talk with someone else who is knowledgeable about these issues and can answer your questions. You do not need a lawyer's assistance to complete this document, but if there is anything in this document that you do not understand, you should ask a lawyer to explain it to you.

The person you appoint as agent should be someone you know and trust. The person must be 18 years of age or older or a person under 18 years of age who has had the disabilities of minority removed. If you appoint your health or residential care provider (e.g., your physician or an employee of a home health agency, hospital, nursing home, or resi-

Source: Texas Civil Practice & Remedies Code § 135.015.

dential care home, other than a relative), that person has to choose between acting as your agent or as your health or residential care provider; the law does not permit a person to do both at the same time.

You should inform the person you appoint that you want the person to be your health care agent. You should discuss this document with your agent and your physician and give each a signed copy. You should indicate on the document itself the people and institutions who have signed copies. Your agent is not liable for health care decisions made in good faith on your behalf.

Even after you have signed this document, you have the right to make health care decisions for yourself as long as you are able to do so and treatment cannot be given to you or stopped over your objection. You have the right to revoke the authority granted to your agent by informing your agent or your health or residential care provider orally or in writing or by your execution of a subsequent durable power of attorney for health care. Unless you state otherwise, your appointment of a spouse dissolves on divorce.

This document may not be changed or modified. If you want to make changes in the document, you must make an entirely new one.

You may wish to designate an alternate agent in the event that your agent is unwilling, unable, or ineligible to act as your agent. Any alternate agent you designate has the same authority to make health care decisions for you.

THIS POWER OF ATTORNEY IS NOT VALID UNLESS IT IS SIGNED IN THE PRESENCE OF TWO OR MORE QUALIFIED WITNESSES. THE FOLLOWING PERSONS MAY NOT ACT AS WITNESSES:

(1) the person you have designated as your agent;
(2) your health or residential care provider or an employee of your health or residential care provider;
(3) your spouse;
(4) your lawful heirs or beneficiaries named in your will or a deed; or
(5) creditors or persons who have a claim against you.

APPENDIX E TO CHAPTER 13
REPORTING CHILD ABUSE—DEFINITIONS OF ABUSE AND NEGLECT

(1) Abuse includes the following acts or omissions by any person:

(A) mental or emotional injury to a child that results in an observable and material impairment in the child's growth, development, or psychological functioning;

(B) causing or permitting the child to be in a situation in which the child sustains a mental or emotional injury that results in an observable and material impairment in the child's growth, development, or psychological functioning;

(C) physical injury that results in substantial harm to the child, or the genuine threat of substantial harm from physical injury to the child, including an injury that is at variance with the history or explanation given and excluding an accident or reasonable discipline by a parent, guardian, or managing or possessory conservator that does not expose the child to a substantial risk of harm;

(D) failure to make a reasonable effort to prevent an action by another person that results in physical injury that results in substantial harm to the child;

(E) sexual contact, sexual intercourse, sexual conduct, . . . sexual penetration with a foreign object, incest, sexual assault, or sodomy inflicted on, shown to, or intentionally practiced in the presence of a child if the child is present only to arouse or gratify the sexual desires of any person;

(F) failure to make a reasonable effort to prevent sexual contact, sexual intercourse, or sexual conduct, . . . sexual penetration with a foreign object, incest, sexual assault, or sodomy being inflicted on or shown to a child by another person, or intentionally practiced in the presence of a child by another person if the child is present only to arouse or gratify the sexual desires of any person;

(G) compelling or encouraging the child to engage in sexual conduct; . . . or

(H) causing, permitting, encouraging, engaging in, or allowing the photographing, filming, or depicting of the child if the person knew or should have known that the resulting photograph, film, or depiction of the child is obscene . . . or pornographic.

(2) "Neglect" includes:

(A) the leaving of a child in a situation where the child would be exposed to a substantial risk of harm, without arranging for necessary

---

Source: Texas Family Code § 34.012.

care for the child, and a demonstration of an intent not to return by a parent, guardian, or managing or possessory conservator of the child;

(B) the following acts or omissions by any person:

(i) placing the child in or failing to remove the child from a situation that a reasonable person would realize requires judgment or actions beyond the child's level of maturity, physical condition, or mental abilities and that results in bodily injury or a substantial risk of immediate harm to the child;

(ii) the failure to seek, obtain, or follow through with medical care for the child, with the failure resulting in or presenting a substantial risk of death, disfigurement, or bodily injury or with the failure resulting in an observable and material impairment to the growth, development, or functioning of the child; or

(iii) the failure to provide the child with food, clothing, or shelter necessary to sustain the life or health of the child, excluding failure caused primarily by financial inability unless relief services had been offered and refused; or

(C) the failure by the person responsible for a child's care, custody, or welfare to permit the child to return to the child's home without arranging for the necessary care for the child after the child has been absent from the home for any reason, including having been in residential placement or having run away.

APPENDIX I

Texas Board of Nurse Examiners (TBNE) Telephone Numbers

General information/Licensing and support services
(512) 835-4880
License verification, endorsement/reciprocity information, prescriptive authority information, advanced nurse practitioner approval status, general information

Education/Examination (512) 835-8650
Registered nurse (RN) nursing programs, extended campuses, National Council Licensure Examination for Registered Nurses (NCLEX-RN) applications, graduate nurse permits, Nursing Practice Act (NPA) questions and practice issues, board rules and regulation inquiries, and declaratory orders

Practice and compliance (512) 835-8686
NPA and rules and regulation violations, complaint and disciplinary action inquiries, monitoring of disciplined RNs, interpretation of NPA and TBNE's rules regarding disciplinary proceedings, ANPs

Accounting (512) 873-6555
Returned checks, refunds, debits

Continuing education (512) 835-8685
Information on the state's requirements for mandatory continuing education for RNs

Sales of lists (512) 873-6554
Computerized lists of RNs on floppy diskettes, magnetic tape, hard copy and/or mailing labels

APPENDIX II

The American Association of Nurse Attorneys

The American Association of Nurse Attorneys (TAANA) is an organization of nurses who are also attorneys. The goals of TAANA are to

- establish a leadership role in health care policy making;
- influence health care social policy, health care legislation, and nursing practice acts;
- educate the membership;
- educate the public about health law issues;
- educate the public about nurse attorneys; and
- serve as a resource, network, and support group for members.

Persons interested in further information about membership, programs, and activities of TAANA may contact either the national or Texas chapter:

The American Association of Nurse Attorneys, Inc.
720 Light Street
Baltimore, Maryland 21230-3826
(301) 752-3318
FAX (301) 752-8295

The American Association of Nurse Attorneys, Inc.—Texas Chapter
P.O. Box 1444
Austin, Texas 78767

APPENDIX III

Criminal Penalties

The penalties for the different crime classifications, which are effective September 1, 1994, are outlined below:

MISDEMEANORS

Class A:	1. a fine not to exceed $4,000 2. confinement in jail for a term not to exceed one year, or 3. both
Class B:	1. a fine not to exceed $2,000 2. confinement in jail for a term not to exceed 180 days, or 3. both
Class C:	1. a fine not to exceed $500

FELONIES

Capital felony:	1. life imprisonment or 2. the death penalty
First degree:	1. five to ninety-nine years in prison and 2. a fine not to exceed $10,000
Second degree:	1. two to twenty years in prison and 2. a fine not to exceed $10,000
Third degree:	1. two to ten years and 2. a fine not to exceed $10,000
State jail:	1. 180 days to two years in jail and 2. a fine not to exceed $10,000

Source: Texas Penal Code §§ 12.21–.23, 12.31–.34.

Notes

1. REGISTERED NURSES—GETTING AND STAYING LICENSED IN TEXAS

1. The Nursing Practice Act is found at *Texas Revised Civil Statutes* arts. 4513–4528.

2. For codified TBNE rules, see 22 Texas Administrative Code chs. 211, 213, 215, 217–219, 221–223.

3. The TBNE's mailing address is P.O. Box 140466, Austin, Tex. 78714.

4. 23 *RN Update* 8 (Dec. 1992).

5. *Id.*

6. *Id.* at 9.

7. Texas Nurses Association, 7600 Burnet Road, Suite 440, Austin, Tex. 78757-1292; telephone: (512) 452-0645.

8. *RN Update*, *supra* note 4, at 9.

9. The following report or data must be furnished by an insurer or the RN to the TBNE within 30 days after receipt by the insurer of the complaint: (1) the name of the person against whom the claim is filed, (2) the policy number, (3) the policy limits, (4) a copy of the petition, (5) a copy of the answer, and (6) other pertinent data and information within the knowledge of the person required to make the report, as the TBNE may require.

The following report or data and information must be furnished by the insurer or RN to the TBNE within 30 days after the date of a judgment, dismissal, or settlement of the suit involving the insured or RN or settlement of any claim on behalf of the insured or RN without the filing of a lawsuit: (1) the date of the judgment, dismissal, or settlement; (2) whether an appeal has been taken and by which party; (3) the amount of the settlement or judgment against the insured

---

Note: the dates for the Texas statutes cited in these notes have been omitted. All statutes cited are current to the date of publication of this book.

or RN; and (4) other pertinent information within the knowledge of the person required to make the report, as the TBNE may require.

10. "Minor incident" is defined as conduct that does not indicate the nurse's continuing to practice professional nursing poses a risk of harm to a client or other person. Texas Revised Civil Statutes art. 4525a, § 6.

2. LICENSED VOCATIONAL NURSES—GETTING AND STAYING LICENSED IN TEXAS

1. *See* Texas Revised Civil Statutes art. 4528c.
2. The TBUNE's address is 9101 Burnet Road, Suite 105, Austin, Tex. 78758.
3. "Disabled person" in this context is defined as any person who has a physical or mental impairment that substantially limits one or more major life activities and who has a record of such impairment. 22 Texas Administrative Code § 235.18.
4. Emeritus status may be granted upon request to a licensee who is in good standing but does not intend to seek gainful employment as an LVN any longer but would like to maintain licensure and continue paying the required fees. The emeritus license cannot be used for employment purposes.
5. *See* Texas Government Code chs. 2001–2006.

3. SCOPE OF PRACTICE

1. Texas Revised Civil Statutes art. 4518, § 5.
2. 22 Texas Administrative Code § 217.11.
3. "Unlicensed person" is defined as an individual who is not licensed as a health care provider, who functions in a complementary or assistive role to the RN in providing direct client care or carrying out common nursing functions. The term includes but is not limited to nurse aides, orderlies, assistants, attendants, technicians, home health aides, medication aides permitted by the Texas Department of Health, and other individuals providing personal care and assistance of health-related services. *Id.* § 218.2.
4. *Id.* § 218.1.
5. *Id.* § 218.11.
6. *Id.* § 218.3.
7. *Id.* § 218.6.
8. *Id.* § 218.9.
9. *Id.* § 218.7.
10. *Id.* § 218.10.
11. *Id.* § 217.6.
12. *Id.* § 218.4.
13. *Id.* § 218.8.
14. Texas Revised Civil Statutes art. 4495b, § 3.06(d).
15. *Id.* art. 4514, § 5.
16. Texas Board of Nurse Examiners "Guidelines for Nurses Administering Medications via the Epidural and Intrathecal Routes for the Purpose of Pain Control," Policy No. 15.17 (approved June 1991).
17. *Id.* "Micro Pigment Implantation," Position Statement 15.20 (Sept. 1991).

18. *Id.* "Performance of Laser Therapy by RNs," Position Statement 15.21 (May 1992).

19. *Id.* "Administration of IV Conscious Sedation by the Registered Nurse," Position Statement 15.18 (Jan. 1992).

20. A copy of these guidelines can be obtained from the American Association of Nurse Anesthetists, 216 Higgins Road, Park Ridge, Ill. 60068-5790.

21. A copy of the ANA guidelines can be obtained from the Texas Board of Nurse Examiners, P.O. Box 140466, Austin, Tex. 78714.

22. 22 Texas Administrative Code § 217.11(15).

23. Texas Revised Civil Statutes art. 4528c, § 1.

24. 25 Texas Administrative Code § 151.

25. "Abuse" is defined as any act, failure to act, or incitement to act done willfully, knowingly, or recklessly through words or physical action that causes or could cause mental or physical injury or harm or death to a resident. These acts include verbal, sexual, mental/psychological, and physical abuse (including corporal punishment), involuntary seclusion, or any other actions within this definition. *Id.* § 151.2.

26. "Neglect" is defined as a deprivation of life's necessities of food, water, or shelter or a failure of an individual to provide services, treatment, or care to a resident that causes or could cause mental or physical injury or harm or death to the resident. *Id.*

27. "Misappropriation of resident property" is defined as the taking, secretion, misapplication, deprivation, transfer, or attempted transfer to any person not entitled to receive any property, real or personal, or anything of value belonging to or under the legal control of a resident without the effective consent of the resident or other appropriate legal authority or the taking of any action contrary to any duty imposed by federal or state law prescribing conduct relating to the custody or disposition of property of a resident. *Id.*

28. A person can be placed on the registry by waiver if she was found to be competent before July 1, 1989, after completing a nurse aide training course of at least 100 hours' duration and has completed the documentation required by the Department.

29. A nurse aide can be placed on the Texas registry by reciprocity when she is currently on the nurse aide registry in another state that has a program in compliance with the Omnibus Budget Reconciliation Act and has completed the documentation required by the Department.

30. 25 Texas Administrative Code §§ 145.251–.265. For information relating to correctional institution medication aides, see *id.* § 145.264.

31. An application will be disapproved if the applicant has been convicted of a felony or misdemeanor or if the crime directly relates to the duties and responsibilities of a permit holder or involves moral turpitude.

32. Texas Revised Civil Statutes art. 4495b-1 (Physician Assistant Licensing Act); 22 Texas Administrative Code §§ 185.1–.16.

33. Texas Revised Civil Statutes art. 4512i (Midwifery Act).

34. Opinion of Texas Attorney General No. H-1293 (1978).

35. "Heritable disease" is defined as "an inherited disease that may result in mental or physical retardation or death." Texas Health & Safety Code § 33.001(1).

36. 25 Texas Administrative Code § 37.53 (Tex. Dep't of Health, Newborn Screening Program).

37. Texas Health & Safety Code § 33.014.

4. ADVANCED NURSE PRACTITIONERS

1. 22 Texas Administrative Code § 221.1 (Bd. of Nurse Examiners, Advanced Nurse Practitioners).

2. *Id.* § 221.3 (Categories of Advanced Nurse Practitioners).

3. *Id.* § 221.7 (Identification of Advanced Nurse Practitioners).

4. *Id.* §§ 221.1–.2, .4–.6.

5. If there is proof of current certification in an appropriate area of practice by a national or state organization whose certification examination is recognized by the TBNE, the TBNE will waive the requirement to review the transcripts and course descriptions from the ANP educational program. *Id.* § 221.2(b).

6. The TBNE does have statutory authority to make and issue rules regarding ANPs when the rules are reasonably related to and referable to the provisions of the Nursing Practice Act. Bellegie v. Texas Bd. of Nurse Examiners, 685 S.W.2d 431, 433 (Tex. App.—Austin 1985, writ ref'd n.r.e.).

7. 22 Texas Administrative Code § 221.9; *see also id.* § 221.8 (practice as ANP must be appropriate to ANP educational training).

8. *Id.* § 221.8(b) (Functions of Advanced Nurse Practitioners) (emphasis added). The ANP rules that were challenged in 1985 and found to be proper did not include diagnosing as a function of ANPs. Rule 388.06.00 reads in part: "The advanced nurse practitioner may act independently or in collaboration with the health team in the maintenance of mental and physical health; in the prevention of illness; in management, observation, and counsel of the ill and injured; or in supervision and teaching of nursing." *Quoted in* Bellegie v. Texas Bd. of Nurse Examiners, 685 S.W.2d 431, 432 n. 2 (Tex. App.—Austin 1985, writ ref'd n.r.e.).

9. 22 Texas Administrative Code § 221.8(d).

10. Texas Revised Civil Statutes art. 4518, § 5.

11. *Id.* art. 4495b, § 1.03(12).

12. *See id.* art. 4518, § 5.

13. *Id.* art. 4495b, § 3.06(d)(1).

14. *See* Opinion of Texas Attorney General, Nos. H-1293, H-1295 (1978).

15. Texas Revised Civil Statutes art. 4495b, § 3.06(d)(1).

16. 22 Texas Administrative Code § 221.8(c).

17. Opinion of Texas Attorney General No. H-1295 (1978).

18. Texas Revised Civil Statutes art. 4495b, § 3.06(d)(5)(A) (emphases added).

19. A medically underserved area is an area in Texas that the secretary of the Department of Health and Human Services designates as having a shortage of personal health services or a population group that has a shortage of such services. The area can be either urban or rural. *Id.* art. 4495b, § 3.06(d)(5)(D)(vi).

20. A health manpower shortage area is either (1) an area in Texas, either urban or rural, that the secretary of the Department of Health and Human Ser-

vices determines has a health manpower shortage and that is not reasonably accessible to an adequately served area; (2) a population group that the secretary of Health and Human Services determines has a health manpower shortage; or (3) a public or nonprofit private medical facility or other facility that the secretary of Health and Human Services determines has a health manpower shortage according to federal guidelines. *Id.* § 3.06(d)(5)(D)(v).

21. Rural Health Clinic Services Act of 1977, Pub. L. No. 95–210.

22. Texas Revised Civil Statutes art. 4495b, § 3.06(d)(5)(D)(iv).

23. *Id.* § 3.06(d)(5)(D)(iii).

24. *Id.* art. 4495b, § 3.06(d)(5)(D)(i), art. 4514, § 6.

25. *Id.* art. 4495b, § 3.06(d)(5)(D)(iii).

26. 22 Texas Administrative Code § 193.8(a) (Bd. of Medical Examiners, Delegation of Drug Orders to RNs).

27. *Id.* § 193.8.

28. *Id.*

29. Texas Health & Safety Code § 483.022.

30. *Id.* § 483.048.

31. Texas Revised Civil Statutes art. 4542a-1, § 40(h). Drug-product selection as authorized in this section does not apply to enteric-coated tablets; controlled release products; injectable suspensions, other than antibiotics; suppositories containing active ingredients for which systemic absorption is necessary for therapeutic activity; and different delivery systems for aerosol or nebulizer drugs. This provision shall not apply to any drug product that is determined to be generically equivalent to the brand prescribed. *Id.* § 40(*l*).

32. 22 Texas Administrative Code § 193.8(g).

33. Texas Revised Civil Statutes art. 4542a-1, § 40(h).

34. Texas Health & Safety Code § 483.024.

35. *Id.* § 483.049.

36. *Id.* § 483.025.

37. 22 Texas Administrative Code § 193.8(h).

38. *See* Texas Revised Civil Statutes art. 4525.

39. *See* Hood v. Phillips, 554 S.W.2d 160 (Tex. 1977); Snow v. Bond, 438 S.W.2d 549 (Tex. 1969).

40. *See* King v. Flamm, 442 S.W.2d 679, 681 (Tex. 1969) (one who holds himself out as a specialist is generally expected to possess a higher degree of skill and learning than a general practitioner).

41. *See* W. Page Keeton et al., Prosser & Keeton on the Law of Torts 187 (5th ed. 1984) (there are minimum requirements of skill and knowledge that anyone who holds himself out as competent to treat human ailments is required to have).

42. Banti v. State, 163 Tex. Crim. 89, 289 S.W.2d 244 (1956).

43. Opinion of Texas Attorney General No. H-1293 (1978).

44. Texas Health & Safety Code § 81.090(a), (c).

45. *Id.* § 81.091.

46. A "financially responsible adult" means "a parent, guardian, spouse, or any other person whom the laws of this state hold responsible for the debts incurred as a result of hospitalization or treatment." *Id.* § 81.091(h).

47. *Id.* §§ 33.011–.014.

48. 25 Texas Administrative Code § 37.53 (Tex. Dep't of Health, Newborn Screening Program).

49. Texas Health & Safety Code § 192.003.

50. *Id.* § 192.005(a). In addition to providing the paternity consent form, the hospital, physician, midwife, or person acting as a midwife may, on the birth of the child, provide written information, including an application for child-support services, furnished by the attorney general, to the mother regarding the benefits of having her child's paternity established and of the availability of paternity establishment services. *Id.* § 192.003.

51. *Id.* § 192.005(d).

52. *Id.* § 192.003(d).

53. *Id.* § 192.002.

54. *Id.* § 192.004.

55. *Id.* § 195.003.

56. *Id.*

57. *Id.* § 195.004.

58. *Id.* §§ 193.003–.004.

59. *Id.* § 193.004(b).

60. 25 Texas Administrative Code § 181.7.

61. Texas Health & Safety Code § 673.003.

62. *Id.* § 673.002(a).

63. Texas Code of Criminal Procedure art. 49.04(a)(8).

64. Texas Family Code §§ 34.02–.03.

65. 25 Texas Administrative Code § 97.11.

5. NURSING NEGLIGENCE INSURANCE

1. Sheryl Seutz-Harter, "Professional Liability Insurance," *in Nursing and the Law* 193 (Professional Education Systems, 4th ed. 1991).

2. The American Association of Nurse Attorneys, Inc. (TAANA), *Demonstrating Financial Responsibility for Nursing Practice* 7 (1989). The reader can purchase this pamphlet from the national chapter of TAANA: 720 Light Street, Baltimore, Md. 21230-3826; telephone: (301) 752-3318.

3. Seutz-Harter, *supra* note 1, at 193.

4. Carmelle Cournoyer, *The Nurse Manager and The Law* 267 (Aspen Publishers, 1989).

5. Seutz-Harter, *supra* note 1, at 199.

6. TAANA, *supra* note 2, at 8.

7. G.A. Stowers Furniture Co. v. American Indem. Co., 15 S.W.2d 544 (Tex. Comm'n App. 1929, holding approved).

8. TAANA *supra* note 2, at 5–7.

9. *Id.* at 1.

10. *Id.* at 3.

11. Texas Property Code chs. 41, 42.

12. Federal Tort Claims Act, 28 United States Code §§ 1291, 1346, 1402, 1504, 2110, 2401, 2402, 2411, 2412, 2671–2678, 2680.

13. Driskill v. State, 779 S.W.2d 945, 947 (Tex. App.—Fort Worth 1989), *aff'd in part, rev'd in part*, 787 S.W.2d 369 (Tex. 1990).

14. *See* Armendarez v. Tarrant County Hosp. Dist., 781 S.W.2d 301, 306 (Tex. App.—Fort Worth 1989, writ denied).

15. Texas Civil Practice & Remedies Code § 101.027(c).

6. NURSING NEGLIGENCE

1. Texas Revised Civil Statutes art. 4590i, § 10.01.

2. Hellman v. Mateo, 772 S.W.2d 64, 66 (Tex. 1989); Neagle v. Nelson, 685 S.W.2d 11, 12 (Tex. 1985).

3. Melendez v. Beal, 683 S.W.2d 869 (Tex. App.—Houston [1st Dist.] 1984, writ ref'd n.r.e.); *see also* Jim M. Perdue & Paula Sweeney, *Medical Malpractice and Hospital Liability Law in Texas—Plaintiff's Perspective* G-6 to 36 (State Bar of Texas Prof. Dev. Program, Advanced Personal Injury Law Course, 1992).

4. Nichols v. Smith, 507 S.W.2d 518, 519 (Tex. 1974).

5. Texas Revised Civil Statutes art. 4590i, §§ 1.03(3), (4), 10.01.

6. Texas Civil Practice & Remedies Code § 74.001.

7. *Id.* § 33.001.

8. *Id.* § 33.012(a).

9. *Id.* § 33.013.

10. *Id.* § 33.015.

11. Hood v. Phillips, 554 S.W.2d 160, 165 (Tex. 1977) (standard for medical doctors articulated).

12. Texas Revised Civil Statutes art. 4590i, § 4.01(a).

7. CONSENT

1. Texas Revised Civil Statutes art. 6701*l*-5.

2. Offenses under chapter 49 of the Texas Penal Code include public intoxication, consumption or possession of alcoholic beverage in a motor vehicle, driving while intoxicated, flying while intoxicated, boating while intoxicated, intoxication assault, and intoxication manslaughter.

3. Texas Code of Criminal Procedure art. 21.31.

4. 25 Texas Administrative Code § 97.13.

5. Texas Health & Safety Code § 81.009.

6. Terry Tottenham et al., *Texas Medical Jurisprudence* 88–90 (Fulbright & Jaworski, Austin, Tex., 9th ed. 1992).

7. A "child" is "a person under 18 years of age who is not and has not been married or who has not had his disabilities of minority removed for general purposes." Texas Family Code § 11.01(1).

8. Tottenham et al., *supra* note 6, at 86.

9. Texas Family Code §§ 12.04(3), (6), 14.02(a), (b), .03, .04; Tottenham et al., *supra* note 6, at 86.

10. Texas Family Code § 35.01.

11. *Id.* § 35.02.

12. *See id.* § 35.03(a)(4).

13. *Id.* § 35.03(f).

14. *See id.* § 35.03.

15. *Id.*

16. Tottenham et al., *supra* note 6, at 89.

17. "Cannot be contacted" means (1) the location of the person is unknown; (2) a reasonable effort made by persons listed in the text accompanying note 17 to locate and communicate with the person to obtain the consent has failed and not more than 90 days have passed since the effort was made; or (3) the person who may consent has been contacted and the person refuses to consent or fails to carry out consent for the minor or refuses delegation, and the person does not expressly deny authority to the grandparent, adult brother or sister, or another person as listed in the text to consent for the minor. Texas Family Code § 35.011(d).

18. *Id.* § 35.011.

19. *Id.* § 35.013.

20. *Id.* § 35.012(a).

21. *Id.* § 35.012(b).

22. *Id.* § 35.04.

23. *Id.* § 35.03(g), (l).

24. *Id.* § 35.03(a), (g).

25. Gravis v. Physicians & Surgeons Hosp., 427 S.W.2d 310, 311 (Tex. 1968).

26. Texas Health & Safety Code §§ 313.001–.007; *see also* Karen Zemis, "Surrogate Consent for Treatment of Incompetent Patients," *State Bar Health Law Section Report* 10 (winter 1994).

27. An "adult" is defined as "a person 18 years of age or older or a person under 18 years of age who has had the disabilities of minority removed." Texas Health & Safety Code § 313.002(1).

28. "Incapacitated" means "lacking the ability, based on reasonable medical judgment, to understand and appreciate the nature and consequences of a treatment decision, including the significant benefits and harms of and reasonable alternatives to any proposed treatment decision." *Id.* § 313.002(5).

8. INFORMED CONSENT

1. Andrews v. Ballard, 498 F. Supp. 1038, 1045–51 (S.D. Tex. 1980).

2. Schloendorff v. Society of New York Hosp., 211 N.Y. 125, 105 N.E. 92, 93 (N.Y. 1914).

3. Andrews, 498 F. Supp. at 1045–48.

4. Texas Revised Civil Statutes art. 4590i, § 1.02(b).

5. Texas Department of Health, 1100 West 49th Street, Austin, Tex. 78756; telephone: (512) 834-6650.

6. *See* Texas Revised Civil Statutes art. 4590i, § 6.07(b); Peterson v. Shields, 652 S.W.2d 929, 931 (Tex. 1983).

7. Texas Revised Civil Statutes art. 4590i, § 6.02.

8. Ritter v. Delaney, 790 S.W.2d 29, 30 (Tex. App.—San Antonio 1990, writ ref'd).

9. *Id.* at 31; Nevauex v. Park Place Hosp., 656 S.W.2d 923, 925 (Tex. App.—Beaumont 1983, writ ref'd n.r.e.); Johnson v. Whitehurst, 652 S.W.2d 441, 445 (Tex. App.—Houston [1st Dist.] 1983, writ ref'd n.r.e.); Forney v. Memorial Hosp., 543 S.W.2d 705, 707 (Tex. Civ. App.—Beaumont 1976, writ ref'd

n.r.e.); Ross v. Sher, 483 S.W.2d 297, 301 (Tex. Civ. App.—Houston [14th Dist.] 1972, writ ref'd n.r.e.); Weiser v. Hampton, 445 S.W.2d 224, 231 (Tex. Civ. App.—Houston [1st Dist.] 1969, writ ref'd n.r.e.).

10. Ritter, 790 S.W.2d at 31–32.

11. The Medical Practice Act, which allows physicians to delegate medical acts provides: "[A] person licensed to practice medicine shall have the authority to delegate to any qualified and properly trained person or persons acting under the physician's supervision any medical act which a reasonable and prudent physician would find is within the scope of sound medical judgment to delegate if, in the opinion of the delegating physician, the act can be properly and safely performed by the person to whom the medical act is delegated and the act is performed in its customary manner, not in violation of any other statute, and the person does not hold himself out to the public as being authorized to practice medicine." Texas Revised Civil Statutes art. 4495b, § 3.06(d)(1).

12. *Id.*; Opinion of Texas Attorney General No. JM-173 (1984).

13. "A person to whom a physician has delegated a medical act to perform is not guilty of practicing medicine without a license unless the person acts with knowledge that the delegation and action thereunder is a violation of [the Medical Practice Act]." Texas Revised Civil Statutes art. 4495b, § 3.07(i).

14. *Id.*; Opinion of Texas Attorney General No. JM-173 (1984).

15. Smogor v. Enke, 874 F.2d 295, 297 (5th Cir. 1989).

16. *See* Texas Revised Civil Statutes art. 4495b, § 3.06(d)(1).

17. *See* J. Fiesta, "Informed Consent Process—Whose Legal Duty?" 22 *Nursing Management* 17 (Jan. 1991).

18. Rogers v. Duke, 766 S.W.2d 547 (Tex. App.—Houston [1st Dist.] 1989, no writ).

19. Campbell v. Pitt County Memorial Hosp., 84 N.C. App. 314, 352 S.E.2d 902, 903–04 (N.C. Ct. App. 1987).

20. *Quoted in id.*, 352 S.E. 2d at 908.

21. Texas Revised Civil Statutes art. 4590i, § 6.07(a)(2).

22. Barclay v. Campbell, 704 S.W.2d 8, 11 (Tex. 1986).

23. M. Sweeney, "Your Role in Informed Consent," 54 *RN* 55, 57 (Aug. 1991).

24. *Id.*

25. Gravis v. Physicians & Surgeons Hosp., 427 S.W.2d 310, 311 (Tex. 1968).

26. Emidio Bianco, "Consent to Treatment," *in Legal Medicine: Legal Dynamics of Medical Encounters* 278 (Mosby-Year Book, St. Louis, Mo., 2d ed. 1991).

27. Sweeney, *supra* note 23, at 58–59.

28. *Id.*

29. Allen v. Roark, 625 S.W.2d 411, 416 (Tex. App.—Fort Worth 1981), *modified on other grounds*, 633 S.W.2d 804 (Tex. 1982).

30. Sweeney, *supra* note 23, at 58.

31. Fiesta, *supra* note 17, at 18.

9. DRUG THERAPY

1. *See* Texas Health & Safety Code ch. 481 (Texas Controlled Substances Act).

2. Terry O. Tottenham et al., *Texas Medical Jurisprudence* 143 (Fulbright & Jaworski, Austin, Tex., 9th ed. 1992).

3. *See* Texas Health & Safety Code ch. 483 (Texas Dangerous Drug Act).

4. "Illegal" means not in the usual course of business or practice or in the performance of official duties. *Id.* § 483.042(b).

5. Texas Health & Safety Code ch. 431.

6. Texas Alcoholic Beverage Code ch. 40.

7. Texas Health & Safety Code § 481.071.

8. 21 United States Code § 333(e).

9. Texas Health & Safety Code §§ 439.011–.017.

10. *Id.* § 431.114.

11. Texas Revised Civil Statutes art. 4495c.

12. Texas Board of Nurse Examiners, "Administration of IV Conscious Sedation by the Registered Nurse," Position Statement 15.18 at 1 (Jan. 1992).

13. *See* Texas Revised Civil Statutes art. 4495b, § 3.06(d).

14. A copy of the AANA's guidelines can be obtained from the American Association of Nurse Anesthetists, 216 Higgins Road, Park Ridge, Ill. 60068-5790. The following discussion draws heavily from these guidelines, which are used with permission of the American Association of Nurse Anesthetists.

15. *See also* Susan S. Murphy, "IV Conscious Sedation," *Texas Nursing* 8 (Jan. 1993).

16. Texas Health & Safety Code §§ 439.001–.005.

17. Tottenham et al., *supra* note 2, at 143.

18. Texas Revised Civil Statutes art. 4495b, § 5.09(c).

19. Texas Health & Safety Code ch. 777.

20. *See Id.* ch. 467.

21. "TPAPN: Nurses Helping Nurses" brochure (Jan. 1993).

22. *Id.*

23. *See* Eleanor J. Sullivan, "Cost Savings of Retaining Chemically Dependent Nurses," *Nursing Economics* 179 (July/Aug. 1986).

10. DOCUMENTATION

1. W. Roach, Jr., et al., *Medical Records and the Law* 14 (Aspen Publication, Rockville, Md., 1985).

2. *Id.* at 26–27.

3. *Id.* at 14–15.

4. Paul Greve, "Documentation: Every Word Counts," *RN* 56 (July 1992).

5. Stephen Bergerson, "More about Charting with a Jury in Mind," *Nursing* 53 (1988).

6. Ellen Eggland, "Charting: How and Why to Document Your Care Daily—And Fully," *Nursing* 79 (Nov. 1988).

7. Roach, *supra* note 1, at 49.

8. *Id.* at 70–71.

9. Greve, *supra* note 4, at 56.

10. Walter Killian, "Good Record Is Good Defense," *American Nurse* 32 (May 1991).

11. Patricia Iyer, "Documenting Discharge AMA," *Nursing* (Sept. 1992) (citing "Better Documentation," *in Clinical Skillbuilders* 30 (1992)).

12. Roach, *supra* note 1, at 25 (citing Joint Commission on Accreditation of Hospitals, *Accreditation Manual for Hospitals* 85 (1984)).

13. Ann Bailey-Allen, "Interrogatories," *Orthopedic Nurse* 62 (Mar./Apr. 1989).

14. *Id.* at 63–64.

15. Helen Creighton, "Legal Significance of Charting—Part II," *Nursing Management* 15 (Oct. 1987).

16. Roach, *supra* note 1, at 38–40.

17. *Id.* at 137 (citing American Hospital Ass'n & National Safety Council, *Safety Guide for Health Care Institutions* 33 (1972)).

18. Roach, *supra* note 1, at 139.

19. Bergerson, *supra* note 5, at 54.

20. Greve, *supra* note 4, at 56.

21. Texas Revised Civil Statutes art. 4495b, § 5.08.

22. Texas Rules of Civil Evidence 509.

23. For the law regarding mental health patients, consult chapter 611 of the Texas Health & Safety Code and rule 510 of the Texas Rules of Civil Evidence.

24. Texas Revised Civil Statutes art. 4495b, § 5.08(g), (h) (1994); *see also* Vicki Brann, "Shhhh! Confidentiality in the 90s," *Texas Nursing* 6 (Nov./Dec. 1993).

25. Brann, *supra* note 24, at 6.

26. *Id.*

27. Texas Revised Civil Statutes art. 4495b, § 5.08(j).

28. *Id.* § 3.06(d)(1).

29. 22 Texas Administrative Code §§ 193.2, .4.

30. *Id.* § 193.2.

11. AIDS AND HEPATITIS B

1. 56 *Federal Register* 64,175 (1991) (to be codified at 29 Code of Federal Regulation 1910); OSHA Instruction CPL 2–2.44B.

2. Texas Health & Safety Code §§ 81.050, .101–.109, 85.201–.206.

3. David Butler, "Recommendations for Preventing Transmission of Human Immunodeficiency Virus and Hepatitis B Virus to Patients during Exposure-Prone Invasive Procedures," 40 *MMWR* RR-8 (July 12, 1991); *see also* David Butler, "HIV: Reconciling Texas Law, OSHA Regulations & CDC Guidelines" I-68 (Univ. of Houston Law Foundation Health Law Inst., May 1993).

4. Butler, *supra* note 3, at I-32.

5. 42 United States Code § 12112(d).

6. "Interpretive Guidelines on Prevention of Transmission of HIV and Hepatitis B Virus by Infected Health Care Workers," 18 *Texas Register* 1202 (Feb. 23, 1993) (Tex. Dep't of Health); *see also* Butler, *supra* note 3, at I-28.

7. Butler, *supra* note 3, at I-32.

8. *Id.* at I-36.

9. 42 United States Code ch. 126.

10. *Id.* § 12111(5). The act will apply to employers of 15 or more employees beginning July 26, 1994.

11. 29 *id.* §§ 701–796i.

12. Texas Labor Code ch. 21.

13. Americans with Disabilities Act, 42 United States Code § 12112(c).

14. Texas law states a patient can be tested for HIV without his consent if the infectious disease protocols are followed and the identifying patient information is destroyed when the testing is completed and the exposed person has been notified of the result. Texas Health & Safety Code § 81.107(b). The federal OSHA regulations, however, disagree with this Texas law; the federal regulations should win out, which state that patient consent must be obtained before patients are tested for HIV. OSHA Instruction CPL 2-2.44B, at 21.

15. 56 *Federal Register* 64,014 (1991).

16. *Id.* 64,009.

17. A copy of the OSHA rules can be obtained from the OSHA Office of Publications, U.S. Department of Labor, Room N3101, 200 Constitution Avenue, N.W., Washington, D.C. 20210; telephone: (202) 523-9667.

18. Butler, *supra* note 3, at I-68.

19. 37 *MMWR* 378–379.

20. The BBP rules require the employer to attempt to obtain the consent of the source individual before testing, but such consent is not mandated under Texas law. 29 Code of Federal Regulations § 1910.1310(f)(3)(ii)(A); Texas Health & Safety Code §§ 81.102(a)(4)(D), .107. Consistent with the Texas Health & Safety Code, the BBP rules further authorize testing of the source individual without the patient's consent if the consent is not required by state law. 29 Code of Federal Regulations § 1910.1310(f)(3)(ii)(A); Butler, *supra* note 3, at I-70.

21. Texas Health & Safety Code § 81.105.

22. Butler, *supra* note 3, at I-71.

12. EMPLOYMENT ISSUES

1. *See* Stuart Johnston, Jr., "Texas Law Relating to Employer Drug and Alcohol Investigations," *in Texas Employment Law* 133 (Sterling Press, San Antonio Tex., Spring 1991).

2. *See* National Treasury Employees Union v. Von Raab, 489 U.S. 656 (1989); Skinner v. Railway Labor Executives Ass'n, 489 U.S. 602 (1989); J. Devereux Weeks, "Public Employee Drug Testing under the 4th Amendment after *Skinner* and *Von Raab*," 24 *Urban Lawyer* 515 (Summer 1992).

3. Texas Health & Safety Code § 481.133.

4. Employee Polygraph Protection Act of 1988, 29 United States Code §§ 2001–2009.

5. Texas State Employee Union v. Texas Dep't of Mental Health & Mental Retardation, 746 S.W.2d 203 (Tex. 1987) (public employee can be tested only when intrusion of privacy is reasonably warranted for achievement of compelling government objective that can be achieved by no less intrusive, more reasonable means).

6. Kenneth Carr & Randolph Grambling, "Employment Agreements," *in TAB Employment Law Handbook* 1-1 (Tex. Ass'n of Bus., Austin, Tex., 1991).

7. Philip Pfeiffer & Xavier Rodriguez, "The Employment-at-Will Doctrine," *in TAB Employment Law Handbook* 2-1 (Tex. Ass'n of Bus., Austin, Tex., 1991).

8. Hauck v. Sabine Pilot Serv., 687 S.W.2d 733 (Tex. 1985); *see also* Pfeiffer & Rodriguez, *supra* note 7, at 2-2.

9. Texas Labor Code § 451.001.

10. Texas Health & Safety Code §§ 242.121–.134.

11. Texas Government Code §§ 554.001–.009.

12. Winters v. Houston Chronicle Pub. Co., 795 S.W.2d 723 (Tex. 1990).

13. Hancock v. Express One Int', Inc., 800 S.W.2d 634 (Tex. App.—Dallas 1990, no writ).

14. 29 United States Code § 660(c).

15. *See* Texas Revised Civil Statutes art. 4525b (Nursing Practice Act).

16. Patricia Becker, "Peer Review," *State Bar Health Law Section Report* 4 (Summer 1992).

17. *See id.* at 4–6.

18. Fair Labor Standards Act, 29 United States Code §§ 206–207.

19. Texas Labor Code ch. 61.

20. 29 United States Code § 651 et seq.

21. Texas Penal Code § 48.01.

22. Americans with Disabilities Act, Pub. L. No. 101–336, 104 Statutes at Large 327; Rehabilitation Act of 1973, 29 United States Code §§ 701–796i; Age Discrimination in Employment Act of 1967, 29 United States Code §§ 621–634; Civil Rights Act of 1964, 42 United States Code § 2000e-2(a); Texas Commission on Human Rights Act of 1983, Texas Labor Code ch. 21.

23. Texas Revised Civil Statutes art. 4512.7.

24. N. Ebe et al., "The Cutting Edge: Developing Issues in Labor and Employment Law," *Matthews & Branscomb Annual Seminar* 23 (Matthews & Branscomb, San Antonio, Tex., Sept. 1989).

25. Texas Labor Code chs. 201–217; *see also* James Neel, "Unemployment Compensation," *in TAB Employment Law Handbook* 9-1 (Tex. Ass'n of Bus., Austin, Tex., 1991).

26. Texas Labor Code chs. 401–417, 451, 501–506.

27. Employee Retirement Income & Security Act (ERISA), 29 United States Code §§ 1001–1461.

28. Consolidated Omnibus Budget Reconciliation Act (COBRA), 42 United States Code § 1395 et seq.

13. ETHICAL ISSUES

1. Texas Family Code § 12.03.

2. Texas Revised Civil Statutes art. 4495b, § 4.011.

3. "Guidelines for State Court Decision Making In Life-Sustaining Medical Treatment Cases" (12 State Justice Inst. 1992) (hereinafter "Guidelines").

4. *In re* Quinlan, 70. N.J. 10, 355 A.2d 647 (1976).

5. "Guidelines" 1–23.

6. M. Bearden, "Termination of Treatment and Withholding of Treatment: An Update" E-1 (Univ. of Houston Law Foundation Health Law Inst., May 1993).

7. *Id.*

8. *Id.*

9. *See* Texas Health & Safety Code §§ 672.001–.021 (Natural Death Act).

10. A "competent" patient is one who possesses the "ability, based on reasonable medical judgment, to understand and appreciate the nature and consequences of a treatment decision, including the significant benefits and harms of and reasonable alternatives to a proposed treatment decision." *Id.* § 672.002(2).

11. A "terminal condition" is "an incurable or irreversible condition caused by injury, disease, or illness that would produce death without the application of life-sustaining procedures, according to reasonable medical judgment, and in which the application of life-sustaining procedures serves only to postpone the moment of the patient's death." *Id.* § 672.002(9).

12. *Id.* § 672.003(e).

13. 42 United States Code § 1395cc(f) (Patient Self-Determination).

14. 40 Texas Administrative Code §§ 19.205(b), .217, .219 (Tex. Dep't of Hum. Serv.).

15. "Qualified patient" means "a patient with a terminal condition that has been diagnosed and certified in writing by the attending physician and one other physician who have personally examined the patient." Texas Health & Safety Code § 672.002(8).

16. Child Abuse and Neglect Prevention and Treatment Program, 45 Code of Federal Regulations § 1340.15.

17. *Id.* § 1340.15(b)(3)(i).

18. Texas Family Code § 34.012(2)(B)(ii), (iii).

19. Texas Civil Practice & Remedies Code ch. 135.

20. *See* Texas Health & Safety Code § 672.002(6).

21. Bearden, *supra* note 6, at E-3, E-6.

22. Texas Penal Code § 22.08.

23. Texas Health & Safety Code § 672.017.

24. *Id.* § 672.020.

25. *Id.* ch. 692.

26. *Id.* §§ 241.027–.028, 241.051–.057, 311.021–.024.

27. 42 United States Code § 1395dd.

28. Texas Family Code § 34.01.

29. *Id.* § 34.07.

30. Leota Alexander, "Chapter 34: Report of Child Abuse," 21 *Texas Tech Law Review* 1697, 1698 (1990).

31. *Id.* at 1701.

32. *Id.* at 1701–02.

33. *Id.* at 1702.

34. *Id.*

35. *Id.*

36. Texas Family Code § 34.02(a).

37. "Professional" is defined as "an individual who is licensed or certified by the state, or who is an employee of a facility licensed, certified, or operated by the state, and who in the normal course of official duties, or duties for which a license or certification is required, has direct contact with children. 'Professional' includes teachers, nurses, doctors, and day-care employees." *Id.* § 34.02(d).

38. *Id.* § 34.03.

39. *Id.* § 34.032.

40. *Id.* § 34.031(a).

41. Texas Human Resources Code § 48.036(a).

42. *Id.* § 48.0361(a).

43. *Id.* § 48.002(2).

44. *Id.* § 48.002(3).

45. *Id.* § 48.002(4).

46. *Id.* § 48.036(a).

47. *Id.* § 48.039.

48. *Id.* § 48.036(b).

Index